JAMES CARVILLE is an American political consultant, commentator, educator, actor, attorney, media personality, and prominent liberal pundit. He gained national attention for his work as the lead strategist of the successful 1992 presidential campaign of Bill Clinton. Carville was a cohost of CNN's *Crossfire* until its final broadcast in June 2005. Since then, he has appeared on CNN's news program *The Situation Room*, and, since 2009, has hosted a weekly XM Radio program, *60/20 Sports*, with Luke Russert, son of the late Tim Russert, who hosted NBC's *Meet the Press*. Carville, who is married to Republican political consultant Mary Matalin, has taught political science at Tulane University since 2009.

STAN GREENBERG is a leading Democratic pollster and political strategist who has advised the campaigns of Bill Clinton, Al Gore, and John Kerry, and hundreds of other candidates and organizations in the United States and around the world. A political scientist who received his B.A. from Miami University and his Ph.D. from Harvard, Greenberg spent a decade teaching at Yale before becoming a political consultant. His 1985 study of Reagan Democrats in Macomb County, Michigan, became a classic of progressive political strategy, and is the basis for his continuing argument that Democrats must actively work to present themselves as populists advocating the expansion of opportunity for the middle class. Greenberg is married to Congresswoman Rosa DeLauro, who represents Connecticut's Third Congressional District.

Praise for *It's the Middle Class, Stupid!*

"A wonderful takedown of how the middle class has been left feeling betrayed and screwed over by both political parties in the last thirty years, and how we need to turn things around quickly to restore the health and prosperity of the American middle class before it is too late."

—*The Huffington Post*

"Top-gun political strategist, ever controversial Ragin' Cajun James Carville and pollster nonpareil Stan Greenberg deliver the message that could keep Obama in office: *It's the Middle Class, Stupid!* But class warfare isn't the answer (nuts!); it's for both parties to admit their failures and for regular people to get involved in taking back their country from bigwigs in Wall Street and Washington."   —*Vanity Fair*

"For many Democrats [this] will be *the* playbook on how to talk to voters about economic issues. . . . Democrats and Republicans alike in the elite and political class should pay heed: these pages contain more than a little truth."   —*National Journal*

"Political guru James Carville and savvy pollster Stan Greenberg team up for a presidential campaign–oriented book that will be part of the media circus surrounding the election."   —*Booklist*

"A recipe for President Barack Obama's re-election . . . Very timely . . . Impressive."   —Associated Press

"For political junkies who enjoy straight-talk policy discussion."
—*Kirkus Reviews*

ALSO BY JAMES CARVILLE

40 More Years

Take It Back (coauthored with Paul Begala)

Had Enough? (with Jeff Nussbaum)

Stickin': The Case for Loyalty

Buck Up, Suck Up . . . and Come Back When You Foul Up
(coauthored with Paul Begala)

. . . And the Horse He Rode In On

We're Right, They're Wrong

All's Fair (coauthored with Mary Matalin)

ALSO BY STAN GREENBERG

Dispatches from the War Room

The Two Americas

The New Majority

Middle Class Dreams

Legitimating the Illegitimate

Race and State in Capitalist Development

Politics and Poverty

IT'S THE MIDDLE CLASS, $$STUPID!

JAMES CARVILLE

and STAN GREENBERG

A PLUME BOOK

PLUME
Published by the Penguin Group
Penguin Group (USA) Inc., 375 Hudson Street
New York, New York 10014 USA

USA / Canada / UK / Ireland / Australia / New Zealand / India / South Africa /China
Penguin Books Ltd, Registered Offices: 80 Strand, London WC2R 0RL, England
For more information about the Penguin Group visit penguin.com

Published by Plume, a member of Penguin Group (USA) Inc. Previously published in a Blue Rider Press edition

First Plume Printing, February 2013

The Library of Congress has cataloged the Blue Rider Press edition as follows:

Carville, James.
It's the middle class, stupid! / James Carville and Stan Greenberg.
p.   cm.
ISBN 978-0-399-16039-4 (hc.)
ISBN 978-0-14-219695-3 (pbk.)
1. Politics, Practical—United States.   2. United States—Politics and government—2009–
3. United States—Politics and government—2001–2009   I. Greenberg, Stanley B., date.   II. Title.
JK1726 C37   2012   2012018191
320.51'30973—dc23

Original hardcover design by Meighan Cavanaugh
Printed in the United States of America
10 9 8 7 6 5 4 3 2 1

PUBLISHER'S NOTE
While the author has made every effort to provide accurate telephone numbers and Internet addresses at the time of publication, neither the publisher nor the author assumes any responsibility for errors, or for changes that occur after publication. Further, the publisher does not have any control over and does not assume any responsibility for author or third-party Web sites or their content.

To

Earl Long

and

Robert F. Kennedy

CONTENTS

INTRODUCTION

We could not be happier with the election. We are happy with the campaign President Obama's people ran, how Obama battled back, and the big choice he put before the voters. He illuminated the very different paths our country could take, only one of which could ensure the middle class's future. That's the single biggest challenge facing the country and that is the mandate of the election.

James That's only possible because President Obama kicked Romney's ass in the election. Simple as that. In the days before the election, we recorded a video, and I said, "I feel very good. If there were a play opening tonight, the title would be *The Ass-Whopping Cometh*." And what was that sound you could hear election night? It was the sound of two-by-fours hitting heads around the country.

Stan By now, people think that's just James, over-the-top. But James is actually very cautious and a little crazy when he thinks a race is coming down to the wire. In the 1992 Clinton campaign, on Election Day he put on white gloves and could be found in a fetal position on a couch in the war room. That's some kind of ritual for him, but I hadn't seen it before.

James We finished our last Democracy Corps poll on the Sunday night before the election, and it showed Obama four points ahead of Romney. All the pundits and media are saying, "It's a toss-up race, anybody can win." And I said, "I think it will be a big win."

Stan Our poll showed the race 49 to 45 percent—3.8 points to be exact—and we were out there, we thought. But we just believed our polling was reading America right. As of this writing, the margin was 3.4 points and inching up. And given everything that's happened to the country, that's a big win.

And Obama won 332 Electoral College votes—winning every state he won in the 2008 landslide, except Indiana and North Carolina. With that, it has begun to dawn on Republicans that they have only won a plurality of the national presidential vote in one election since 1988. They are a party of whites, and maybe just older whites in the Border States and Deep South, Appalachia, and the Mormon West. Obama won only 28 percent of the white votes in those areas, but this narrowing of support is costing them everyplace else.

James This confirms two of my books: *40 More Years* and this one, *It's the Middle Class, Stupid!* The long-term trends are just against them.

Like I said in my 2009 book, the underlying composition of the electorate tends to favor the Democrats. And I think the campaign did a really good job of playing into that. I think they recognized it and played into it. I thought the president's immigration strategy, where he said they were going to stop arresting people, was a good strategy. And Romney couldn't do it. It boxed him in. I think that was the right thing to do politically and the right thing to do morally. So they did some smart things and that was a big component.

I think in terms of non-Southern, non-Appalachian whites,

Obama did better than most people think. And I think that George Bush had a lot to do with that, too. I really think people remember.

Stan Campaigns cannot help but reveal Republicans' view of America. They're banking that old white guys can elect a president. But they're banking this is a much whiter country than it is—or they can just keep everyone else from voting. They're saying to a generation of voters: "We don't want Hispanics and African Americans. Our future is white people."

James They're saying, "We want more coal and less immigration." That's not a very attractive idea to people. Then there's their weird obsession with rape—I can't imagine how much that's hurt them. And then you have John Sununu basically saying black people are incapable of having a judgment outside of their race—a very telling moment. We've had the war on women, war on science, war on fact checkers, war on pollsters, and now we have a war on Nate Silver. So now they're against people predicting election outcomes. They're going to run out of opponents.

President Obama won an Electoral College landslide and 51 to 47 percent victory—against the great odds posed by prolonged high unemployment, lack of income gains, a barely perceptible recovery, and political gridlock that kept his job approval at just 50 percent at best. He won because he was able to engage the diverse national coalition of Latinos, African Americans, and Asians, young people, and unmarried women who formed nearly half the electorate, despite the fact that these groups suffered the brunt of recession and have benefited least from the halting recovery.

Mitt Romney has a theory of the case: Obama just bought off those people. "What the president's campaign did was focus on certain members of his base coalition, give them extraordinary financial gifts from the government, and then work very aggressively to turn them out to vote," Romney said on a post-defeat conference call with donors. That was all too reminiscent of the secretly recorded video where Romney said the 47 percent "dependent upon government, who believe that they are victims, who believe the government has a responsibility to care for them, who believe that they are entitled to health care, to food, to housing, to you-name-it" will never vote for him.

Romney elaborated after the election. For young people, "forgiveness of college loan interest was a big gift"; for women, "free contraceptives were very big with young, college-aged women"; for African Americans, "you can imagine for somebody making $25,000 or $30,000 or $35,000 a year being told you're now going to get free health care, particularly if you don't have it, getting free health care worth, what, $10,000 per family, in perpetuity—I mean, this is huge." "Likewise with Hispanic voters, free health care was a big plus. But in addition, with regards to Hispanic voters, the amnesty for children of illegals, the so-called Dream Act kids, was a huge plus for that voting group."

Well, he was right. The 47 percent did not vote for him, and we took some perverse pleasure in watching his vote heading down to 47 percent.

Mitt Romney didn't lose because Obama managed to turn a majority of the country into a dependent class. He lost because Obama managed to turn the election into a battle for the future of the middle class. As we wrote in this book, Obama struggled when he was making the case for economic progress and asking for more time to finish the job, but not when he made the election about what was happening to the middle class and his plans for change. Right at the beginning of his speech before the Democratic National Convention, Obama declared that we will have "a choice between two different paths for America." Put simply, "ours is a fight to restore the values that built the largest middle class and the strongest economy the world has ever known."

And Obama waged class warfare and won.

James No, no. Not class warfare! Didn't the pundits and elites tell us that's a sure sign of a losing, divisive campaign? We had that argument in this book, Stan.

Stan Yes, we wrote in this book that the most successful Democratic campaigns waged class warfare and proposed raising taxes on the rich. Obama did both.

They successfully defined Mitt Romney as an out-of-touch rich guy who does not care about the "47 percent," shipped jobs overseas as CEO of Bain Capital, wanted to return to "trickle-down economics" and cut taxes for the rich, and wanted to "reform" Medicare in ways that would damage middle-class retirement. When we asked voters in big national surveys right after the election about their three biggest doubts about Romney, being for the rich and out of touch with average people encompassed half of the total responses.

Among James's more outlandish challenges in this book, he urged Obama to go to the Democratic National Convention and declare, "I will raise taxes on the rich and Romney won't. That's the choice." Indeed, Obama insisted "everybody pay their fair share and get a fair shake," while proposing higher taxes on the wealthiest as a central plank in his economic plan.

In one of the more striking findings in our post-election survey, Obama and Romney battled to a draw on who voters trusted to handle taxes. Do not listen to the pundits and consultants who tell you voters will punish Democrats when they raise taxes, and that should tell you something serious about the policy mandate ahead.

Romney finally shook up the race in the first presidential debate when he contested the choice that Obama posed while lamenting that Obama had failed the middle class. "The policies of the last four years have seen incomes in America decline every year for middle-income families, now down $4,300. . . . It's just a tragedy in a nation so prosperous as ours that these last four years have been so hard."

That, too, was his closing argument when he campaigned in the battleground states. "[A]lmost every measure the president took made it harder for the economy to recover and it hurt our fellow Americans. . . . One in six Americans are poor, and the middle class, even those that have jobs, the middle class is being squeezed with lower incomes every year and higher prices from everything to health insurance to gasoline and electricity bills. It's been tough for middle-income [Americans]."

The president probably spent too much time defending the past and arguing to let him finish the job, as he did in one of his closing stops in Des Moines. "We've made real progress these past four years, but Iowa, we're here tonight because we've got more work to do. We're not done yet on this journey." There are still some who have not found work or remain in poverty.

But he went to the main closing argument: "We know this nation cannot succeed without a growing, thriving middle class and sturdy ladders for everybody who is willing to work to get into that middle class." The voter has "a choice between going back to the top-down policies that caused the mess we've been fighting our way out of for four years—or moving forward to a future that's built on a strong and growing middle class."

When the dust settled on Election Day, Obama established a near double-digit advantage over Romney on "restoring the middle class"

51 to 42 percent. The advantage was triple Obama's margin in the vote and tracked his vote at 51 percent. He made the election about the middle class, and it allowed him to win in very tough times.

In his press conference after the election, he affirmed that was his mandate. "I've got one mandate. I've got a mandate to help middle-class families and families that are working hard to try to get into the middle class. That's my mandate. That's what the American people said. They said: Work really hard to help us. Don't worry about the politics of it; don't worry about the party interests; don't worry about the special interests. Just work really hard to see if you can help us get ahead—because we're working really hard out here and we're still struggling, a lot of us. That's my mandate."

We spoke with voters in our surveys right after the election: "Barack Obama and Mitt Romney said in their campaigns that this election is about the future of the middle class. That was the big choice. Now that the election is over, which three of the following are the most important for us to focus on?" Their answer was pretty clear and not very consistent with the elite consensus that long-term deficits are our main problem. Right after they elected Barack Obama, they told us in no uncertain terms: create jobs and get the economy moving; protect middle-class retirement benefits including Medicare, Medicaid, and Social Security; and invest more in education. Reducing the debt for future generations was also very important, but not for those who voted for or considered voting for Obama. And by two-to-one, voters say the top priority should be growing the economy rather than reducing our deficits.

Reflecting the election campaign, over 60 percent of voters say any bipartisan bargain to reduce the deficit over ten years must raise taxes. The mandate of this election about the middle class is to increase taxes on the top earners and protect Medicare and Social Security.

It is pretty stunning that voters remained clearheaded when the big special interests spent so much money to steal this election from the ordinary voter. The campaigns and outside groups spent a breathtaking $6 billion at the federal level, more than $1 billion of it by super PACs. In our surveys, voters told us they are fed up with super PACs and big money politics, which they believe simply undermine democracy. In an otherwise intensely partisan and divided electorate, concerns about money in politics unite voters across parties and demographic groups. Voters are open to major reforms to change it.

We began our policy recommendations in this book with cleaning up money and politics—and we have no doubt that it is still true: We will not get changes in policy that help the middle class unless we address the moneyed interests that dominate what happens in Washington.

Most important is President Obama's opportunity to appoint new Supreme Court justices that can overturn the obscene campaign finance rulings that have given corporations as much constitutional protection as individual citizens and have allowed our democracy to become so polluted. We should move ahead with a constitutional amendment as well, and we stand by the tough reforms laid out in this book. With the backdrop of such massive giving and spending, we found voters are even more supportive of a plan that allows candidates for Congress the option of having the small donations from people in their home state matched with public funding, as long as candidates take no contributions over $100.

The biggest challenge ahead is how to produce economic growth, and, just as important, an economic growth that enriches everyone. That is the starting point for everything else.

The public mood on the macro economy and job market ticked up just before people were voting on Election Day, driven by increased optimism but not necessarily by improved pocketbook-level experiences. People are still struggling with health insurance, stagnant or declining wages, keeping up with grocery bills, and making mortgage payments. Remember, real income went down right before the election and is likely to be challenging in the years ahead. Obama won reelection on the middle class, but on the economy in general and on jobs, Romney finished with an advantage. Voters will be rooting for the president, but they are still uncertain of his plans for a growing economy and rising prosperity for all.

More than ever, we think the policy agenda laid out in this book is the mandate. In these times, if your mandate is the middle class, then you have to aggressively address health-care costs, protect middle-class entitlements, invest in infrastructure and education at minimum to make America strong, and rally the country to break the gridlock.

James We've got to ask ourselves: What about the debt? Someone's going to read this book and say, "They talk about all this, but didn't their polls show the debt was the main concern?"

I should answer my question. "It's health-care costs, stupid!"

Stan Right, we know that getting health-care costs down is the only way to be serious about deficit reduction. We devoted a chapter to doubling down on heath-care reforms and taking on the special interests to bring changes that can shift the curve.

Voters do want to address the deficit, but their starting point is higher taxes on the rich; indeed, four in ten voters want a 50-50 Clinton formula, where every dollar of spending cuts is matched by a dollar of taxes on the wealthy. And people get it when you make clear the consequences of drastic, immediate spending cuts and make the case for investing for the long term. A majority of the public rejects a call for austerity in favor of this economic argument:

"We should avoid immediate drastic cuts in spending, and instead, we need serious investments that create jobs and make us more prosperous in the long term that will reduce our debt, too."

James   And you would not do any short-term stimulus spending?

Stan   We know that voters are skeptical about short-term stimulus spending that is not grounded in long-term investments for the country that will make us more prosperous with less debt. But "serious investments" that "make us more prosperous in the long term" wins the public argument by 51 to 42 percent—and those margins have been growing going into this period of debate about the economy and debt.

The citizenry is ready for serious reform and serious investment and measures that address how to raise incomes going forward. Simply continuing where we started before the recovery will not get us on a trajectory that breaks the pattern that has left the middle class in trouble after three decades.

Right after the election, we tested some bold policy ideas from Jacob Hacker and Lawrence Mishel, and they show a country ready for a very different policy agenda that can shift the prospects for the middle class.

- Clean up lobbyists, and prevent government staff from cashing in on their connections to the private sector by closing the revolving door between the government and lobbying firms (81 percent favor, 68 percent strongly favor).
- Strengthen Medicare by controlling health-care costs, putting in place new budget goals, and cutting waste on payments to providers, not cutting benefits to beneficiaries (78 percent favor, 51 percent strongly favor).

- Raise the top tax bracket to 40 percent for those with incomes over $1 million, which would fix inequality in the tax code, help pay down the deficit, and strengthen the safety net for the middle class (64 percent favor, 49 percent strongly favor).

- Put limits on corporate executive pay and encourage pay for performance through increased transparency and disclosure requirements, so that CEO compensation more closely aligns with the long-term interests of the company and not short-term profit motives (67 percent favor, 48 percent strongly favor).

- Raise the minimum wage to ensure everyone can make a living wage (69 percent favor, 47 percent strongly favor).

- Provide $55 billion over the next three years to rehire teachers and modernize schools (65 percent favor, 43 percent strongly favor).

The election mandate was about the middle class, but we are only now beginning to raise the policy options that can really get us out of the three-decade trajectory.

James And what about climate change? Is it still the case that it doesn't exist? Is it not a threat to the middle class?

Stan It's a threat to the globe, it's a threat to the people, it's a threat to the country. We've got to do something about it. If I am looking at the president this year in terms of what he does, I think climate has got to be part of what he does on energy, part of what he does with infrastructure. It's got to become a new consciousness that we recognize is happening and begin to address in everything we do.

James Stan, watch the polls. With extreme weather year after year, there is a growing conviction that this is real and damaging. No one who lived through Hurricane Sandy, nor anyone who lived through Katrina, is going to have to be persuaded of that. If you think this stuff is going to stop, that the next four years won't look like the past three years in terms of climate events, you're probably okay. But I think Sandy changed some attitudes. We're getting once-a-century events every few years now, and soon they may well be annual occurrences.

The more I know about this stuff, the utterly more frightening it is. I mean, the case that it's happening is indisputable. And the case for the reason that greenhouse gases are the cause of it is very compelling. Not only is it compelling, there isn't another good theory.

The middle class is the heart of our country, and it is not rhetoric to say our future depends on our getting the job done for all those hardworking people, like our parents and families who invested everything in us. We worked valiantly to make the middle-class agenda number one and the mandate, but as we know all too well from President Clinton and every president since, you will certainly be surprised by big things that take over. Your mandate sometimes fades from view as we seek to grapple with ever-changing issues. George Bush never figured on 9/11.

Who expected the "October surprise" of Hurricane Sandy? That is why James raised climate change as part of the mandate. Our leaders will have to consider new kinds of investment and new ways to budget our extreme weather, which, as he knows all too well from New Orleans, seems to go out of its way to hit hardworking people and the poorest the hardest. Just look at New Jersey and New York.

But in the end, we do not think the future of the middle class can be pushed off the agenda. They are now the future and too many candidates have been elected saying they will roll up their sleeves and work for them. Our attempt to succeed as a country in an ever more globalized world is not going to fall off the agenda either, and America cannot lead in fact and by example with a hollowed-out middle class. That's not the American way.

That is why we wrote this book and why the political and policy agenda is even more important now.

IT'S THE MIDDLE CLASS, STUPID!

1.

WE ARE WRITING THIS BOOK BECAUSE WE FAILED AND THAT'S NOT GOOD ENOUGH

There's no other way to put it. We failed. It is as simple as that. Both of us have spent our lives focused on what's happening with working people and seeing them get a fair shake for a hard day's work—seeing them get the chance to move up the ladder and be honored. We put the middle class at the center of the world, because you can't have an America without a middle class.

Well, we failed, and we have got to do better, and that's why we are writing this book.

You need to understand the Democratic Party and why people have been drawn to it over many decades and through so much of our history. Some joined because it was the party of working people that would stand up for the little guy against the big shots. Some joined because it was the party that stood up for the poor. Some because it was the party of rights for women, Latinos, immigrants, gays and lesbians, each in their time—the party tolerant of the country's growing diversity. Some joined because it was more supportive of abortion. Some because of the environment and climate change. Some because of spending on the arts or whatever.

Those are all good and important reasons to embrace the Democratic Party, but they are not what has animated us through all the years of struggle. Our passion for Democratic politics began with race and racial equality. That shaped us like no other issue and upended the political world like no other. But, like Robert Kennedy, we quickly came to believe that our party would only succeed and have purpose if we put work, work values, and hardworking people of whatever color at the center of our efforts. Given our country's history, that might take a lifetime.

The two of us could not be more different. James is tall and bald. Stan is a short guy who had a 'fro. And you could not have constructed more divergent personal journeys to our common passion. Stan grew up in working-class big-city neighborhoods and galloped through Harvard and Yale before putting his spotlight on the Reagan Democrats, the disaffected working class that felt betrayed by the Democratic Party. James grew up in small-town Cajun Louisiana, joined the Marines, and barely got passing grades in law school before he started running and winning campaigns. Both of us became convinced that Bill Clinton was the extraordinary politician who was trusted by African American voters and instinctively understood he had to honor and win over the "forgotten middle class" to lead the country.

James   I grew up in Carville, Louisiana, in Iberville Parish, sixty-five miles north of New Orleans. Carville was barely a blip on the map back then, and the only thing that stopped folks passing straight through was the stop sign in the middle of town.

Carville was named after my paternal grandfather, who was accorded that honor because he was the postmaster, one of the three generations of our family to hold that position. He also owned a country store, which was a big deal in a place like Carville. The store and the post office were adjacent. I remember in my daddy's time when he ran the store, if you wanted to buy a three-cent stamp, which was what a first-class stamp cost for most of the fifties (it went up to four cents in 1959), my dad would say, "Fine, here's your stamp." Then if you wanted a loaf of bread and a quart of milk, he'd walk you next door and sell you that. My momma, Miss Nippy, worked selling encyclopedias door-to-door. They were hardworking people.

My dad reckoned up two tills each night, one in the store and one in the post office. I think Washington got what was coming to it and the Carville kids got the rest. Mom and Dad could never make a lot of money when they had eight kids going in and out of the store: we pretty much ate up everything they had. I helped myself to a lot more soft drinks, candy, cookies, and sandwiches than I did stamps. I didn't have much use for those.

It's my guess that Carville was about 85 percent black, and for the first ten years of my life it was segregated. Whites and blacks went about their business separately. It might have been hard for an outsider to figure that Carville was divided along racial lines, because there weren't actually any amenities to segregate. My father, Chester, employed a black man in his store—something you never saw in the South—and we never used racial slurs in my family on instruction from my parents.

Because the biggest employer around was the federal government—the National Leprosarium in town was the nation's premier center for the treatment of Hansen's disease—Carville was a different kind of place, and it's safe to say I grew up in one of the more egalitarian places in the rural South, which might not be saying much.

But after the Supreme Court ruled in the landmark *Brown v. Board of Education* case in 1954, everything changed. Once segregation was declared unconstitutional, people paid more attention to what had been the norm around town for many years. After taking segregation for granted for generations, whites became fearful of what a newly empowered black minority might mean, because we knew that black people were going to assert their constitutional rights. Perhaps the prevailing sentiment was that if blacks weren't so pushy, life would continue as it had before.

Few times in life can you pick out an experience that forced you to alter an opinion you held. I can identify one right here. When I was sixteen I borrowed a copy of *To Kill a Mockingbird* from the mobile library. I'd asked for a book about football but I guess the lady could tell I needed some educating. I got so engrossed in Harper Lee's classic that I stuck it inside a different cover and read it under my desk during lessons at school. When I finished, I realized that whatever preconceptions I had about race, I was wrong—dead wrong.

My great-grandfather was born in Ireland; he came over to Wisconsin when he was twelve years old and he was in a regiment at the end of the Civil War. As a Republican in the era of Reconstruction in the South, he was with the good guys; Lincoln, the Great Emancipator himself, was of course a Republican. My great-grandfather actually served in the Louisiana legislature and in the very short administration of P. B. S. Pinchback (1872–73), the first African American governor of any state.

The Republican inclinations of the family at that time have left a legacy that lives on in me. Don't be alarmed, my Democrat friends: that legacy is just my name. My daddy's name was Chester and my actual name is Chester James Carville. We were both named in honor of Chester A. Arthur, the twenty-first president of the United States—and a Republican—who assumed office in 1881 after the assassination of President Garfield. Presidential names are a Carville tradition. In my great-grandfather's day, people who were pro-Union tended to be very patriotic, and they would show this by naming their kids after presidents. My great-grandfather was John Madison Carville (after the fourth president) and his brother was Garfield (after number twenty, the assassinated one, and another Republican).

By the time I was growing up, Democrats and Republicans were standing for very different principles, and I could see which side was going to represent me. I understood from reading *To Kill a Mockingbird* that things had to change and I knew that the federal government had to make things change. It wasn't as if Congress could pass a law in Washington and segregation would simply wither away. There were riots when James Meredith tried to enroll at the University of Mississippi in 1962 and it took five hundred U.S. marshals and a detachment of Army engineers to allow this brave pioneer to take his rightful place at school. My already existing interest in politics had a point on which to focus, and my views have remained the same ever since.

My understanding that black people were getting a bad deal ensured that I became a national Democrat because of the party's commitment to civil rights. I helped organize the first chapter of college Democrats at Southern University, the historically black university in Baton Rouge. A group of us went up there to help students start their chapter in 1964 when I was at LSU and we may have been the first LSU students ever to set foot there. I campaigned for Hubert Humphrey when he passed through our mutual alma mater in 1964 and I still have a letter he wrote me at the time.

In 1966, ahead of being drafted, I joined the U.S. Marines. Whenever there's a war, the Carvilles join up; that's just what we do. Serving in the Corps was very formative. The military doesn't tolerate any racial BS and there wasn't any institutional segregation, although the white guys hung out with the white guys and the black guys hung out with the black guys, by and large. I was in the Corps through 1968. When I left the Corps, integration was moving forward, especially in the schools, and I wanted to be a part of the deal. So I taught science, about which I knew little, at a public school for boys in Vacherie, Louisiana, in 1969, which was the first year of complete integration in the state. The ratio of white students to black students at the school was maybe 60:40.

I developed a fascination for the machinery of politics from what I saw at the Louisiana state legislature, in Baton Rouge. I had a summer job running checks around town for a local bank, and it was a treat to get assigned a delivery to the legislature, which was part theater and part circus. I'd watch a session for a few minutes from the gallery, and one time I saw Governor Earl Long marching down the halls, trailing cops and reporters and functionaries behind him like he was the most important man in the world. It was the coolest thing I'd seen in my life.

To this day, Earl Long remains one of my great American political heroes. Earl was governor three times, elected in 1939, 1948, and 1956; the last of these terms coincided with my teenage years, and the rebel in me liked his iconoclasm. In Louisiana, you were in one of two camps with regard to Earl and his brother Huey, who'd died in 1935: while my family was against Earl Long, I appreciated his sense of humor and his cleverness. Earl's every instinct was populist, and he distrusted corporate power with every bone in his body. That point of view appealed to this young man.

In 1959, William Shawn, the editor of the *New Yorker*, sent the great reporter A. J. Liebling down to Baton Rouge to write about Earl because the governor had been committed to a mental hospital. Among the issues politicians had with Earl was that he was insufficiently dogmatic on the question of segregation. About an hour after arriving in Louisiana, Liebling proclaimed that in fact the only sane person in the state was the governor and that everyone else was nuts.

Liebling wrote five pieces about Earl for the *New Yorker*, and they were published in book form as *The Earl of Louisiana* in 1961, after Earl had died. That book had a profound effect on me. Earl's story unfolds before your eyes, and it's like a Greek tragedy. His political demise was largely centered on race. Liebling writes a wonderful account of Earl having a set-to in the legislature with a really odious character named William Rainach, who Earl called "pinhead Willie." Rainach was blatantly removing blacks from voter rolls, and Earl called him on it. Earl was very drunk at the time, but he told Rainach that one day, when he'd gone back to where he came from, he'd sit out on his porch and look up to God. "And when you *do*," Earl yelled, "you got to recognize that *n*———*s* is human beings." Despite the crassness of the language, and Earl's mental state, Liebling wrote that Long was protecting black voters' rights in a way no other southern politician of the time would have dared to do.

My political career started that same year I saw Earl Long in the flesh: 1959. Using my newly minted driver's license, I motored around Iberville Parish, stumping for a state legislature candidate named Price LeBlanc. Not for the last time, the guy I campaigned for lost the race. I lost a lot more races once I finally graduated from

LSU undergraduate and law school and went to work in the law. I helped a guy at my law firm run for the public service commission, but he lost. I campaigned for a woman running for judge in Baton Rouge, and for E. L. "Bubba" Henry, who ran for governor of Louisiana in 1979, but they lost too.

My lack of success (if that's the word) didn't deter me from jumping out of the law in 1980 and going to work for the political consulting firm of Gus Weill and Raymond Strother. I assisted on the campaign of Billy Tauzin, who was elected to the U.S. House of Representatives in 1980, and was campaign manager for Baton Rouge mayor Pat Screen, whose office I went to work in. But I realized what I really wanted to do was run political campaigns, and in 1982 I told myself I was either going crazy, going to jail, or going out of town. Option three looked a little more attractive than the others, so I left. Peter Hart and Mark Shields, two well-known Washingtonians, got me a job running the 1982 Senate campaign of Virginia lieutenant governor Richard Davis, which we lost by only a few thousand votes.

By now I was nearing forty and hungry for success. I was hungry, period. I was out of work and I got a job managing the Senate campaign of Texas state senator Lloyd Doggett. We won the primary, won the runoff, and got slaughtered by Phil Gramm in the general election.

Then I was out of work again, and getting desperate, when I was hired by Bob Casey Sr.'s 1986 campaign for Pennsylvania governor against Bill Scranton; it would be my first big come-from-behind win. I ran Casey's campaign with Paul Begala, and I think it was during this gubernatorial race that my liberalism underwent a major shift toward economic issues. It was a kind of turning point. Casey was pro-life and socially conservative, but he was a strong union supporter and very liberal economically. Casey sympathized with the people in Pennsylvania who were losing their jobs in the steel industry, and he had a very detailed plan to put people back to work.

Casey had already stood for governor three times and lost, and Scranton was saying that the state of Pennsylvania needed a winner, not this guy who'd lost three times. To which Casey said that he knew what it was like to get knocked down and get back up off the canvas: the view from down there could teach a man a lot. There were plenty of people in western Pennsylvania who were on the floor but were showing great courage and determination in trying to get up. Casey wasn't the most articulate guy, but he really connected with people with that.

Another campaign that shifted in my focus was Harris Wofford's special Senate election victory over Dick Thornburgh following John Heinz's death in 1991. Wofford was a very soft-spoken guy who told us about meeting an ophthalmologist from suburban Philadelphia who said, "You know, I want to tell you this: If a criminal has a right to a lawyer, why doesn't a working person have a right to health care?" Boom: we ran that right into the Senate, and that's when I got a call from Bill Clinton.

Stan Until I got to high school and moved to the suburbs, my family lived in a series of small row houses, first in Philadelphia and then, from the time I was age five, in Washington, D.C. My father worked on the line at Westinghouse, then started and lost two small retail shops before convincing the American Instrument Company in the D.C. area to take a chance on this self-taught engineer. While he took a lot of night classes, he didn't go to college and get a degree, because his father used all the family money to bring Jews from Russia to escape Hitler's reach. He brought our own family members whenever possible but he also assisted many others who appealed to him for help. My father resented that choice and never made very much money, but he was intense and smart, worked hard, was a whiz at mathematics, invented many things, and became well-known in environmental sciences. He invented the first germproof cabinet and the device that measures the toxicity of materials on airplanes.

But for all that, he really put his energy into pushing and following his kids, whether he was filming my brother playing quarterback on his school team, or interrogating my teachers about why I had gotten an F in civics or why I wasn't taking calculus. Along with a close band of young families, he founded and built the synagogue directly across the street from where we would live. He became the president for many terms, and my mother, who was a bookkeeper, served as president of the sisterhood. I accompanied my father to New York when he interviewed candidates for rabbi, and learned pretty quickly that people think they know as much as religious authorities about what is true or false, right or wrong.

We rented a house in an all-black neighborhood in Washington—the "'hood" of our day—right by the Tivoli Theater and just up Georgia Avenue from Howard University. Back then, I never set foot in the more affluent areas of the city that I now inhabit. I am sure this was all my parents could afford, but it was also walking distance from an Orthodox synagogue—a necessity for my grandparents, who lived with us.

These formative years were dominated by race and desegregation. Washington was a very southern city, and segregated; that included the schools. It is hard to believe now, but whenever I visited my relatives in Philadelphia or New York City, they mocked my southern accent. I went to an all-white school across the alley from our house, but the black kids went to another, Barnard Elementary School, farther away. All my friends were black. I don't have any recollection of white kids until we moved to a mostly working-class white and Jewish neighborhood when I was in the third grade. But when the U.S. Supreme Court ruled that Washington's school segregation was unconstitutional, I was bused to the school that my black friends had been attending—and they protected me. I was also short and very fast. "Busing" was a term of art. They literally picked up two sixth-grade classes with all the white pupils and moved them intact to the black school. Previously, I had walked to school, but now I had to take two city buses to get there. I remember at the time dancing with the only black girl in the class when I saw she was sitting alone, and collecting the money from the other pupils to buy our black teacher, Ms. Dillard, a clock radio as an end-of-year gift and wondering why she was crying so hard.

My parents and everybody else I knew was a Democrat, but I don't remember politics ever being discussed. We mostly argued about my brother or me dating a *shiksa*, a non-Jewish girl, or whether I would finally start reading books. My mother would give me a dollar every time I read a book, but when I started devouring them, my mother paid for every other book; when I got to college, all my book bills went directly to them. I never hung out with the smart kids until my senior year, and never considered going anywhere but to a state school.

My parents never volunteered in a political campaign; it was enough just to vote. I was conscious of a few Communists in one strand of the family, but my father kept us out of their Jewish youth groups, given his concerns about keeping his security clearance during the McCarthy era.

The summer before I went away to college, I worked in a factory owned by the company where my father was employed. It was in rural Maryland, and virtually all the workers were from West Virginia—except for the blacks, who worked only in the shipping department. I volunteered every evening after work at the NAACP office on U Street and helped organize the March on Washington, which I watched from the organizing tent on the mall. But these were hot times at work, and I stayed inside with the black workers when the whites went out to Route 1 to jeer at the marchers coming down from New York.

By the time I arrived at Miami University in Oxford, Ohio, I was ready to take off: I became active in the Young Democrats, wrote a weekly column for the paper, and organized a speakers program called Voices of Dissent that brought the head of the Communist Party and the publisher of the *National Review* to campus. The latter offered to help when some state legislators and the alumni association tried to stop it. I headed up a movement to overturn the rules that allowed men later hours in the dorms and barred women from living off campus. Seeking to overturn the university's legal principle of acting in loco parentis, I had stickers printed, "One Man, One Mother."

I was consumed with studying government. In the summer, I worked in the War on Poverty VISTA office in D.C. and did volunteer work at the Young Democrats—and wound up going to the Democratic National Convention and dating the best friend of Lucy Johnson, which got me into the family quarters of the White House. I later told President Clinton about making out in the solarium where we were meeting. But by 1965 I was picketing the White House to protest the Vietnam War. For all the upheaval and tragedy, we were fortunate to be shaped by such times.

I went to Harvard for my PhD and, after three years, went to teach at Yale. I joined the Harvard strike and class boycott over Vietnam, but mostly I put my efforts into helping Robert Kennedy's campaign by developing a computer program with fellow students to determine where a visit by the candidate would have the biggest impact, particularly in the white Catholic areas of Indiana, Wisconsin, Oregon, and California. Many more of my fellow students backed Senator Eugene McCarthy ("Get Clean for Gene"), the first presidential candidate to break on the war and win the campuses and affluent suburbs. That was the defining choice of my generation of emerging activists. Bill Clinton, too, backed Robert Kennedy, who was adored by black Americans and whose call for greater personal responsibility enabled him to win in the Catholic neighborhoods as well. I was not very conscious of it at the time, but that cross appeal is what drew me to him.

During my time at Harvard, I ran a one-hundred-city study for the War on Poverty on poor people's attitudes, ultimately focusing on five neighborhoods: three black ones in Atlanta, Philadelphia, and Detroit; a Latino one in San Jose; and a poor white one in Hamilton, Ohio. My dissertation started as a series of surveys, but for my first book, *Politics and Poverty*, I went to live in these cities and conducted in-depth, in-person interviews to reveal more of the texture of people's thinking. I had learned a lot from James Q. Wilson, my dissertation adviser at Harvard, about understanding urban life and the seriousness of crime, and from Robert Dahl and Bob Lane, my colleagues at Yale, who had written classic works after observing New Haven's ethnic politics and conducting in-depth interviews to understand working-class thinking. I read avidly the work of Antonio Gramsci, the Italian Communist, who wrote about the durability of capitalist countries, primarily because of "hegemonic ideas" that win the support of key elements of the working class.

I taught a course at Yale with John Wilhelm on organizing city neighborhoods. John would organize Yale's employees and head the national hotel and restaurant workers' union. In fact, he commandeered the phones that I had installed in the basement of our house for polling to canvass employees and win the union recognition election at Yale. As a result, I was hardly the administration's favorite professor. I organized a work-study program at Yale with Mayor Charles Evers, the first black mayor of Fayette, Mississippi, and supervised our work-study students there: I would rent a car and drive to Natchez and other towns that figured in our civil rights history.

I also was recruited by Rosa DeLauro to help with polling and the get-out-the-vote effort for the local reform candidate for mayor— who, to everyone's surprise, defeated the party machine's candidate. We would marry after a few years—my second marriage, during which I would learn about the real America. Rosa's family was from Wooster Square, the heart of New Haven's Italian American community, where her father and mother had served as ward chair and members of the board of aldermen. Rosa would ultimately be elected to Congress. They all taught me a thing or two about the centrality of hard work and putting everything into seeing your kids get up that ladder.

My opus as an academic was *Race and State in Capitalist Development*—the inelegantly titled book that took me to Alabama, South Africa, Israel, and Northern Ireland. I wrote about how emerging business organizations, unions, and commercial farmers used ethnic divisions to protect their interests—contrary to conventional wisdom that economic growth breaks down barriers and promotes integration. What I really got hooked on were my interviews with white trade unionists in the steel and mining industry in Alabama; mostly Afrikaans-speaking union leaders across the gold mining, auto, and textile sectors in South Africa; and Jewish leaders of Histadrut, the general workers' union in Israel. Some were full of animosity for other groups, but mostly they were not; in any case, you did not need ethnic or racial animus to understand the choices they were making. I identified with the Histadrut's call for "100 percent Jewish labor" on the kibbutzim and moshavim to allow Jewish emigration to Israel and to teach Jews to respect labor. But mostly what I learned was to push away preconceptions and prejudices and listen to people, particularly working people, who everywhere struggle to survive and get any leg up that they can.

Chris Dodd foolishly decided to exploit my emerging talents in his first race for the U.S. Senate, as did Bob Carr to win back his Michigan congressional seat. There, the United Auto Workers and the state Democratic Party asked me to figure out why they got slaughtered in the Catholic, middle-class, and UAW-dominated suburban of Macomb County, which had given John Kennedy his biggest margin in any suburb. I called these defectors "Reagan Democrats" and it stuck, because I reflected their cry of frustration and pointed a path back. After hearing the moderator read a quote from Robert Kennedy about equal opportunity, these disaffected workers shouted: "That's bullshit. No wonder they killed him." They had voted for Reagan and Wallace not because they had shifted their own thinking but because they believed the Democratic Party had betrayed them. They wanted to know when the Democrats would be for the middle class again.

The Democratic Party in Washington scorned my work. With worries of another Jesse Jackson candidacy for president, the chairman of the Democratic National Committee declared me persona non grata, but not the Democratic Leadership Council, which had been founded by southern and moderate politicians, and not the National Education Association, which was then at the periphery of the union movement. Joe Lieberman paid attention when he surprised everybody and defeated Lowell Weicker for the U.S. Senate, carrying working-class towns that national Democrats had been losing.

And so did Bill Clinton, who told people he read my article on reaching Reagan Democrats three times. In his announcement speech in front of the Old State House in Little Rock, Arkansas, he declared, "This is not just a campaign for the presidency—it is a campaign for the future, for the forgotten middle-class families of America who deserve a government that fights for them."

So that is where James Carville and I met and started working together, talking every day, yet apparently for naught. With the middle class now on life support, we clearly have both failed. Well, they can't settle for that, after years of hard work, and neither can we. That's why we're writing this book.

2.

WHO'S MIDDLE CLASS AFTER ALL?

James We know it can be a complicated issue and not everyone fits in a neat statistical box. It's not such a common feature of middle-class life to grow up in a town named after one of your ancestors and be named after a president, and the truth of the matter is, relative to the rest of the town, I had it better than most everybody.

The family kept one car. We had a nice home with four bedrooms and two bathrooms, but because there were so many of us, we had to double up to sleep (or, in my case, triple up, as I shared a room with two of my brothers). By today's standards, we were of very moderate means, but compared to the rest of the town we were almost affluent. In rural south Louisiana circa 1960, we had two bathrooms when a lot of people had none.

I came into the world on a U.S. Army base, at Fort Benning, Georgia, because my dad was stationed there in the infantry. Later, as the postmaster, he was a government employee. I never remember thinking that Daddy was earning a superior living when he went from running the public-sector post office to running the private-sector small store, or a diminished living when he went back to the public sector. For the life of me, I don't understand why the labor of the policeman, the soldier, the park ranger, or the street cleaner is any less sacred than that of the person who owns the dry cleaner or the hash house or anything else, but that's just me.

At the time, because I had gotten out of the Marine Corps, I was benefiting from the G.I. Bill, which paid me a check for $300 a month—not bad pocket change to be carrying around. In addition, I had a part-time government position working for the district attorney where I would answer calls on a tip line people used to phone in information on crimes they knew about. In the summers I had a very good job in the private sector working on a dredge boat. One summer we worked the Mississippi River, shifting silt and keeping the shipping channels open; another summer we rebuilt part of a public beach between Pompano Beach and Ft. Lauderdale in Florida.

Before I started practicing law in Baton Rouge, I did my stint teaching eighth-grade science at the school in Vacherie, which completes my story through my time in the legal profession. Eventually I started working on political campaigns and ended up where I am today.

It never struck me at the time that I was earning an inferior living by being a deckhand on a dredge boat that had a government contract. The beach we worked on in Florida was public: anybody could go on it. You could be poor, middle-class, or rich, and I guess I should have realized it was nothing but a lot of shiftless people sitting out there on the beach. The state could have charged them a fee, because they were sucking on one version of the government sugar tit, as we were building up a beach for their recreation on the government's dime. The work I did on the Mississippi River was nobler, because we were making sure goods could move freely around the country. As I've grown older, I've found out that it's just a little more complicated than that. In the world as understood by right-wing television and talk radio, I was probably a more honorable person then, even if I was still middle-class.

Stan If you had asked me "What are you?" when I was growing up, I would have told you I was Jewish and belonged to Shaare Tefila, the synagogue, meaning we were not Orthodox, where a barrier separated men and women? I was from my neighborhood in Riggs Park and later Silver Spring, meaning I went to Paul for junior high and Montgomery Blair for high school—and very self-consciously: not Wilson or BCC, where the richer kids went at the time. As I got older, I was conscious and a little in awe of friends' big stand-alone houses where kids didn't all sleep in the same room. My father was a professional in a low-paying position, earning $10,000 when he started and only $20,000 when he retired. My mother always worked as a bookkeeper and insisted that I take two years of typing and shorthand, so I could always get a job. My brother and I were the first in our family and neighborhood as far as I knew who went to college, but it was a given that we would and that we would become doctors or lawyers and marry Jewish, which was the consuming identity issue in our family.

My friends' fathers were making their way as a kind of petit bourgeoisie and aspiring middle class: one was a dental technician making false teeth; a number had small businesses; one had a shoe store on Georgia Avenue in the black neighborhood and owned a piece of land near Griffith Stadium where the Senators and Redskins played. At some point I worked under age and under the table at each of those places. My next-door neighbor who was Italian and one of my best friends was Johnny Boccabella, who went to Catholic schools and, later, we assumed was the John Boccabella who signed with the Chicago Cubs and played catcher. I was in *Bye Bye Birdie* and *Li'l Abner* with Goldie Hawn in high school and we double dated, but I remember how we all thought she had made a bad life choice when she went to Broadway to be a dancer rather than going to college.

My parents—who worked really hard to own a house with a very small yard and, despite that, were deeply involved in our lives—had a presumption that we would work hard and excel at school, that we would go to college and join a profession and do well by some un-stated standard, and that we would raise Jewish children who would do the same.

So, were we middle-class? I presume we were, but I dare you to take any simple measure to that conclusion. My father worked on the line at Westinghouse and owned two failed small retail stores along the way, while my mother retired as a bookkeeper, and I worked various jobs from a young age: as a parking attendant, as a sales clerk, and as a factory worker. We never had any money, but my parents retired with more money in the bank than I had for a very long time.

Almost 58 percent of Americans in the middle of this prolonged economic crash call themselves middle-class.[1] Think of that: In what other country would that be true?

The number who says they are "poor" is at 7 percent, double what it was almost a decade ago—which is about half of the number who are actually poor (as defined by the government, based on income). A solid and unchanging quarter of the country says they are "working-class." The middle comprises at its core the

39 percent who say they are simply "middle-class" and 9 percent who are "lower-middle-class." The "upper-middle class" stands at 11 percent—and likely stands together attitudinally and politically with the self-reported rich. They apparently took a big hit, as they are half the size of what was reported in polls in 2002. Two percent of Americans say they are "wealthy"—unchanged and double the 1 percent that we know really runs the country.

However you cut the pie, half the country calls itself middle-class and three-quarters of the country are made up of the working class and the middle class combined. We embrace the larger number, because Americans themselves embrace the identity up and down the class ladder, however you define it. Half the country hasn't finished a four-year college degree. That includes people who dropped out of high school, high school graduates, people who have gone to a tech-

Three-quarters middle and working class

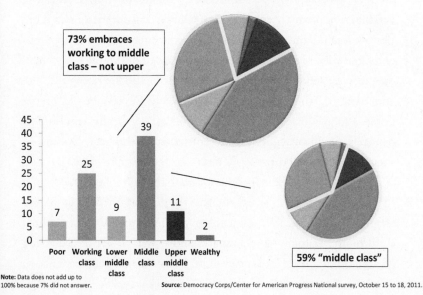

73% embraces working to middle class – not upper

59% "middle class"

Note: Data does not add up to 100% because 7% did not answer.

Source: Democracy Corps/Center for American Progress National survey, October 15 to 18, 2011.

nical school to learn e-commerce or to be a mechanic, or finished the program at the New Orleans Culinary Institute or the nursing program at a junior college, like Gateway Community College in New Haven. Yet, more of those people call themselves middle-class than working-class.

Four in ten of those earning under $20,000, who could hardly afford anything like what we associate with a middle-class life, described themselves as middle-class.[2]

If you ask us what incomes qualify you to be middle-class, we look at a broad range: essentially, anybody earning under $125,000. That describes around three-quarters of the electorate, or even more. We do not even ask about income in our own Democracy Corps polls or use it as a way to separate out voters because it is subject to so many other factors, like age, how many people live in the house, whether one gets income from interest and dividends or salary, whether you are in debt and have a mortgage, and whether you are retired or still getting a paycheck. A widowed retiree receiving $30,000 who owns her condo near Tampa will face issues that are very different from those facing a single woman with that same income but with two children and a mortgage and who lives anywhere on the West Coast. The poverty level nationally for her is $17,300, and Bank of America has probably already forced her out of her home. Our widow with Medicare covering her health care bills is probably doing okay. So we use education as the best measure of social class and standing.

When we do focus on income, we go to the midpoint or median—the income level that has exactly half the country earning more and 50 percent earning less. That takes you to $50,000. If you take a third of the households below and above that to get at America's great middle, you are looking at a middle income range from $28,636 to $79,040.[3] But the kind of family it is matters a lot. The median income today for one-parent families with two children is $25,200.

That gets your attention. For two-parent families with two children, the median income is $80,600.[4] If you live in a place like Vacherie, Louisiana, with dirt-low housing prices, low utilities bills, and low taxes, the median income looks very low by national standards; but if you live anywhere near a big city in California, the median will be dramatically higher.

But we tend to trust the voters on this kind of thing. If they earn less than $30,000, they estimate that it takes about $50,000 to earn a "middle-class lifestyle in their area"; but if they earn between $100,000 and $150,000, they think they will need around $80,000.[5] People are pretty smart.

So there are families somewhere in the country who earn as little as $30,000 and as much as $125,000 who qualify to join our not-very-exclusive club of middle-income earners. But then again, if you are a newly arrived Dominican immigrant working legally at a retail job in New York City, your median pay is $9.50 an hour, and most places don't offer you health insurance or paid sick leave, and you may well be working a second job. You are not even close to living above the poverty level, so we say: Screw it. You're in our middle class. Since we hope our policies will benefit the poor, the working class, and the great middle, we take in fully three-quarters of the country.

James and I have had this unbelievable window into what's happened to the middle class—a decade of intense discussions and monthly national surveys conducted by Democracy Corps, an organization we created but that is only sustainable because of some unique supporters, like Steve Bing. With Democracy Corps, we are continuously educated by everyday people.

When we interviewed young people, Latinos, and folks without a four-year college degree over the last few years, they underscored how tough it is in this world and how ambiguous are all these distinctions and lines as people struggle to stay afloat and stay at the same economic level as their parents or neighbors. Their eloquent statements below about being middle-class tell us a lot more than the numbers.

> "I used to think of myself as middle-class but I would say that now I'm more struggling middle-class—closer to a lower end. . . . I think that's different now just for the fact that I haven't had a raise in about three years, so the price of living has gone up but my salary has not gone up. I haven't been able to invest as much as I wanted to. I have lost money in the market more than anything. So now it's more like save, save, save, because you never know when you're not going to have a job anymore."—Woman, Latino, age 30, non-college-educated

> "I mean, I think one big quality that kind of needs to be looked at is where people live, because . . . considering where I live, it's, like, if I lived somewhere cheaper I would probably actually be middle-class. Like, I made $37,000 last year, so that's not too bad, but I mean, considering where I live, like, I'm pretty poor; I'm probably, like, the lower class."—Woman, Latino, age 25, non-college-educated

> "I like to think of myself as middle-class only because I grew up in a middle-class neighborhood here in Illinois. Both of my parents worked and between the two of them they made over $70,000 a year, which back then would be considered middle-class or upper-middle-class. Nowadays I don't know what that would be construed as. But

even though I don't make the type of income that one would need to make to be considered middle-class, I still think of myself as that. . . ."—Woman, white, age 40, non-college-educated

"Right now I'm working-class. I used to be middle-class."—Man, white, 45, non-college-educated

"Middle-class, just because neither of my parents have blue-collar jobs. They both have white-collar jobs."—Woman, white, age 25, non-college-educated

"Well, I kind of think of those two as the same, but definitely working-class. I couldn't not work and, you know, I'm kind of lower than mid-dle-[class], but I live in a decent neighborhood and, you know, pay my bills. And I feel that I'm pretty similar to most of the people out there and maybe better off than a lot, so I'm definitely right in the working middle class. . . ."—Woman, white, age 45, non-college-educated

"You know that everybody that's poor wants to be middle-class and people that are middle-class, maybe we used to aspire to be rich, but today we're aspiring just to hold on and make sure our kids are there too."—Man, white, non-college-educated

"I consider myself the lucky class. I've got a healthy family, I'm breathing. . . ."—Man, Latino, age 25, non-college-educated

President Obama ran for office on a platform that included cut-ting middle-class taxes—any household earning less than $250,000, or 95 percent of the households—and voters heard that: "I can see him caring about the middle class. . . . Like, all his policies sort of resonate with the average person, making the average person's life better." We can live with that $250,000 limit because after the accelerating inequality of the last few decades, that's where the money is.

To get into the top 1 percent, you need to earn at least $385,000 a year, and the median is $1.5 million. One of the 1 percenters told *New York Times* reporters that, with property values and taxes so high in Nassau County, Long Island, and other such places, "it is barely a living." Although such 1-percenters may well think of themselves as part of the middle class, our guess is that the reporter didn't get to talk to a lot of those folks, who are more guarded: as one person commented, "It's not very popular to be in the 1 percent these days, is it?"[6]

The reason we don't dwell very much on these distinctions is that we have always accepted that being middle-class is an identity, a way of life, an idea and aspiration and set of values—and something uniquely American, shaped by our half century of post–New Deal and post–World War II history. It should be pretty clear by now that we think being middle-class starts with hard work and a sense of responsibility, family, and an unbelievable commitment to making sure the kids get along and rise up the ladder. It starts with the belief that, in America, the middle class formed the heart and soul of the country and prospered as the country prospered and saw each generation do better. This was America's formula in the time of our parents and families. While I am sure that there was always a sense that society rewarded the wrong values and didn't appreciate the hard work of the great middle, that grievance has become consuming as our country has taken some wrong turns.

What's missing in all the numbers is the pain and anguish of the middle class. They are deeply troubled by what they see happening— to themselves and the country—and we intend to give them a voice.

3.

THE MIDDLE CLASS: ISN'T IT THE ENGINE OF AMERICA?

Over the last several years, our conversations with people across the country have revealed some interesting things about what it means to be middle-class in America at this moment. At the core of working- and middle-class identity right now is the idea that those in the middle "really have to work hard" for what they get: they exist from paycheck to paycheck, without any cushion against an emergency. Many feel like they are slipping lower economically, that they don't have a lot of help, and that they are just trying to hold on to their middle-class identity. Some have just enough to "breathe," to eat out sometimes, and to build up a nest egg—but it is a losing battle. The people we talked to told us that the middle class is the "engine of the country" and "what makes America America," yet "the middle class is disappearing," leaving America a country divided into rich and poor, the way it was in England or in some Third World countries. They aren't giving up on the American Dream, but it is being downsized and becoming harder and harder to reach, especially for their kids.

When Stan first began writing about middle-class anger and James began working to win their votes almost three decades ago, people talked about a disappearing middle class, squeezed by rich and poor just as they speak of it now, but with one stark difference: back then they complained that elites and government were rigging the game in favor of black people. Affirmative action. Welfare. Participants in Stan's first focus groups in Macomb County in 1985 were not subtle on this point. It started with the man who said he didn't get the loan because "I was an average American white guy." Another stated that when he applied for a job at one company, the personnel office told him "[The] government has come down and said that I can't have the job because they have to give it to the minorities." Another said, "I got an attitude toward business, government, and anybody in control, anybody in authority, because they shit all over me." As for getting a business loan, he quoted the banks as saying: "No go. Forget it. You just ain't the right color, pal."[1]

But for all the talk about Barack Obama and the importance of race, the subject hardly ever comes up in our interviews and groups. Occasionally, somebody brings up the illegal immigrants and the burden on schools and hospitals, but it is not a consuming issue in this context. Some lament that "I don't get my money for free" or talk about not being eligible for college aid, but their focus is their own desperate finances, not some privileged group. One young woman described how her family couldn't get financial aid because they earned more than $60,000 a year yet faced daunting rising costs, saying, "If you want to fund your child's education, then you need to eat dog food all year so you can do that."[2]

The middle class is struggling today because of declining wages, reduced benefits, and crushing costs for the essentials of life. It is the three decades of income squeeze that now drives middle-class identity. They are being screwed because the country's losing ground, not because they think some other group is screwing them—unless it's the 1 percent. But we'll get to that.

Stan When I began listening to the disaffected voters in 1985, my work was supported by the Michigan Democratic Party and the UAW. In recent years, it has been groups like Women's Voices. Women Vote, founded by Page Gardner, who supported our work of the new electorate and their struggle in these tough times. And Page was a lonely champion of the Macomb County studies.

James You're talking about 1985 and the focus being on race. I remember the Jesse Helms campaign ad from 1990. It showed a white man's hands as he crumpled up a rejection letter for a job he was best qualified for but went to a "minority" because of quotas. The voice-over said the senatorial race came down to one idea: the African American candidate Harvey Gantt was for racial quotas and Helms was against. It was scaremongering. Today, not even the most cynical win-hungry political consultant would run that ad. I think it would backfire if it was run in North Carolina.

There are plenty of qualified men, slightly older men, who have applied for many, many jobs. Try telling *them* that a black man got the job every time! What happens is that companies are going with younger, less-qualified workers because they're cheaper. The costs, especially the health care costs, are much less. If there's a fifty-year-old applying for a job and a twenty-two-year-old applying for the same job, you better believe that job is going to the twenty-two-year-old. Every second in corporate America, some fifty-year-old loses his or her job and the company hires two young people at half the cost or less. The new race is health care costs.

Stan And everything is tough. "You have to really work for your money and nothing really comes easy; it seems like everything is tough," a non-college-educated nurse in Raleigh, North Carolina, told us. "Yeah, working-class and middle-class, to be honest, I think that's the same thing."[3] One young man from Chicago said, "I've got a healthy family, I'm breathing. . . . I would have to consider myself partly middle-class [just] because . . . my job is pretty secure and I'm able to make just enough to put food on the table and pay the bills."[4]

There is a division in their minds between working-class and middle-class based on what kind of cushion you have, which has real consequences in these times. A white non-college-educated woman from Iowa put herself squarely on the working-class side: "Yeah, working-class, absolutely . . . because we basically live paycheck to paycheck, you know. If we didn't work, I mean, everything would fall apart. We don't have . . . I mean, you're supposed to have a cushion, [but] we don't have that cushion, we can't afford it and [my husband and I] both work."[5]

There is a consensus on what the other side of the line looks like for the middle class—and it's not paved with gold but characterized by having some extra cash and being able to pay your bills, put away some savings, take vacations, and go out to a nice place sometimes.

"I would think that a working-class person is somebody who most likely has a family, so they can't support the whole family on what most people are getting paid; and middle-class people, I would assume, probably have more than one income if they're a family and, if not, then they at least make enough to support themselves and have extra cash, save money, and take vacations and things that people in the middle class do."—Woman, Latino, age 25, non-college-educated

"Well, I think [middle-class people] are stable at least and they can afford it when something comes up, an emergency situation; they can probably afford it without depleting themselves. . . . I think they're a little more financially stable than the working class."—Woman, white, age 50, non-college-educated

"[If] you're middle-class, you've got a little bit to play with at the end of the month."—Man, white, age 45, non-college-educated

"I used to be middle-class and now I'm working-class. . . . I don't have any disposable income at all; everything that I have, it's in one hand and out of the other, and before it seemed like I would be able to go out to nice places and pay my bills and still have some money left."—Woman, Latino, age 50, non-college-educated

"No, we'd be working-class . . . because of the income bracket that I'm in and the fact that I don't . . . I mean, everything that I've had I've had to work hard for it, you know; I don't have any large reserve or any kind of reserve that I could just say, 'Oh, well, I've got this to fall back on' or whatever. No. I would think people in the middle class have more of that going for them than those in the working class do."—Woman, Latino, age 35, non-college-educated

"I would say the middle class are a little more comfortable where you're situated and you don't have so much stress worrying about your bills. . . . With my family, we're getting by, but it's not easy." —Woman, white, age 40, non-college-educated

Some look across that line and see their parents and that generation that has held on to being middle-class, while they themselves are sinking: "I'm definitely working-class . . . ," a non-college-educated Latino woman informed us. "I . . . live from paycheck to paycheck, definitely . . . I just . . . consider my parents more middle-class: they've got their nice little nest egg and have been able to do things like that and have that little bit of savings."[6]

And some see economic conditions around them deteriorating so badly that they think they may still be middle-class even though they've got none of the cushion or nest egg that they associate with the middle class. Because she could not get ahead of her expenses, one Latino woman called herself working-class but granted, "with everything going on, I may be middle-class."[7] A non-college-educated woman in Fox Lake, Illinois, was experiencing the same slide downward: "A lot of the middle class, with the way the economy has done over the last couple of years, have now found themselves no longer in the middle class but actually in the lower class."[8]

In our national surveys, we ask people to give a gut reaction to the term "middle-class future." Using a thermometer scale where 100 degrees means very warm and favorable and zero means very cold and negative, voters give "middle-class future" a mean temperature of 45.1 degrees—meaning many more people have negative reactions. Just over a quarter of voters at the outset of 2012 were upbeat about the middle class's future. It is interesting that most young people and African Americans were positive, undermining any simple connection between being hit hard by the crash and views about the future. With a longer perspective on income and job decline, white working-class voters had the bleakest outlooks: twice as many were negative rather than positive about where things were going for the middle class.[9]

It is not a very big leap to the new common sense: that "the middle class is disappearing," with big implications for the country. "[If] the middle class keeps disappearing, we're going to have the haves and the have-nots," a Latino woman in Sacramento observed. She used to believe "that it can't happen, and now I see it happening. I see people losing jobs. I see outsourcing jobs. [We're] losing money and the middle class keeps being hit."[10] A man in suburban Chicago got it too: "The middle class seemed to be disappearing more and more and it just tended to be going to more of a, if you want to say, two-set class." Speaking for his group, he added: "You know, this is interesting how we all say the same thing over and over again and it's such a non-sexy issue, but every one of us feels it. You know, our parents' aspirations. [What] we aspire for our kids. . . . we see this turning into England or every place else in the world that isn't America."

Because in America, the middle class "kind of makes the country, you know, the world go round."[11] Without them, "the economy in America can't function like that," a steelworker in Fox Lake, Illinois told us.[12]

> "Well, I mean, that's what made America America, is the middle class. You've got the rich and you've got the poor and there's a really huge gap. So you've got to be somewhere in the middle. . . . The middle class basically is the backbone of America: without a middle class there is no class [system] and you'll either have the super-rich and then you'll have the super-poor, and really, the economy in America can't function like that." —Man, white, age 35, non-college-educated

It is not surprising that a large majority of the public—65 percent, according to one recent survey[13]—believes the country is in decline.

That is the context—to them a rising middle class is closely associated with a rising America.

An America with a disappearing middle class might also be an America without an "American dream"—but most are not yet ready to go there; nonetheless, the dream has definitely been battered and clearly downsized. A decade ago, as the Clinton era came to an end, a stunning three-quarters of Americans said they were satisfied with "the opportunity for a person in this nation to get ahead by working hard." But before the financial crisis that dropped to two-thirds and afterward to 55 percent. This year, just half the country believes it is still true that "if you work, you'll get ahead"—a pretty muted endorsement for American opportunity.

Two-thirds think that it is harder to reach the "American dream" today than it was for their parents, and three-quarters believe it will be harder for their children and grandchildren to succeed; both figures rose sharply during the economic crisis. This has to have impacted how they think the rich got to be rich: just 43 percent say it was due to "their own hard work, ambition, or education."[14]

What is the American dream? Well, it is no longer the Horatio Alger–type rags-to-riches story; only 6 percent of Americans still hold that view, a number that, not surprisingly, is in decline. What dominates people's conceptions of the American dream right now is being able to provide a good life for their families—fully 45 percent, up 9 percentage points in a year—which reflects the struggle of working-class and middle-class people to provide and care for their loved ones. This is a point of great stress. About a third (approximately 34 percent) of those surveyed associate the well-being of their families with financial security, up 5 percentage points in a year, reflecting the genuine financial challenges facing most families. About an equal number choose freedom and opportunity.

Not that many people are able to freely choose good jobs and to

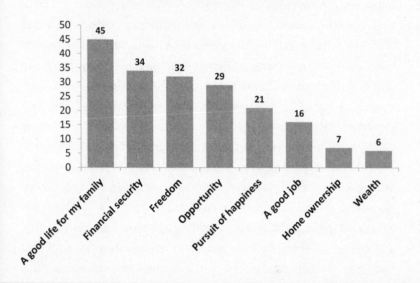

What is the American dream?

A good life for my family	45
Financial security	34
Freedom	32
Opportunity	29
Pursuit of happiness	21
A good job	16
Home ownership	7
Wealth	6

Source: From the Second Annual State of the American Dream Survey, March 5 to 15, 2011, Xavier University Center for the Study of the American Dream.

own their own homes, given how challenging both have proved in the last few years.

People are developing their own strategies to survive and find a way to do better, and their views of the American dream are a work in progress. We have conducted research over the full three years of the financial collapse, starting in 2009. In the early period, when people thought at least the recession times would come to an end soon, there was more optimism, and the American dream was for them the light at the end of the tunnel. Early on, people even saw an upside in the tough times: they began saving more, became less materialistic, and took on less debt.[15] As Obama was coming into office and before the waves of foreclosures, Stan's firm conducted research with Public Opinion Strategies for the Pew Research Center. At that time, many people mentioned that home ownership seemed to embody security, autonomy, independence, family, future wealth, and happiness. In focus group exercises in 2009, when asked to define the American dream, people wrote: "owning a home and having 2.5 kids"; "happy family, living in a nice home with a white picket fence"; "home ownership, self-employment, freedom"; and "family, home, stable income."[16] Many mentioned "freedom to pursue anything you want," "becoming something from nothing," and "opportunity to be anything you want to be." And of course more simply cited money and success: "money in the bank"; "being successful"; "money, power, respect, honesty, responsibility, travel."[17]

But with the extended period of high unemployment and income decline, the American dream became less dreamy and a lot humbler. Some still spoke of the dream as owning and providing a good home and giving their kids a college education "to give them the opportunity to get a really good job or have a business or to be successful," along with the hope that doing so "wouldn't be costing them [the respondents] every cent that they make and that they would be able to eat well and healthy and, you know, just have a nice comfortable life."[18]

"Well, the American dream just means providing for your family and not having to worry day-to-day, knowing that things are not going to be bad, obviously, and just being enough to provide for your family, enough to get a vacation and, you know, have a car and . . . [not] have to work to, you know, like, eighty hours a week or sixty hours a week, just work but at the same time enjoy life." —Man, white, age 21, non-college-educated

"The American dream to me would be being able to live a comfortable life and provide for yourself and your family, and not have to worry really about 'Where are we going to get our next whatever?'— that kind of thing. It doesn't necessarily mean having to have really extravagant luxuries or anything like that but being able to provide, to have a roof over your head. At this point in time that's the American dream."—Woman, Latino, age 35, non-college-educated

"The American dream is to take care of your family, the people around you, and . . . to earn a decent living."—Woman, white, age 30, non-college-educated

"I think that for most people it's having a family you can provide for and being reasonably comfortable. Not live exorbitantly but not be too concerned with survival. You know, just 'comfortable' seems to be the operative word in our society."—Woman, white, age 25, non-college-educated

"What it means to me is having a job, and that job being stable and not worrying whether or not you're going to get a pink slip in a week or a month and, you know, having the freedom and the money to do what you want to do, whether it be to take your kids to a movie or buy a new car or go on a vacation or whatever. That to me is what the American dream is: having enough money to move comfortably, you know, but obviously not living outside of your means but being able to live comfortably, to be able to do the things you want to do with your family or with your significant other."—Woman, white, age 40, non-college-educated

"I mean, I used to own my own business and I had what I thought was the American dream a while back. . . . If people lose sight of that and think that there's no possibility of that, then yeah, it's going to become very mundane and they are going to become very unhappy people."—Man, white, age 45, non-college-educated

The people who are most optimistic are minorities and immigrants, who have been hit very hard by the weakened economy but still have a certain confidence that America delivers for those who work hard.[19] That means, of course, that the white working-class voter and aspiring middle class are the least optimistic about the future, but they just aren't ready to throw in the towel. There is something un-American about doing so.

We asked people an unusual question in our one-on-one, in-depth interviews: "How would America work without the American dream?" The question stopped them. The idea of taking it away led them back to it, for all the problems involved. What are you asking? they seemed to say. No, that's "unimaginable" or too "depressing" or "No, I don't think it works without it."[20]

"It's something that people just look for; you know, it's a goal, it is the dream, it's something to look forward to, to work towards in a positive way."—Woman, white, age 25, non-college-educated

"I think it would fall flat. I don't think it would have a chance. You've got to have dreams and you've got to have goals."—Woman, white, age 50, non-college-educated

"If you don't have hope, you have nothing. Do you know what I mean?"—Woman, white, age 40, non-college-educated

"It would be all depressed and we would have nothing to look forward to, you know? I mean, as long as you have your dreams and you can try to go after them, then that gives you motivation to do things."—Man, white, age 35, non-college-educated

One Latino man with some college education saw the crash putting the dream in a more realistic context:

"Well, people need to dream. I'm just glad that it's back to being somewhat of a dream and not still a nightmare. Like, people go to sleep at night and they're happy to wake up the next morning, or at least not as miserable. They're not afraid that they're going to get fired, they're not afraid that they've just lost $3.5 billion overnight. They're not afraid to leave the house. People start going to parks instead of the movies. People start taking their kids outside instead of buying them a new Xbox. I mean, this crash just set us in our place. We were like an arrogant bully in school and Casey Heynes came by and started to body slam us and put us in our place."

But an America put in its place would not be exceptional; it would be like any other country, but worse. "I think if we didn't have it, then we would be another China," a non-college-educated white woman in Fox Lake told us, laughing as she said it. "I think that we could quickly slip back into being some Third World country."[21] And a non-college-educated Latino woman in Anaheim said, "If we didn't have an American Dream, I think we would be just like every other country . . ."[22] According to one Latino man, "That's why people migrate, so they can have better opportunities for their family."[23] In other words, America would lose its freedom, its attraction, and we would be a country where background, ancestry, and class mattered above all.

"Oh, I think that would be terrible. I mean, you'd have problems. People would, you know, if there was no American dream, not a lot of people would be coming to this country: nobody would. We don't want it to be like a communist country where you have to generally follow the rules of what the person who's in charge tells you what to do."—Man, Latino, age 30, non-college-educated

"I think it would become sort of like the rest of the Central American countries, that they are all in chaos. There is a very big distinction between the two. There would only really be two classes."—Woman, Latino, age 30, non-college-educated

So there is nothing like taking away the dream that brings out an underlying consciousness that shapes the middle-class aspiration. Americans insist on a path to something more idealized, even in very tough times.

We agree with them. It is that kind of thinking that affirms our conclusion: we have failed but must attempt to right it in this book.

James We know what the American dream was circa 1965. Dad worked and got two weeks' vacation and the family owned a house and a car and there was health care available and Dad retired in his sixties with the kids safely through college. We also know that the country has fundamentally changed. The dream of 2015 will not be the same as the dream of 1965. But what can we tell people the dream has become?

Back in the sixties, you wouldn't even consider asking people if they would be the beneficiaries of their own hard work. It wasn't something that anyone questioned. The American way has always been to reward people who work hard: it's a core value. Well, if you look at the last three decades, working hard hasn't paid off.

The American dream was about participating in the riches of the country, and more and more, people in the middle class are being told that they don't get the chance to participate anymore. The country hasn't been able to grow its wealth equally, it hasn't been able to offer people a way into the middle class, and in a huge number of cases it hasn't been able to stop families from falling out of the middle class. How's that for a dream: I dream that I won't fall out of the middle class, because that's about as high as people are being allowed to aspire to!

Stan I was very late for Vice President Joe Biden's speech to the Democratic House members' retreat in Cambridge, Maryland, last January because I was finishing up editing this closing final paragraph. It wasn't quite right. But amazingly, when I walked sheepishly into the main ballroom full of members of Congress, he was shouting out, "Do you know what they don't get?" He was talking about the Republicans, of course, but you could feel that his message was really about the elites and the privileged. "What's at stake here is about restoring the bargain with the middle class." It is about the "connective tissue that holds this country together." A job is more than "what you get paid. . . . A home is a lot more than about whether it is rational to rent. . . . This is just Joe Biden and the way I grew up. The two dreams are you get to own a home and send your kids to college. Take those out and you take out what we're about as a country, about community, about my kids being able to do better than me." And you know what? "They are tired of being tired."[24]

I did not make this up, and he is right. Americans are just not going to give up on working for a good job, a house, and college for their kids. That is the bargain, and from now on, it is the "middle-class dream" that we will work to see fulfilled.

4.

WHAT'S HAPPENED OVER THE LAST THREE DECADES, AND NOW

Stan We met in Washington, D.C., with Larry Mishel, head of the Economic Policy Institute, to get the "facts" about the American story over the last three decades. We shared our angst about the fundamental destabilization of the middle class, and I challenged Larry, "Could you pull together 15 graphs that tell that story?"—a challenge he clearly relished.

When we got the graphs by e-mail, I printed them out and spread them across a king-size bed in my hotel room and James did the same in his, just to take it all in. The totality stopped us cold. The two of us study these problems every day, but looking at that mélange of graphs, we felt like we were looking at a different country in a different time.

James If you look at the totality of the data relating to how the middle class has been faring over the last 30 years, there is a depressing sameness to most of it. Clearly, the financial crisis that began in 2008 hit the middle class real hard, but we can see that most of the forces degrading the day-to-day fortunes of middle-class people were already in place, many of them appearing during the eight years of the George W. Bush administration.

When the financial crisis struck in 2008, it had the effect of hitting somebody suffering from pneumonia with a pickup truck. It may have looked like the trouble started when Lehman Brothers filed for bankruptcy protection in September 2008, but probably 75 percent of the country had been exasperated since 2001. It wasn't as if these tens of millions of families were just diddy-bopping along, doing fine, minding their own business, when they got suckerpunched out of left field. They were already wobbling and the financial crash was the event that finally pushed them over the side.

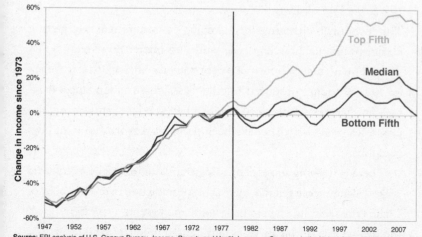

The Postwar American Story
All rise together until the late 1970s

Source: EPI analysis of U.S. Census Bureau, *Income, Poverty and Health Insurance Coverage in the United States: 2010 – Historical Income Tables*, Table F1: Income Limits for Each Fifth and Top 5 Percent of Families, and Table F 5: Race and Hispanic Origin of Householder – Families by Median and Mean Income, Excel spreadsheet accessed November 23, 2011.

Stan I got stuck staring at the first graph. That's the whole story. In post–World War II America we grew the middle class and we grew together. Everything we've done was rooted in that story and reality. Our parents created it and we took advantage of it—and government made it possible for each generation to get on the ladder. But as we neared 1980, the country changed, never to go back. The top 20 percent are on their way and the top 1 percent beyond them, but for the median household—the core of the middle class—the good days are behind them. This is not what America is about.

If you are a low-income household—the bottom 20 percent—you make less now than you did in 1973. If you are in the middle, you grab the few years of gains—the second half of the 1980s and nineties—but nothing since 2000. When it's all said and done, you make only 10 percent more in real dollars than what you earned more than thirty years ago, in 1980.

Change in Work and Jobs

The economy is changing. It is damping down any chance of getting ahead, no matter how hard you work, no matter how many hours you put in, no matter how much debt you take on. In postwar America, our economy produced middle-class jobs in abundance—and by some accounts a majority of jobs in 1980 could support middle-class lifestyles—but they have been replaced year by year with low-paid jobs.[1]

There is nothing more depressing than looking at the entry-level wages of new college and high school graduates over this period. That is the front line where hard work and parents' aspirations meet the real world. In the 1970s, a high school graduate could start out making $13.15 an hour in current dollars, but that has sunk inexorably lower over the years, to just $10.95 an hour in 2011. That was the three-decade pattern before wages went down another dollar an hour after the financial crisis hit.

In the 1970s, new college graduates started at around $18.50 an hour—a damn good premium for getting a college education. But the payoff did not come until the second half of the 1990s, under President Clinton, when new college grads saw real gains in starting wages. But more important, new entrants have not seen any increase in their starting compensation for the last decade. A new college grad is getting double the high school grad, but both are stuck in our new economy.

A critical part of the transformation of jobs and work is what has happened with health insurance and pension coverage. What is a middle-class job after all? Well, health insurance is the starting point—and indeed, at the beginning of this period (in 1980), almost

Entry-level wages of high school and college graduates, 1973 to 2011

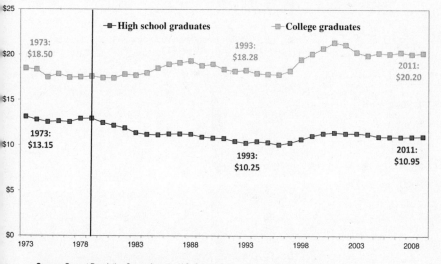

Source: Current Population Survey from the U.S. Census Bureau, Outgoing Rotations Group.
Note: Results in 2009 dollars, adults ages 19 to 25.

two-thirds of high school graduates got health insurance with their first job. The trend paused under President Clinton, but that was just temporary. Before the crash, barely 30 percent of high school graduates had employer-provided health insurance. As bad as that was, we have basically fallen off the cliff: now just over 25 percent of high school graduates are covered under their employers' plans.

In 1980, 80 percent of college graduates started out in jobs with health insurance. They did the prudent thing. But they have lost ground steadily, too, falling sharply under George W. Bush and then dropping to 65 percent after the crash. These are better numbers than for high school graduates, but for everyone the trend is down. Not reflected in these stats is the fact that those employees who do receive health insurance are paying far higher contributions for it.

We would utter "Disgrace!" but then we would not know how to

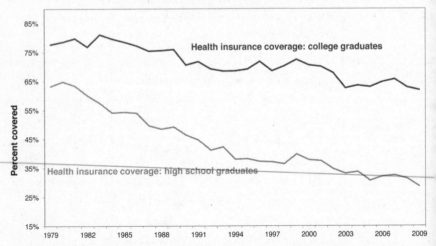

Health and retirement security are eroding
Health insurance coverage for recent graduates, 1979 to 2009

Source: EPI analysis of the Current Population Survey from the U.S. Census Bureau, annual income supplement.
Note: Sample is of private wage-and-salary earners ages 23 to 29 who worked at least 20 hours per week and 26 weeks per year. Coverage is defined as being included in an employer-provided plan where the employer paid for at least some of the coverage.

begin to describe what has happened to pensions over the last 30 years. Just 40 percent of high school grads got starting jobs with pensions in 1979, but even that has been cut in half. About half of college graduates got starting jobs with some kind of pension, and that held up through Bush, but they have lost ground too.[2]

But also part of the idea of being middle-class is working and saving so your kids can go to college. That is a key principle in the middle-class story and key to our whole experience. But the cost of attending a four-year college is up 72 percent just since 1990—up 140 percent since 1980—and the middle class is paying an increasing percentage of their income to send their kids to college. For middle-class families, the cost of one year of tuition equals about half of their household income.[3]

James It has been ingrained in the psyche of the country that an education is a ticket to the middle class. You can expect to do better if you get educated. If you want to do better than your parents, or if you want to continue to enjoy a good middle-class lifestyle, whatever your aspiration, there are two things you have to do. First, you have to get an education. Yet we're making it harder and harder for people to get an education. The second thing you have to do is work hard. People are certainly taking that to heart and working their socks off, but their wages are going down. They have to work for a hundred years to save the money to send Junior to college.

These principles have been instilled in us: Get a good education and work hard. So, what have we done? We've made education more expensive and work has become less rewarding, so it's harder to get a good education and people are working more hours and they're not getting any more for it.

That's what's behind all these charts. We're attacking the fundamental idea of America that has persisted since about 1900, when the country developed a mass system of public education. That fundamental idea paid off really well for us until about 1973.

This is the real sucker punch we've been hit with. While the cost of a college education has skyrocketed, its value has fallen. At some point, the lines will cross and college won't be worth it.

Working Longer and Taking On Debt

Stan So, how do you survive or claw your way up to prosperity? Well, you work longer hours and you take on more debt. That is the center of the new story of America's middle class.

If those in the middle feel crushed, it is because they are. Long hours and diminishing returns have become *the* story of the middle class—and the increase in hours in the middle is really staggering. They are now working an average of 200 more hours per year (or the equivalent of five additional workweeks) than they did in 1979.

And those in the upper middle class—the households in the 60th and 80th percentiles—are working even longer hours: on average, more than 300 more hours per year than in 1979. To be sure, this is largely due to a massive increase in two-earner households: between 1970 and 1993, the proportion of dual-income households increased from 39 to 61 percent.[4] But even with two incomes, many of these families have not seen real wage increases, despite the fact that they are working more—in some cases more than double—the hours.

There is a widely shared presumption that those at the top got there and stay there and earn their increasingly outsized incomes by working hard. But the data tells a different story. Since the late 1970s, the average hours worked by the highest-income households has

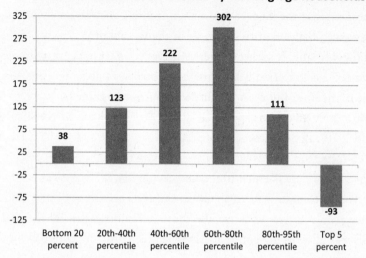

Growth in annual hours worked by working-age households

Source: EPI analysis of Current Population Survey from the U.S. Census Bureau, annual social and economic supplement data.

actually *decreased*: those in the top 5 percent now average almost 100 fewer hours per year than they did in 1979. But those in the middle— the ones whose incomes we have watched stagnate over the last 30 years—*are* working harder. And they're doing it for less and less.

James This is one chart that grabbed my attention even more than the rest. I stared at this chart the first time I saw it and I doubted that the data could actually be correct. But it is. Amid the statistics on declining real wages and rising costs of health care and education was this graph showing the 60th to 80th percentiles of middle-class households by income working an additional 302 hours a year, or about 6 hours a week, but the top 5 percent isn't all in: they worked 93 *fewer* hours a year.

It's pretty clear to me that the middle class does the work in this country. Middle-class people are trying to find overtime, or they're working two jobs, and they're still going backwards. And it's not just the fact that the richest are making more—they're also working less—and that is just rubbing salt in the wound. But if you want to know why the American voter is obsessed with debt, you should stare at this graph on debt. Sure, household debt grew as a percentage of income after the war, but so did income and the overall economy. And Americans' personal debt loads stabilized in the 1960s and 1970s. But as incomes stopped rising in the 1980s, families covered their rising needs with debt—crashing through the 100 percent line (where debt is equal to income) as George W. Bush was taking office, accelerating during the Bush era, and crashing with the crash. Increased debt was what families used to maintain the illusion that this was all working and that America was a growing country. This is sobering.[5]

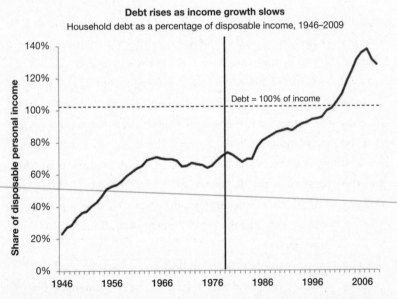

Debt rises as income growth slows
Household debt as a percentage of disposable income, 1946–2009

Source: EPI analysis of U.S. Federal Reserve Board, Flow of Funds Accounts of the United States.

Productivity Theft and Inequality

Stan Now for the theft.

People are barely getting paid more, working much longer hours, losing benefits, dealing with rising costs, tapping into their savings, and taking on debt—and, in the spirit of America, they are steadily becoming more productive. The productivity of the American worker rose steadily in the post–World War II period, regardless of the ups and downs of the economy. Up until 1980, wages and productivity went up together. Companies felt they had to pay more as they made more. But the deal stopped in 1980. Since then wages stalled and productivity continued to rise, meaning corporations and employers have taken much more money as executive compensation, profits, and dividends.

We have witnessed the theft of productivity that has taken place

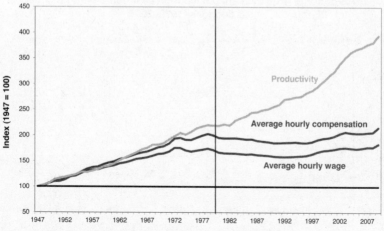

Worker productivity outpaces earnings

Source: EPI analysis of Bureau of Economic Analysis and Bureau of Labor Statistics data.

over the course of a generation. The idea that workers share in the good fortune they helped create for their employers has been replaced by a culture that rewards CEOs with outsized and outlandish compensation that is out of proportion to performance.

James This proves that America is now a country where work is not being rewarded, if you think of income as being the main reward for work. Work is essential to life. Between the ages of five and sixty-five—or sixty-eight, to be more realistic—we are either educating ourselves, i.e., training for a job, or we're already in a job. Many people are fortunate to have any job, but if you are particularly lucky, your job is also your career, with an upward trajectory in satisfaction, responsibility, and reward. For the very few, a career is also a vocation, something you love doing.

In the final speech in the 1993 documentary *The War Room*, about Bill Clinton's campaign for the presidency in 1992, I alluded to the fact that, other than love, labor is the most important thing a person can give of themselves to others. Well, people are working harder in

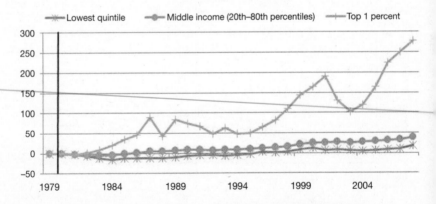

Percentage growth in annual income, by income percentile over 3 decades, 1979–2007

Source: Economic Policy Institute, analysis of Congressional Budget Office Data, 2012.

the middle income ranges in this country—they're giving more of themselves—and they're not getting the reward for it.

Stan The tragedy of this period is what has happened to the middle class—what they have to do to maintain the dream of being middle-class. The hours and debt tell you everything—but what tells you the real deal is that increasingly productive work has stopped producing wage gains. The top 1 percent and senior executives were allowed, regardless of who was president, to take almost all the gain, changing the character of the country.

Many people say that the growing gap in wealth has more long-term consequences than rising income disparity. We don't have to choose between the two. Both are a problem, and worsening. In this period, the ratio of wealth of the top 1 percent in relation to the median person's wealth went from 131:1 to 225:1. We focus more on

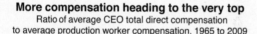

More compensation heading to the very top
Ratio of average CEO total direct compensation
to average production worker compensation, 1965 to 2009

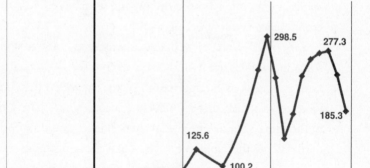

Source: EPI analysis of *Wall Street Journal*/Mercer, Hay Group (2010).
Note: Point markers denote where ratio is known.

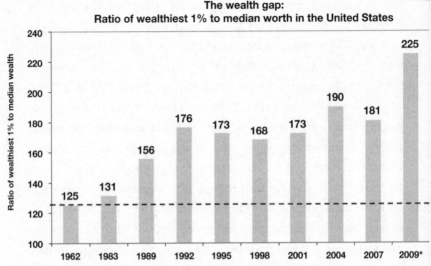

The wealth gap:
Ratio of wealthiest 1% to median worth in the United States

*2009 data is estimated based on asset price changes from the Federal Reserve Flow of Funds data.
Note: Wealth defined as net worth (household assets less debts).
Source: EPI analysis of Survey of Consumer Finances and Flow of Funds data.

income and benefits because we believe government can actually do something to impact those things, and we take seriously the public's ambivalence about targeting wealth.

James Even the most liberal among us is going to concede that some individuals are going to make more than others. I do not believe it's the skyrocketing wealth of the 1 percent that is the major issue; it is the fact that middle-class incomes have barely risen at all in the same period. The rise in the top level would not be nearly as corrosive to the whole of society had there been any meaningful gain in middle-class incomes that trickled down over the past 35 years. It simply didn't happen. CEOs were making 300 times what an average worker was earning.

$8,757 a year. We know from EPI calculations that if America had continued to grow the way it did up until 1980 and shared its bounty, the median family would be earning $8,757 more each year.

There is a material price for the way America has been allowed to develop, but as we will see below, there are pervasive consequences.[6]

Consequences

Stan Casualty number one is the prospect of secure retirement for the middle class—nearly the point of all this for our parents and most of our peers. As they near retirement with reduced savings and more debt and stagnant wages, people are depending more and more on Social Security and Medicare. Many continue to work, accounting for a quarter of the income of those over 65 years, with Social Security the dominant income source. That clearly raises the stakes as one thinks about the budget decisions ahead. The elite

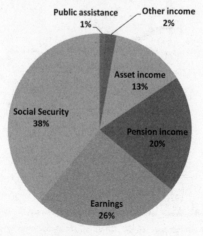

Income sources for persons aged 65 or older as a share of aggregate income

Public assistance 1%
Other income 2%
Asset income 13%
Social Security 38%
Pension income 20%
Earnings 26%

Source: U.S. Social Security Administration, 2004.

should tread carefully when talking about the need for "shared sacrifices."

This three-decade-long era has taken a big toll on the work and family lives of middle-class America—and those without college degrees and with the lowest incomes have been especially hard-hit. The "traditional American family" has crashed across all racial groups. In *Coming Apart: The State of White America, 1960–2010*, an otherwise exasperating and doctrinaire book, Charles Murray sets out some inescapable results of what has happened to lower-income and working-class whites, his "bottom 30 percent." Their marriages have fallen apart. Looking at his graphs, more than 80 percent were married in 1960, but barely half are married now—while marriage has stabilized for those at the top. The concept of "never married" hardly existed in 1960. Now a quarter of working-class white adults have never married. Divorce has accelerated for those in the "bottom 30 percent" while stabilizing for those at the top. The

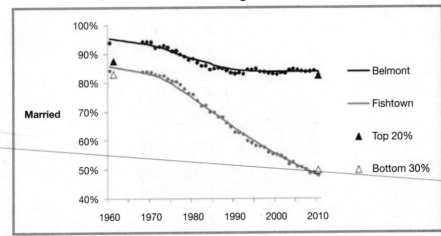

Marriage

Note: Sample limited to whites ages 30–49. "Married" refers to persons married and not separated.
Source: Charles Murray's analysis of IPUMS data that appeared in *Coming Apart: The State of White America, 1960–2010.*

White nonmarital birth ratio by mother's education

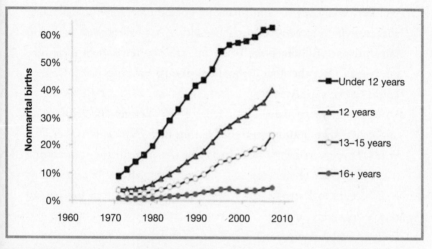

Note: Murray's analysis of alternate years of the Natality Public Use Files of the Centers for Disease Control, beginning with 1970. Sample limited to white women.
Source: Charles Murray's analysis from *Coming Apart: The State of White America, 1960–2010.*

number of children born outside of marriage has accelerated over this period—not for those with at least a four-year degree, but for everyone else, and much more for those with the least education.

As a result, lower-income and working-class whites report that they are less happy in their marriages and just less happy overall. They are substantially less involved now in their communities, their civic organizations, even their churches: more than 55 percent attended church regularly in the late 1970s, but now it is closer to 40 percent. They are increasingly less trustful of others—the opposite of what we observe among those at the top 20 percent. It is hard not to be alarmed by this fall from grace, dramatic even by the norms of the 1960s and 1970s—trends that Murray says put at risk "the American project."[7] Even without all the ideological garb, this era has left a lot of wreckage.

So it's no wonder that the totality of what has happened to the middle class has played itself out in the real bottom line: how long you live. We now live with forms of worsening economic inequality that were hard to imagine three decades ago—except with regard to racial disparities, which we have spent the better part of a century addressing. But the new inequalities about who lives for how long could not be starker.

In the early 1970s, the top half of the income spectrum lived about two years longer than the bottom half: 79.6 years versus 77.7 years. There was a gap, but it was not that big. In the intervening 30 years, however, the top half has extended their life expectancy by 5.8 years to a striking 85.4 years. Great. The bottom has gained barely another year of life: 78.9 years.

It all adds up, it seems, in the most fundamental way.

What is most perverse about the consequences is what has happened in education. As we know, education was supposed to be the

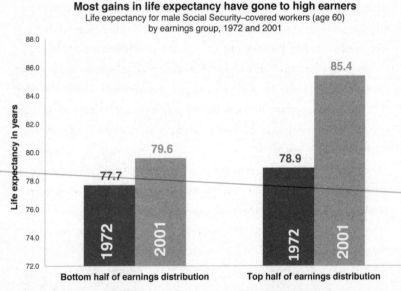

Most gains in life expectancy have gone to high earners
Life expectancy for male Social Security–covered workers (age 60)
by earnings group, 1972 and 2001

Source: EPI analysis of Waldron (2007).

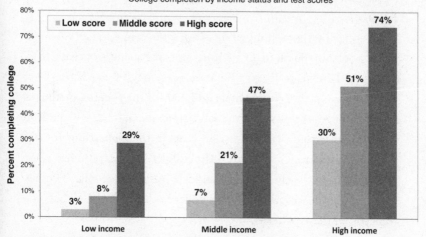

Low-scoring students from high-income families more likely to complete college than high-scoring low-income students

College completion by income status and test scores

Note: Low income is defined as bottom 25%, middle income is middle 50%, and high income is top 25%.
Source: Fox, Connolly, & Snyder (2005).

great social and economic equalizer. Killing yourself so your kids could get a good education was part of the deal, but what we are now seeing is that education may be reinforcing and accelerating inequality. If you have a high income and your children have good test scores, they will most likely complete college—about 75 percent of those children will finish school. But what if your kids have just mediocre scores? If they come from money, they still have a 50 percent chance of completing college.

The picture is much different for less affluent students. If you are middle-income—even if your kids get high test scores—there is just a 50 percent chance that they will complete college. If their scores are anything less, they are finished: only one in five will get their degrees. Let's not even talk about what happens to those with low incomes. Far from a great equalizer, the education system is actually part of the problem. Family preparation and the ability to

afford tuition are now so essential to academic success that our supposed "meritocracy" actually perpetuates, rather than mitigates, inequality.

Among the more compelling observations in Charles Murray's
awful book are the mutually reinforcing consequences of rising SAT
scores at the elite colleges, which are reaching 700 at Harvard but
near 400 at North Carolina State and 350 for high school graduates
who do not go to college. At the same time, the number with college
degrees has tripled over the last 40 years in the highest-income zip
codes—communities that are attracting a higher proportion of
graduates from the elite colleges and elite business schools.[8] There is
a deepening segregation of the college-educated elites that en-
trenches all these patterns.

James If you want to go to college, it's better to be rich than
smart. What we're doing is stacking the deck. If the Republicans
succeed in getting rid of the estate tax, and public contribution to

Correlation of Intergenerational Earnings

Source: New America Foundation analysis of OECD data.

higher education is continually reduced (which we will talk about more in the next chapter), then we are puncturing equality.

Stan Virtually every developed country except Great Britain and Italy has greater social mobility than the United States. In Denmark, there is about a 15 percent correlation between parents' income and that of a child; in the United States it is nearly 50 percent. Income is now destiny in this new period.

James This all has big consequences for American exceptionalism and the American dream. If you work it, educate it, innovate it, enterprise it, you move up in America. We are a country where children are brought up with a belief in the possibility of social mobility. Except, it is not true.

The great thing that we always believed about America is that even if you were not born wealthy, you still had a great chance to make it; but as we have seen, that just isn't true anymore. Not only is that idea no longer true, we seem to be doing everything we can to make it worse—to institutionalize inequality and make it permanent. We live in a country where people aspire to be successful, and that's great; but we're falling back toward the middle of the pack in equality when, throughout our history, that equality has been our greatest asset.

How George W. Bush Made Everything Worse

James The fact is, these problems were exacerbated by the policy decisions made in the Bush years. Start with the 2001 and 2003 tax cuts, which reduced taxes, including the top rate from 39.6 percent to

35 percent and reduced the estate tax, adding $1.7 trillion in deficits to 2008 and widening the inequality gap substantially.[9] (The Medicare prescription drug benefit didn't help, either.)

At the end of 2001, Osama bin Laden and his lieutenants were holed up in caves at Tora Bora in southern Afghanistan, but we didn't deploy ground troops and he escaped. Then we invaded Iraq and divided our military focus, so instead of being in a position to win one war, we ended up where we are today, where neither position looks favorable, and at the cost of more than 6,400 American lives and over $1.3 trillion.

Admittedly, missteps in financial affairs were made in the previous administration, but Bush "embraced a governing philosophy of deregulation," as *Time* magazine put it, holding the SEC back from supervising mutual funds and hedge funds.[10] So the marketplace was allowed to work its magic, and we all know what happened next. Every time the Bush administration had a choice in military and fiscal matters, they made disastrous decisions.

Under Bush, everything was politicized. This is, I think, my favorite story about the Bush years: The Coalition Provisional Authority ran Iraq and its members were recruited under the watch of a White House liaison at the Pentagon. Were they most interested in employing people who could help run Iraq? No, they looked for good, loyal Republicans. Candidates were asked "if they supported *Roe v. Wade* and if they had voted for George W. Bush." Résumés of highly qualified people were thrown in the trash because their allegiance to Bush's vision was "uncertain."[11] No wonder it all went so well!

Under Bush, the country took a sharp turn in the wrong direction. When President Clinton left, we had a projected surplus of $5.6 trillion over ten years, but Bush bequeathed Obama a $1.3 trillion deficit, projected to $8 trillion over ten years.[12] Just think what we could have done with that money. We could have made significant steps toward rebuilding the middle class with a tax policy that meant the less you make, the more you take home, and not one that fattened up the top 1 percent. There could have been real investment in the middle class—in education, in jobs, in the infrastructure, in reducing health care costs. Instead we have stayed far longer than we should have in what most would say was a war of necessity in Afghanistan, and undertook another war that has bled us dry.

You can argue if you like that Alan Greenspan bears more responsibility for the economic decline than George Bush, because Greenspan kept interest rates artificially low for so long. There's one fact I know separates the two men: at least Greenspan admitted he erred, which Bush has never done. In October 2008, Greenspan testified to Henry Waxman's House Committee on Oversight and Government Reform and talked about the free market ideology that had guided him for forty years, including more than twenty at the Fed. "I found a flaw in the model that I perceived as the critical functioning structure that defines how the world works," he said.[13] In other words, Greenspan was saying: I goofed.

The only time there has been appreciable income growth for the middle class was in the nineties. So, what did the Republicans do? They decided they were going to favor tax cuts for rich people, engage in unnecessary wars, and pursue a health care policy that benefited drug companies. In January of 2001, they had every chance in the world to make decisions that would have continued the modest progress of the Clinton years, but they decided they were just going to favor rich people and turn their back on middle-class people. President Bush left us with a huge mess that we're still trying to deal with, and the American people for sure don't want to go back to that way of doing things.

5.

THE ATTACK ON HIGHER EDUCATION

James When I ask myself what institution has made the most difference in my life, and the one I most care about, it's clearly Louisiana State University. I attended the university as an undergraduate and a law student. My mom and dad had eight kids, and six of them went to LSU. Between them, these eight kids have gone on to give my parents twenty-three grandchildren, and of these no fewer than thirteen are LSU grads, two of whom have postgraduate degrees, with another on her way. Considering that three of the twenty-three kids aren't old enough to attend college yet, the Carvilles are currently running a 65 percent strike rate at LSU.

I'm not going to claim LSU is the best state university in the country; it's not. I won't even say it's the most improved, although by some important measures, like graduation rates, LSU and the University of Maryland can legitimately make that claim. What I am going to say is that LSU is the most indispensable state university in the country. Louisiana doesn't have a Michigan State to rival its Michigan, or a Clemson to rival its South Carolina, or an Auburn to rival its Alabama; in Louisiana, LSU is it.

If you live in Louisiana, and you're a doctor, a lawyer, an MBA, an engineer, or an entrepreneur, the chances that you went to the state university are probably as high as, if not higher than, anywhere else in the country. LSU is important for its work on some very specific issues that are of vital importance to Louisiana, like coastal deterioration and hurricane protection, and year in, year out, some of the best people in the world are working on them in Baton Rouge. If you ask what the greatest environmental disaster in the country is, most people would be shocked to know that it's the ongoing deterioration and destruction of the Louisiana coastline. LSU scientists have been studying it for decades; they have conducted a lot of the solid research post-Katrina and again following the BP oil spill in 2010. To put a number on it, the university says that more than 1,700 LSU graduates hold the title of president, CEO, owner, or founder, and nearly one thousand of them live in Louisiana.[1]

Paying for college tuition is one of the burdens that is killing the middle class today, but when I was at school, the cost of going to LSU was minimal. I attended LSU Law School in the early seventies and my tuition was $95 a semester. I was awarded a small scholarship, but even without that, it was not a crippling amount of money. When I told the students in the political science class I teach at Tulane that I paid my tuition from the billfold in my pocket, they laughed. But I think they were more rueful than amused.

Back then the student loan as we know it today was in its infancy. Guys like me might get helped out by a family member, and I had the backing of a check from the G.I. Bill: $300 a month, which was a fortune (the equivalent of $1,700 today). Tuition was historically very low: books cost more than the tuition did. The point is that it was not surprising that everybody in Louisiana got the chance to go to LSU. The truth was, my parents couldn't afford to send me anyplace else. And there was no question that this was where I was going to go. The school wasn't that difficult to get into, and it wasn't that expensive, so it functioned as a kind of equalizer. It was the ticket to the middle class for thousands of kids. Increasingly, that's no longer the case.

LSU is suffering from the same funding cuts that are affecting state universities all across the country. In a three-year period, general state appropriations to LSU were reduced from $245 million to $153 million, a drop of $92 million. In early 2012, another $8.1 million in cuts was announced. In 2011, less than 39 percent of LSU's operating budget is coming from the state; two years ago it was 58 percent. The consequences for the area are serious. The university has cut programs, consolidated colleges, and cut faculty by 10 percent. The faculty also hasn't had a raise in three years.[2] LSU is a vital part of the Baton Rouge–area economy; the university generates $1.3 billion a year in revenue and supports twenty-two thousand jobs; and LSU students inject $600 million a year into the local economy.[3]

LSU has traditionally been a low-tuition, highly state-supported school. By any measure—and we don't need charts to convince you of this—Louisiana has been one of the poorer states in the union. But in large part because of oil and mineral wealth, LSU has always been fairly well supported by the state. The response to falling revenue has been that the university should follow the model of a private school, or a semiprivate one, like the University of Michigan or the University of Virginia, where the tuition has been increased dramatically to make up for the lack of state funding. On the surface, that seems like a reasonable reaction to the same kind of crisis that any number of other universities have faced, but LSU is a special place.

The state is underfunding the university, and we are losing people left and right because of this. And because we have decided we want to be a low-tax state, depriving LSU of the kind of revenue needed to fund new programs and attract and keep talented academicians, we are not only not making those kinds of investments in higher education, we are dramatically cutting the investment. I have no idea why anybody would consider this part of a sound long-term plan to reverse the fortunes of a historically poor state.

It's also the case in Louisiana that any student with a 3.0 grade point average can go to LSU on a subsidy from the state, i.e., for nothing. So my daughter can go to LSU for free, even though it's absurd that somebody making a fair amount of money can send his or her children to college for free. It just strikes me as wrong that rich people's children can go to LSU for nothing, and at the same time we are cutting state financial support for the university.

I didn't mind tuition being subsidized for my daddy's kids; I do mind it being subsidized for my own kids. There is every rationale in the world for subsidizing the higher education of the eight children of a small-town postmaster. There is no rationale at all for subsidizing the tuition of two kids whose father appears on cable TV.

It's one thing to waive the cost of tuition for someone who has a 3.5 grade point average and whose family has a limited income, but if you do that for everybody with a 3.0, it just becomes an entitlement. This also encourages state schools to favor the admission of out-of-state students: if they keep in-state tuition really low, they're going to take anybody they can from across the state line who is willing to pay more to attend.

When LSU was expanded greatly in the thirties, the state had a severance tax on oil and gas revenue that kept tuition at universities low; the same tax was used to keep property taxes on homes low as well. However, the severance tax revenue on gas drilling has fallen, as gas prices have remained low.

It was Huey Long who applied severance tax revenues to LSU; under his governorship, the university grew mightily in size and academic achievement, and for the first time it acquired a national reputation. Long made sure the university was adequately funded, increasing appropriations from $1 million in 1931 to $2.87 million in 1935. Being Huey Long, he focused his attention on areas of academic life like the band and the swimming pool, making sure each was large enough to match his ambition. He funneled money into the university's infrastructure, building dorms and music and arts buildings, increasing the size of the football stadium, and constructing a field house. He established a medical school and a PhD program, and enrollment grew to the point that LSU went from being the eighty-eighth largest university in the country to the twentieth, and eleventh among the state schools.

According to T. Harry Williams, Long's biographer, "This rapid growth was in part a result of LSU's new reputation, but largely it was a reflection of economic conditions. LSU charged practically no tuition and provided a generous number of scholarships to needy students. It was well on the way to achieving the goal Huey had set for it—to make its facilities available to every poor boy and girl in the state."[4]

Huey Long's vision is now under threat.

This is happening across the country, and there seems to be little outrage about it. We understand the seriousness of the economic situation of the country, but if we continue to cut education funding, we are burning our own seed corn. Nationally, politicians seem to

have convinced people that there is waste and bloat in higher education, and some of the attacks on higher education have taken hold
with people.

A lot of the people in Louisiana who should be more outraged
are sending their kids to other schools anyway.

The truth is that these kids are graduating into what is now a
brutal job market and is going to be for some time. We're not sure
exactly what it is, but something is seriously wrong when you have
this willingness to disinvest in the exact kind of people you need to
move the individual states along, and with them the country.

What does this change mean? Graduates are entering a more
viciously competitive world—and competitive not just in terms of
other college graduates in the United States but in regard to people
around the world as well. The working world that James Carville en-
tered is an entirely different world from the one that exists today.
Kids today are going to need more tools to stay afloat, and as you cut
the quality of the education that they get, they're less prepared to
compete. In addition to that, there are fewer trained people at the top.

What this also means is that you just don't develop the same standard of expertise at the state level. Whether it's managing water
resources, controlling coastal erosion, dealing with environmental
disasters, training large swaths of the workforce, cultivating the kind
of teachers you need to train people, developing the expertise of primary care physicians, or fostering a steady stream of entrepreneurs,
management experts, and finance people who spend their time
developing medium and small firms around the state—all of that is
going to pay the price for short-sightedness. And almost all of that
expertise is created at LSU.

The Republican Party is operating on the principle that you can
cut your way to prosperity. Sometimes the consequences of that
don't manifest themselves within a year, but they do become appar-

ent over a long period of time. The Republicans would undermine the chances of a middle-class family to have it as good as their parents did. How can you lie to people about income mobility, yet cut the funding to the very thing that is going to provide any hope for income mobility? Yet that is what we have been doing.

The idea that we are saving money is absurd. Education doesn't cost money, but ignorance does. Does anybody think that the kids who are committing crimes in New Orleans are doing so because they are too educated?

"It Could Be a Lot Worse"

James We see the same situation being played out all across the country. In Pennsylvania, Governor Tom Corbett's proposed 2012–13 budget involves cutting funding to the fourteen universities in the Pennsylvania State System of Higher Education by 20 percent and to four state-related universities—Temple, Penn State, Lincoln, and Pittsburgh—by 30 percent. This follows spending cuts and tuition increases the year before, including 19 percent cuts at the four state-related institutions (the governor had asked for 50 percent cuts). The president of Lincoln University, Robert R. Jennings, who had to raise tuition 7.5 percent as a result, said another cut would be "completely devastating."[5]

Corbett says he wants colleges to be run more like businesses, create more jobs and cut costs, and not raise tuition.[6] Corbett said he was "not necessarily" trying to reduce state contribution to zero and said the money he cut represents about 2 percent of the University of Pittsburgh's budget. "It could be a lot worse," Corbett said.[7]

I think Governor Corbett should run for reelection on that slogan, which would fit just right on a bumper sticker. I have another idea. It seems like we're getting stupider, but just think about how much stupider we could get. So now we have two slogans: "Gov. Corbett: 'It could be a lot worse'" and "Pennsylvania: There's lots of stupid left in us."

The point I would make to him is, okay, go look at for-profit colleges that operate like businesses and tell me that you'd rather have your kid graduate from Kaplan than Penn State. Then just go ahead and send them there, because they operate on the principle of the profit motive, and they're really good at getting people to sign up and getting student loans and milking the government.

I have a good friend who is an esteemed scholar and professor of Roman history at Penn State, a man by the name of Garrett Fagan. His job is not to cut costs; his job is not to create jobs; his job is to teach Roman history. I would argue—and correct me if I'm wrong—that the main function of a college or university is to graduate young women and men with qualifications so they can go out into the workplace, make a living for themselves and their families, and contribute to the economy.

The governor of Pennsylvania's argument is patently absurd and indicative of the appalling lack of understanding of what higher education is about. Kids attend university and benefit from the research and scholarship of the university and its broad-based knowledge. The state invests in these kids who are in their twenties and reaps the benefits for the rest of their lives.

But remember: it could be a lot worse.

Perhaps it's worse in California. In December 2011, the state announced a 27 percent funding cut, amounting to $100 million, on top of an existing $650 million reduction. The $2 billion state contribution was the lowest since 1997–98, even though in 2011, the California state system was serving 90,000 more students.[8] I guess there is some way that could get worse too.

Santorum and Romney Attack Education

This attack on education was conjoined with gusto by the two main candidates for the Republican nomination for president. Given Rick Santorum's portfolio of beliefs, it's easy to see why he would favor ignorance over knowledge. Remember, this is the guy who thinks global warming is a "hoax."[9] Ask Rick about the dangers of the well-known greenhouse gas, carbon dioxide: "Tell that to a plant, how dangerous carbon dioxide is."[10] And he's still talking about undermining the teaching of evolution in schools more than a decade after the failure of his "Santorum Amendment," a proposed tack-on to the 2001 No Child Left Behind Bill that tried to promote the teaching of "intelligent design"—a concept later described by a federal judge barring its teaching as "a religious view, a mere relabeling of creationism, and not a scientific theory."

Santorum wants the federal and state government out of education entirely. He's clearly afraid of the consequences of kids thinking for themselves. During his 2012 campaign, Santorum told Glenn Beck that colleges are "indoctrination mills" for a secular lifestyle and that "62 percent of kids who go into college with a faith commitment leave without it."[11] If Rick thinks it's going to college that makes kids lose faith, he's wrong. In fact, a program on PBS revealed that another statistic from the same report Santorum quoted from shows that among kids who *don't* go to college, 76 percent attend church less. Which means kids in college are more religious than those who aren't in college.[12]

Santorum's morbid fear of thinking led him to launch his famous attack on President Obama: "President Obama once said he wants everybody in America to go to college. What a snob."[13] (The Politi-Fact website found no evidence the president ever said that.) Santorum is holder of a BA from Penn State, an MBA from the University of Pittsburgh, and a JD from the Dickinson School of Law at Penn State. That's one more degree than President Obama. If Obama's a snob, what does that make Santorum?

The same PBS piece that debunked Santorum's "indoctrination mills" statement points out that, far from falling for the secularism embodied by humanities and liberal arts, students are enrolling in programs that will set them on track for money-making careers in finance, medicine, and the law. For years UCLA freshmen have been asked what the most important factor was that encouraged them to go to college. In 2001, the most popular option was "being very well-off financially," whereas "to help others who are in difficulty" topped the list in 1971 (when "being very well-off" was fifth).[14]

You might think such a trend would appease Rick Santorum, not to mention Mitt Romney, a man for whom "being very well-off financially" is clearly important. But education doesn't seem to be something Mitt Romney thinks much about. "Whether it is public or private, traditional or online, college must be available and affordable," he says on his campaign website, but offers no ideas on how to achieve these goals when the trends are obviously going in the other direction.[15] When asked at a town hall meeting in Ohio how a young person might better afford college, Romney's thoughtful and helpful response was that kids should "shop around" for loans and an affordable college or consider joining the National Guard—pretty much the equivalent of saying, "Good luck, kid. You're on your own."[16]

The cause of Mitt Romney's curious hostility to education (for a man who attended Harvard and BYU) was probed in a *New York Times* op-ed piece by Paul Krugman. His conclusion makes unedifying reading:

Over the past 30 years, there has been a stunning disconnect between huge income gains at the top and the struggles of ordinary workers. You can make the case that the self-interest of America's elite is best served by making sure that this disconnect continues, which means keeping taxes on high incomes low at all costs, never mind the consequences in terms of poor infrastructure and an undertrained work force.

And if underfunding public education leaves many children of the less affluent shut out from upward mobility, well, did you really believe that stuff about creating equality of opportunity?

So whenever you hear Republicans say that they are the party of traditional values, bear in mind that they have actually made a radical break with America's tradition of valuing education. And they have made this break because they believe that what you don't know can't hurt them.[17]

To a great extent, if someone is very wealthy, he is able—and his kids will be able—to thrive in an economy with a low-wage, low-education workforce. Under these conditions, in the factory, at the supermarket, in the home, the help is cheap.

The Attack on Education: The Consequences

What are the consequences of this incredible shortsightedness? The nation's ability to compete internationally is being undermined at the same time as the chances for middle-class youth to maintain the standards of living of their parents, and the opportunities for the less well-off sections of society are slowly destroyed. As we've seen, the American ideal of equality has been threatened over the last thirty years, and the potential exists for far worse damage in the future.

Jamie Merisotis is president and CEO of the Lumina Foundation, whose aim is to increase the number of college graduates in this country. Merisotis says that more than 60 percent of American jobs will require some postsecondary education by 2018, while today the number stands at 40 percent. Merisotis's foundation wants America to meet that 60 percent requirement by 2025; meanwhile, in South Korea, 63 percent of young people already have a two- or four-year degree. We used to rank number one in college attainment; now we're at number fifteen.

To produce more graduates at a time of spiraling tuition costs, Merisotis promotes a number of measures. Institutions can be funded on the basis of the number of students they graduate, not the number they enroll (Tennessee parcels out 70 percent of its funding this way), and students can be offered performance incentives. Colleges can actually be smarter about business, buying products together and improving information. Employers need to step in and encourage government to help provide the training our economy requires, and they can help in training the 37 million Americans who have some college credits but no degree.[18]

Education and the Middle Class

James Merisotis cites a giant 2010 study by the Georgetown University Center on Education and the Workforce: "Help Wanted: Projections of Jobs and Education Requirements Through 2018." The study is predicated on two facts: first, "the ability of individuals to connect education, training, and careers has become key to employability and to attaining and maintaining middle class status"; and second, "in spite of its growing importance, our ability to match education alternatives with career option is woefully underdeveloped." Look, we're failing again.

The authors of the study point out that 65 percent of postsecondary education and training takes place outside the college or university in on-the-job training or apprenticeships or in the military, and training is a key component in producing the technologically competent workforce that is vital in an ever-evolving economy. But it's a self-reinforcing cycle, as individuals with a college education are more likely to get formal company training than any other group.

The Georgetown study publishes charts that rival ours in depressing statistics. Their definition of the middle class is the middle four deciles in income (the lower-income class is the lower three deciles; the upper-income class the top three). The study measured education distribution in these three groups in 1970 and 2007. They found that the middle class was split "into two opposing streams of upwardly mobile college haves and downwardly mobile college have-nots."[19] High school dropouts, high school graduates, and those with some college but no degree were headed downward: in 1970, 46 percent of high school dropouts were in the middle class; in 2007 it was 33 percent. In 1970, 60 percent of high school graduates were in the middle class; in 2007 it was 45 percent.

The more education you got, the better off you were. Over the same period, the percentage of people with graduate degrees in the middle class fell from 46 percent to 30 percent, a dramatic decrease. But they weren't getting poorer, because at the same time people with graduate degrees in the top 30 percent rose from 41 percent to 61 percent. In other words, people with graduate degrees were rising out of the middle class and into the more affluent tranches above.

The statistics show that education is the best way to stay in or ascend out of the middle class, even as the value of a college degree is challenged by the stagnation of real wages and the specter of productivity theft. The Georgetown study reveals how much increased education is worth progressively over a lifetime. The authors estimated that a high school graduate could expect to earn $1.77 million over the course of his or her lifetime. With an associate's degree, that person's total lifetime income rose to $2.55 million; with a PhD, it rose to over $4 million; and with a professional degree, it rose to more than $4.65 million.

Looking ahead, the report sees an even greater correlation between success in the workplace and postsecondary education. By 2018, the economy will create 47 million jobs and 63 percent of them will require some college education.[20] And yet, at precisely the time when our position in the world demands that we take action to improve education and training, we're slashing education budgets across the country.

Another way cuts are affecting universities is the closing of entire university departments. Texas wanted to shut down physics departments that were suffering from low enrollment. If the criteria they applied—graduating 25 students in five years—were used across America, 526 of the country's 760 programs would be shuttered.[21] In 2012, I think exactly what this country needs is fewer physicists. Low enrollment is part of a vicious circle. There are fewer graduates teaching physics in high schools, so there are fewer kids who develop an enthusiasm for physics so they go on to study it in college. Closing state programs would concentrate study, and grants, at a few elite colleges. Consider this, from the National Society of Black Physicists:

"College physics programs are the incubators of content-driven K–12 physics teachers that plant the seeds that blossom into future

Texas innovators. Physics graduates are direct contributors to economic prosperity. Even at the BS level a physics degree leads to high-paying jobs that fire the engines of innovation."[22]

It is these engines of innovation that are being threatened all across the country, including at my beloved LSU. As tuition rates inexorably increase at the great state schools, their character inevitably changes. The threat is especially worrisome because of the anti-intellectual, anti-intelligent . . . okay, plain dumb stance of the Republican candidates for president. Higher education, perhaps the key component of middle-class attainment and improvement, is under real attack in this country.

I understand that we're never going to get back to the situation that existed when I went to LSU, when people paid $500 in tuition and had the equivalent of $1,700 a month in walking-around money. But something has to be done to make college more affordable, to help the kids I see around Tulane who are facing a terrible job market with $200,000 in debt on their backs. If universities like LSU stop being affordable, we're creating a knowledge, skills, and jobs gap in this country that hurts us all.

For-Profit Colleges

James One sector of higher education is creating tremendous wealth—if we look at for-profit colleges and what they pay their CEOs. The *Huffington Post* analyzed the compensation of a sample of the highest-paid college employees and found an average of more than $6 million in compensation at for-profit colleges, higher even than the large salaries paid college coaches. Meanwhile, graduation rates are below 50 percent. Gregory Cappelli, co-CEO of the Apollo Group, parent company of the University of Phoenix, topped the list with a compensation package of $25 million, including $19 million in stock—more than the CEO of Coca-Cola receives.[23]

For-profit colleges pay CEOs, but their students stack up debt they can't afford to pay the often higher-than-average tuition. Figures for 2009 show a national student loan default rate for public institutions was 4.6 percent, while the student loan default rate for for-profit schools rose from 11.6 percent to 15 percent. The Department of Education said it had taken measures to protect students from programs that leave students with a lot of debt and poor employment prospects.[24]

Senator Tom Harkin, chairman of the Senate Health, Education, Labor and Pensions Committee, has long targeted for-profit colleges. On the Senate floor in 2011, he pointed to the schools' very high dropout rates. He attacked the aggressive marketing strategies, like the fifty-six-page strategy document that Kaplan University uses to attract veterans, because their funding under the post-9/11 G.I. Bill doesn't count toward the limit of 90 percent of their revenue that these colleges can receive from federal financial aid programs.

This situation is unacceptable. All too often, students at for-profit schools encounter a high-cost, low-value education, a lack of appropriate support services, and executives whose day-to-day priority is squeezing every available dollar from students and taxpayers. It is all the more alarming that active-duty military personnel and veterans, using their hard-earned benefits, are often victims of these for-profit schools.[25]

Despite greater scrutiny being directed at for-profit colleges, the trend toward these models needs to be reversed in public-sector education. These schools derive up to 90 percent of their revenue from federal student loans and Pell grants. That's what running something like a business means: get as many subsidies as you can, and make profits for the shareholders.

While the head of the University of Phoenix makes $25 million, Dr. Charles Lockwood, dean of the College of Medicine at Ohio State, makes $710,000. And who do the Republicans want to penalize? Ohio State. The fundamental question we have to ask ourselves is: Will this country be built by online, for-profit institutions that maximize their returns by getting as many people as possible to take out big student loans, or will it be built by institutions like Ohio State?

Mitt Romney is a big supporter of for-profit colleges, like Full Sail University in Florida, which he touted during his campaign—a place where the tuition is $81,000 for a twenty-one-month course in "video game art" and whose chief executive, Bill Heavener, co-chaired his fund-raising effort in Florida. The *New York Times* reported that the video game course graduated 14 percent of its students on time, 38 percent in total, with an average debt load of $59,000 per student in 2008. Full Sail is owned by a private equity company whose chairman has given $40,000 to a Romney super PAC. At a town hall meeting, a student named Kallie Durkit asked Romney about tuition; Romney suggested for-profits like Full Sail. "When he said that, I was just like, 'You're kidding,'" she told the *Times*. Unfortunately, I don't think he is.[26]

6.

"A 'SECOND OPINION' ON THE ECONOMIC HEALTH OF THE AMERICAN MIDDLE CLASS"; OR, THE FOG MACHINE AND THE DENIAL OF ALL THEIR PROBLEMS

Stan It is hard not to address the breathless excitement of many conservative writers over their recent discovery that the American middle class is actually alive and well—even flourishing. In academia, Richard V. Burkhauser, Jeff Larrimore, and Kosali I. Simon of the National Bureau of Economic Research offered "A 'Second Opinion' on the Economic Health of the American Middle Class."[1] The *Washington Post* editorial page just ran an op-ed piece by Ron Haskins under the headline, "The Myth of the Disappearing Middle Class." It begins by throwing out pretty much everything we have been saying: "President Obama, many Democrats and editorial page writers have been working to convince the nation that it is wracked by inequality, a disappearing middle class and a lack of opportunity." Scott Winship wrote a piece in the *New Republic* headlined to get a response: "Stop Feeling Sorry for the Middle Class! They're Doing Just Fine." And FoxNews.com headlined their contribution, "Sorry, Mr. Biden Most Middle Class Americans Are Better Off Now Than They Were Thirty Years Ago."

Well, I guess we got it wrong. We could have saved ourselves a lot of time.

James These are all examples of something you see more and more in modern politics—what has been quite accurately referred to as the fog machine. What the fog machine does is work to deny that a problem exists. Everything we have been saying about the middle class has been denied at one point or another. And the fog machine operates in so many other areas, too, especially on controversial subjects like climate change.

The fog machine operates on a cycle. First, they just deny. Whatever it is, it doesn't exist. The middle class is in crisis? No, it isn't. If they can't keep a straight face when confronted with facts on the issue, then they can admit, "Okay, maybe there is something to it. But if there is, the government's to blame, not us. And if that's the case, well, there's just nothing we can do about it. The fix is too costly and the government is just going to get in the way." On other occasions, the fog machine says, "No, it's not a problem, it's actually a good thing," or "Yes, it is a problem, but it's your fault." In the end, the fog machine is never responsible for anything.

So let's deny that the middle class is in trouble, as these people—and we all know who they are—are doing. I want to enumerate other areas where the deniers are working hard. If you say the climate's changing, the first thing the machine says is, "It's doing no such thing, so keep on polluting." Before 2008, people said that the housing market was getting overheated. "No, it's not overheated," the fog machine retorted. Then, when it became apparent that it was so overheated, the lid about to blow off, the fog machine responded with "There's nothing you can do about it," and even "This is actually good for you. This is a creative destruction. It's actually a positive thing that this happened."

It doesn't matter how ridiculous the denial is, you can count on the right wing to push it out there and the mainstream media to give the argument equal time, which is why we have to read this garbage. So if we think this is the end of the middle class, what are they whining about? First of all, there's not a problem with the middle class, but if there is, it's that more of them should get married. And we can say that's absurd, just like we said that it was absurd to say that black people should be blamed for the financial crisis— but they were. Or we say that it's absurd for people to say that global warming is caused by human intervention—but they do. Or that it's absurd for people to say that a country that spends 18 percent of its GDP on health care with a low life expectancy has the best health care system in the world—but they do. They do! And they do it with a straight face!

Stan   To be honest, I am baffled by their excitement about this. I recognize the need to deny that a problem exists if you want to avoid facing it, but their data largely affirms everything we are saying here. Everything.[2] To write those headlines and come to those conclusions, they must ignore key parts of their own recalculations and tables; misread their own and others' findings; refuse to examine the periods that preceded the one they studied; and remain silent on the huge trends that undermine the approved story. At the same time, they quickly concede points that would have dramatic implications if they had not rushed past them. And finally, they put their findings and conclusions about the poor at center stage, as if we should feel guilty for our misplaced focus on the middle class.

James It's classic misdirection. They will do anything to keep this from being the main problem. And then they'll say, which they do, that the number of poor in this country is grossly exaggerated—the government's definition of poverty is wrong. By the time you are tackling that issue, they've moved you decisively off the first problem, or so they hope.

Stan Their key starting point is refuting the concepts of a "middle-class decline" and a "vanishing middle class" and denying the conclusion that "things have gotten worse for middle-income Americans."[3] They have focused like a laser on President Obama's observation in Kansas that "over the last few decades, the rungs of the ladder of opportunity have grown further apart, and the middle class has shrunk." That rallies them to dispute his observations and those of the chair of the Council of Economic Advisors, Alan Krueger, about the growing polarization of the country—that fewer people cluster around the median income and more are at the top and bottom.[4]

That is beside the point. We will give the president a little rhetorical space to describe the problems facing the middle class. The indisputable assertion of this book as well as EPI, CAP, and others is that the incomes of those in the middle in recent decades are barely growing compared to middle incomes during the World War II decades that followed. This stands in sharp contrast to what has happened at the top, particularly the top 1 percent. We never said the middle class "shrank"; in fact we have an expansive view of the middle class, including working people. What absolutely everyone agrees on is that the broad middle faces stagnant, barely rising incomes with no indication that this will improve in the future. That is the crux of the problem.

Burkhauser and his collaborators spend a lot of time factoring in changes in household size, post-tax income, transfers like tax credits and food stamps, and health insurance. Thomas Edsall's *New York Times* essay reviewing the controversy indicates these are legitimate adjustments, but it does not matter in any case.[5] According to their calculations, those in the middle of the income scale saw their incomes rise 37 percent over the last three decades. That is about a percentage point a year and not very different from what we saw in Chapter Four. The results also match for the top 5 percent, as well as the dramatically widening divide in the country during this unique period.

These reports share a common trait: they do not display data or talk about the top 1 percent, who do not get so much as a line in the Burkhauser tables. In fact, in the *Washington Post* op-ed, the writer lists the Democrats' charges, including the country being "wracked by inequality." Well, that "is partly true, mostly because those at the top of the income distribution have pulled away from the rest of us." Well, other than that, Mrs. Lincoln, how was the play?

And most important, despite all this academic rigor, there is no mention of the three postwar decades, when income grew at more than six times the rate of the last 30 years. In the three decades following World War II, income growth was not only stronger than it is now, but all income quintiles also grew together.[6] The current period is an abrupt change from the America of the post–World War II period but conservatives are silent about it.

They are also silent and coy on labeling the periods that make up the three decades—the three "business cycles" of the period: 1979–89, 1989–2000, and 2000–2007. The names "President Reagan," "President Clinton," and "President Bush" do not make it into the article. Try your word search. Yes, income grew 37 percent for the middle over the three decades, but half of that growth in income came in the period dominated by the economic and tax policies of the Clinton administration. The rate of income growth in the Clinton economic period was 16.8 percent, double the average for the two Republican presidents (8.3 percent). I wonder why *that* was not mentioned.

Guess what else? After all their calculations, only during the Clinton period did the Gini coefficient—the standard measure of inequality—improve. The top 5 percent saw a 15.1 percent gain in income—just a touch *less* than the middle, who had gained 16.8 percent. The Reagan period brought a dramatic worsening of these numbers, while the George W. Bush years were just bad for everybody. That was about the time John McCain was saying "the fundamentals of the economy are fine."

Not having unpacked any of that story and its implications for policy, Burkhauser tells a sympathetic interviewer, "No one has the slightest idea what will work. The cupboard is bare." But the op-ed writers on FoxNews.com certainly did, pointing out that "while the Great Recession has certainly taken a harsh toll in recent years, these long-term gains hold vital lessons for politicians to uphold pro-growth policies at a time when they're hearing populist cries to remake the economic order."[7]

James What a relief that is. I guess we really were wrong about the problem. The denials just keep getting bigger and bigger and the deniers bolder and bolder.

Stan One of the most curious elements of this "middle-class crisis" denial is the highlighting of what has happened to the lowest quintile and the poor. The conservative public intellectuals and the op-ed writers are enthralled with the new calculation that takes into account the earned income tax credit and the value of all "public transfers," including food stamps, welfare, Pell grants, Social Security, and other government-provided cash assistance, as well as Medicare and Medicaid: the poorest in the country, they contend, are doing much better than you think. Again, I have no idea whether other calculations account for these or whether this calculation is a full accounting. But the conclusion is amazing: as Ron Haskins wrote in the *Washington Post*, "the bottom 20 percent had about 25 percent more income in 2007 than in 1979. Even the bottom is moving up."[8]

Yes, they moved up, but the only period when that happened was under President Clinton. You should stare at their charts on pages 33 and 35 of Burkhauser's paper. They are right. The income of the bottom quintile went up 23.2 percent in the Clinton economic period, but only .4 percent under Reagan and 2.2 percent under George W. Bush. The great expansion of the Earned Income Tax Credit along with wage gains allowed the bottom 20 percent to make real gains. It is the only period when the bottom made significantly more gains, by these calculations.

You would think that somebody would notice that this has implications for those thinking of voting for the Paul Ryan budget, which demolishes the food stamp program and seeks to get rid of refundable tax credits and limit the Earned Income Tax Credit.[9] These commentators are utterly silent on this subject.

For others in this camp, like Scott Winship, who writes in the *New Republic* and the *National Review*, "the attention we insist on paying to the overstated problems of the middle class come at the expense of the more critical challenges facing the poor." He argues that the president's alarming tone will have the "shameful effect of unnecessarily raising Americans' economic anxiety levels" and delaying "a full recovery," and will dampen the hopes of those who wish to transcend their disadvantages. Pretty astonishingly, he argues that the "scare-mongering targeted at the middle class" will reduce "support for policies that would disproportionately help the poor." Why? He says the real debate will be "over which economic problems merit the most attention in a nation that cannot afford to help everyone."[10] It seems he does not want the national debate to center on the middle class.

And if you have the right ideological filter, you realize that our safety nets—their value richly demonstrated in the work of Burkhauser and his colleagues—"might simultaneously lift the poor out of destitution yet discourage the upward mobility of poor children." Those transfers and tax credits are inadequate incentives for "work, marriage, and saving." That does not concern the "left," which "does not want to confront the important issues of family instability, criminality, and personal responsibility in limiting life chances."[11]

If we can get off this middle-class kick, we could get to the real problems facing the country.

I won't dwell on these patronizing and out-of-touch characterizations of what is happening in the lives of working people. After all, unemployment is not that widespread, and "middle class anxiety has been relatively muted," Winthrop writes.[12]

We welcome you to visit America sometime.

The Sane World vs. the Fog Machine

THE SANE WORLD	THE FOG MACHINE
The earth was created over billions of years.	The earth was created five or six thousand years ago. (See Republicans in the Tennessee and Louisiana legislatures.)

THE SANE WORLD	THE FOG MACHINE
The earth is getting warmer.	The earth is cooling.
The rich pay too little in taxes in the United States.	If Mitt Romney had to pay any more than 13% tax, he might have to move to the Cayman Islands.
Over-leveraged, unregulated risk taking caused the financial crisis.	Black people caused the financial crisis.
Middle-class families are working harder and longer, and receiving fewer of the benefits of better productivity through rises in national income.	The middle class should be grateful they have a cell phone and drive a Toyota.
The single largest contributor to the budget deficit was the Bush tax cuts.	How can that be possible? Tax cuts increase revenue.
Economic inequality is increasing in the United States.	Social mobility means inequality doesn't matter.
Social mobility is declining in the United States.	People on lower incomes are lazy.
Attacking Iraq was one of the most stupid things we have done in the history of the United States.	It worked beautifully and we should still be in Iraq.
Kids need comprehensive sex education to understand the consequences and alternatives to unwanted pregnancies.	If you tell people not to have sex, that will stop them every time. Abstinence works!

THE SANE WORLD	THE FOG MACHINE
Birth control pills are an effective drug against unwanted pregnancies.	Aspirin is an effective drug against unwanted pregnancies.
If you see someone you know who is not a Christian between Dec. 15 and Dec. 25, you should be polite and say "Happy holidays."	You are attacking Christianity and engaging in a War on Christmas.
Eating too much fatty food is not good for you.	That's just a plot to try to control what you eat.
Unregulated drilling is threatening our coastlines and National Parks.	There's nothing more beautiful than an oil company balance sheet.

It's Not Easy Being Rich

James   Part of the denial of middle-class hardship is to downplay the effects of income inequality. Let's face it: it's tough to be rich. It's hardly worth the extra effort it takes to become super-wealthy, given that poor people can get their grubby hands on pretty much everything that billionaires have. The most asinine newspaper piece I have read in years was written by a guy named Andy Kessler in the *Wall Street Journal*.[13] Thanks to what Mr. Kessler calls "consumption equality," the wealthy work their sixty- to eighty-hour weeks inventing things for the masses, but there's not much they can buy with their money that the middle class can't afford.

"What does Google founder Larry Page have that you don't have?"

Mr. Kessler asks, perhaps rhetorically.[14] A suite at the Super Bowl? You're better off watching on TV. A Bugatti? Why even bother? "Even a $16,500 Ford Focus can hit 80 on the highway or get stuck in the same traffic as the rich person's ride." On he goes. A hip replacement or a stent? You can only afford one, because some rich person invented it for the masses, just like they did with smartphones, hard drives, and affordable air travel.

It shouldn't come as a surprise that Mr. Kessler used to manage a hedge fund. What he spouts is a classic argument for the low-taxes-for-us, low-wages-for-you crowd. We should concur with Mr. Kessler and be grateful for what we have. So what if we're working years longer and our incomes are going down: we can buy that better TV and watch football. Who cares if we can't afford to send our children to college: we can buy them a cell phone, now that they don't cost $4,000, and talk to them as they stand in line for a job interview at McDonald's. And what if your parents, after working their whole lives, lose their health insurance and one of them gets sick? No worries, you can drive them to the emergency room in your Ford Focus and hope to God you don't get stuck in traffic behind some jerk in his Bugatti.

7.

SMARTER THAN YOU THINK: THE FINANCIAL CRISIS

Stan Tim Geithner, head of the Federal Reserve Bank of New York, and Treasury Secretary Hank Paulson huddled increasingly with the CEOs of America's biggest banks to decide how to respond to the increasing vulnerability of investment and national banks in the face of falling home values and progressively worthless mortgage-backed securities. When the Treasury decided to let Lehman Brothers fail in September 2008, all shit broke loose—and the White House accepted it would have to create a bailout fund of some $750 billion, soon to be called TARP, the Troubled Asset Relief Program.

Barack Obama conferred with his team of prominent economic advisers and lent his support for the administration's actions at this time of national crisis, and John McCain called for a moratorium on campaigning and a closed White House meeting with all national political leaders. At that meeting, Obama crisply set out the problem and what should happen and made it clear that the Democrats would support the Treasury. McCain said almost nothing, deferring to congressional Republican leaders—but both leaders rallied support in Congress for the bailout fund. When Secretary Paulson met with the Democratic House leaders in secret session, as we now know from Andrew Sorkin's book and the HBO movie *Too Big to Fail*, Paulson got down on one knee and begged Speaker Nancy Pelosi to support the bailout fund lest the country face Armageddon, as my wife described it at the time.

The surprise defeat of the bank bailout by the U.S. House of Representatives took the Dow stock average down 778 points, another $1.2 trillion in market value, and wiped out trillions in markets around the world. Congressional leaders brought back the members to jam the bailout bill through after ladening it with the traditional pork-flavored goodies to win Senate and House support.

The ordinary citizen understood exactly what was happening: the elites from both Wall Street and Washington, from both parties—i.e., banking and politics, including both presidential candidates—were taking care of all the people who took the country into this crisis. This was an elite, secret deal to use taxpayer money to bail out the irresponsible.

From the very beginning of the financial crisis in the summer and fall of 2008, the voter understood the scope of responsibility for the economic mess. The Pew Research Center asked 1,485 people how much responsibility each of the players should bear for the economic situation, and it is intriguing how much they spread the blame around, starting with themselves. Unlike many of the bankers who continued to justify their practices, their role in bringing on the crisis, and the need for public support, the voter was pretty frank about everyone's complicity in creating the crisis.[1]

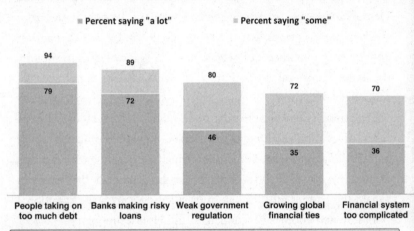

Causes of financial crisis: people, banks, and government

How much do you think each of the following has contributed to the current problems with financial institutions and markets?

■ Percent saying "a lot"   ■ Percent saying "some"

94	89	80	72	70
79	72	46	35	36
People taking on too much debt	Banks making risky loans	Weak government regulation	Growing global financial ties	Financial system too complicated

Source: From Pew Research Center for the People & the Press, October 15, 2008.

From the beginning of the crisis, voters identified two big factors related to debt and leverage: "people taking on too much debt" and "banks making risky loans." Yet in stark contrast to the bankers, the voters started with their own role and responsibility. More than nine in every ten said people had contributed some or a lot to the current problems; almost as many said the banks had. More than 70 percent said both owned a lot of the blame. Voters saw two other factors playing big contributory roles: "weak government regulation" and "growing global financial ties."

It is the ordinary voter who came to the crisis with perspective and a sense of personal responsibility, despite the fact that it was leaders of both parties in Washington and those on Wall Street who struck the bargain that created the financial rules, and acted only when the banks were threatened, even as the economy was rushing to shed hundreds of thousands of jobs a month.

When the job crash hit its worst point in the recession in March 2009, voters could be fairly described as angry. Two-thirds reserved their anger for the big banks and financial institutions and for big corporations. An impressive six in ten said they were angry with the Bush administration, and four in ten blamed consumers. Only half that number, one in five, were angry at the Obama administration.[2]

Democracy Corps began conducting one-on-one in-depth interviews with many of these people about a year into the Obama administration, TARP, and the Economic Recovery Act. What impressed us more than anything else was how sophisticated they were about the character of this crisis, as if they had read Sorkin's book: they spoke fluently about the lack of liquidity in credit markets, the consequence of leverage, the housing bubble and the subprime mortgage crisis, and a lack of government regulation to prevent such excesses.[3]

This took place in a developing culture of overconsumption and overspending, and a lack of oversight and limits, that were fueled by greed—and, in the end, a presumption that different actors play by different rules. This started with the banks that were "at the center of the storm, loaning to people who could not afford it and fueling the fire." People who were doing "everything they can to just pay their bills and break even" faced rising monthly mortgage payments, even as some lost jobs, taking the country to "a breaking point."

"I think, like anything else, the corporations unfortunately did a lot of bad things, especially with free money, and they were giving opportunities—just basically giving all these mortgages and these homes that people couldn't afford to buy. . . . They were just giving them anything to make a buck and nobody cared about the long-term effect or something like that."—Man, white, age 35, non-college-educated

"And these balloon payments on mortgages . . . it's just like it starts at one end and it just trickles down to everybody."—Woman, white, age 50, non-college-educated

"I mean they [Wall Street banks] were just hand over fist making money with the housing instead of saying, 'Okay this is really getting out of hand.' I mean, if you are making all that money, who is going to put a stop to it, you know?"—Woman, white, age 45, non-college-educated

"Homes went for too much. There was just no doubt about it, so there had to be some kind of breaking point. It just couldn't be climbing, so there had to be some kind of breaking point, but it was like the bottom fell out all at once in everything."—Woman, white, age 45, non-college-educated

While people began the story with the banks, they reserved some of their harshest criticism for everyday people—indeed, themselves. Sure, the banks had preyed on them, but many of them had bought bigger houses than they needed or could afford, put luxuries on the credit card, and had given in to their kids' desire for more and more material things. On mortgages, many pushed back against the blame

game: "You can't really blame nobody because everybody is responsible for themselves, [and] everybody is suffering, not just one
person."[4]

"[Everyday] people, they played a part in contributing to it by going
out and buying houses that they couldn't afford. . . . The banks were
actually giving money to people—you know, no money down or doing
the interest-only loans and stuff—and people were living beyond their
means, because, once again, I think everyone just thought it was
going to be here forever. . . . People were just living beyond their
means."—Man, white, age 40, non-college-educated

"They weren't tallying their checkbooks, they weren't watching their
pocketbooks. They were living off of somebody else's money and not
their own. They couldn't afford to borrow the money that they had.
They didn't have the means to pay it back. People were naïve, listening to people—banks and people—say, 'Hey, we will lend you the
money.'"—Woman, white, age 40, non-college-educated

The problem with the banks and crap mortgages was greatly
compounded by consumers' penchant for buying more than they
could afford and depending on debt to do it. They viewed the problem as almost cultural: consumption threatened their families' well-
being. "Our society overspends unbelievably. I mean, we live off of
not . . . what we can buy but what we can make payments on," one
man told us.[5] Another declared, "I think in the United States we are
gluttons."[6] They no longer asked themselves what they could afford
but rather "Can we cover the payments?" But they knew that they
were on the edge of something scary: a Latino man in Studio City,
California, said, "The next thing you know, your payments are all

your income."[7] Some thought the recession had taught us a pretty big lesson: "Hey, if we don't do something, we are going to be living on the street, because we can't live like this anymore," a man in Atlantic Beach, Florida, told us.[8]

The crisis exposed not only their own vulnerability but also the underbelly of corporate America and government. The white working class and non-college-educated spoke with particular intensity, not only about the greed of the big banks that had wrecked the housing sector, but also about the corporations that had laid waste to whole industries and were barely employing Americans anymore. They went for the short-term advantage, the belief was, and did not act for the long term. Since this way of doing business had settled in for some time, they were the most pessimistic about the economy.

"[For] the upper class, everything was laid out for them to . . . play with our money. . . . [The] banks and everything, they just had free rein to do whatever they wanted without any punishment and, you know, caused a lot of things to fall and, you know, they're still getting away with it by . . . getting help and stuff like that."—Man, white, age 35, non-college-educated

"I think there again the key word is 'greed': they've been selling out all our jobs overseas to take advantage of poor people over in other countries where they can pay them a nickel where it would cost them a dollar over here, so everybody's selling out. . . . I think they could do a better job at trying to keep our workers keep the jobs here in America."—Man, white, age 50, non-college-educated

"It seems like corporate America is all about the mighty dollar and not about the long term but today."—Man, white, age 50, non-college-educated

Virtually everyone we spoke to took out their anger on government, which is no small part of the reason why people have trouble turning to government for anything. Some of the anger was just downright libertarian—a Jeffersonian distrust of anything government does—particularly among the non-college-educated, who saw a controlling government and politicians who spent recklessly, said one thing and did another, and worked for the big guy anyway.

> "Well, the only ones that I really know of that seem to be trying is the church groups and stuff: I see them doing a lot of things that are helping people and the government in my eyes has really been losing their control. I mean, they're trying to gain control over everything we do and have and think about and I think they're getting out of control on just sort of a lot of things, I can't say one particular person."—Man, white, age 50, non-college-educated

But many more of them were angry at the government for not doing its job, not seeing the risks, not attempting to limit corporate and consumer excess, and just not getting control of things. They were looking for more government, not less. Some of this sentiment was expressed by the young voters, unmarried women, and minorities who make up a growing progressive bloc of voters. They recalled George Bush's hands-off policies that let companies police themselves, but across all these interviews people were frustrated with the lack of oversight and really angry at government for failing in its responsibilities.

"Well, business is business. If you let the business go wild, it's going to go wild. . . . [It is] going to take the money and run. I think you've got to make sure you stay on top of it. I mean, you've got to have laws, you've got to have protection, you know. You can't, you can't do this because it's going to crash the economy. Look at the bank I was with: it failed."—Man, white, age 35, non-college-educated

"Well, I feel we were taken advantage of by the banks. The laws . . . [Pause] everything crashed. I think somebody should have overseen more of that. [They] are giving out money to these home owners and people that shouldn't have had it. And I just feel somebody should have stepped in and stopped it."—Woman, white, age 50, non-college-educated

"I just think everything that he has done, the Republicans and President Bush, had a lot to do with the banking and he let them do what they wanted to do."—Woman, white, age 50, non-college-educated

"Well, I mean, [Bush] pretty much set up the failure."—Woman, black, age 25, non-college-educated

At crunch time, government bailed out the banks that produced this mess, not the people living the consequences. As a non-college-educated white woman from White Oak, Pennsylvania, put it, "It's pretty simple: government's with them, not us."

"The government decided they wanted to bail everybody out. The only people they are not bailing out is us working class. They are bailing out the banks, they are bailing out the car companies, they are bailing everybody out, but what about me? I'm not getting a dime; all I'm doing is paying more. I'm sick of bailing everybody else out. I'm sitting here and doing nothing while everybody is getting bailed out. These executives are getting a million, two-million, three-million-dollar bonuses. I'm lucky to get a 2 percent raise a year." —Woman, white, age 55, non-college-educated

"But they get the bailouts and what do we get? We get jobs outsourced, we get taxed. Are we responsible for other people, like the bankers and the corporations, for their failures? And there are other insurance companies that went under or that needed bailouts, like [AIG], I think. They relied on us taxpayers to bail them out. But, yeah, I don't like his approach to the economy at all." —Man, Latino, age 40, non-college-educated

When you talked through TARP individually, some people understood why it had to happen, but feelings against the bailouts ran very strong. On our surveys in the years since, around two-thirds have opposed them, even though most of the money was repaid.[9] Voters just thought the bailouts were wrong.

And voters punished both Democratic and Republican politicians who voted for TARP on successive polling days. Ask Utah senator Robert Bennett and Minnesota senator Norm Coleman. Bennett, who voted for TARP, came in third in a field of three candidates in the Senate nomination race at the 2010 Republican convention in Utah. Coleman, who also voted for TARP, lost his Senate seat to Al Franken.

And ask President Obama and the Democrats about the 2010 elections. With TARP and the auto bailout fresh in their minds, less than half the country thought President Obama and the Democrats stood with Main Street over Wall Street.[10]

That does mean that the passage of time has left people in an equivocal frame of mind about who bears responsibilities for that traumatic period in our history. Their views of the actors are set in stone, whatever has transpired in the meantime. In the absence of any real recovery, the voters were impatient and frustrated with President Obama, but to this day they put him at the back of the line of those responsible for the economic troubles. Plain and simple, it was the big banks, the Bush administration, and lack of government oversight that created the mess. Voters held Obama and the Democrats painfully accountable in the 2010 off-year elections, but they were not confused about who produced the financial crisis.

Well into 2011, half the voters in a *New York Times*/CBS poll still blamed Wall Street banks and the Bush administration for the state of the economy, and some cited Congress, but less than 10 percent said the Obama administration owns the crippled economy.[11]

And the same is true of their understanding of America's ballooning federal deficits. They were alert to what happened in the lead-up to the financial crisis, as America waged two wars and added a prescription drug benefit without paying for them. Despite the trillions that Obama added to the deficit during his term in office, voters continue to go back to that history. On the deficit, over 40 percent of voters at the beginning of this year put the responsibility at the feet of the Bush administration—more than twice the number who blame the Obama administration or Congress. That same pattern has held throughout Obama's term in office.[12]

Voters erupted against Congress, politicians, and Democrats in the 2010 off-year election, but there is no indication this has overshadowed the electorate's understanding of the crisis, which no doubt shapes their reactions across a broad range of issues.

But what's good for the goose is good for the gander. The very same considered perceptions of the financial crisis and underlying economy have also made it painfully difficult for President Obama to be heard when he talks about economic progress, the economy being on "the right track," and, above all, the number of new jobs being created month after month. And for the president, nothing is more important than being heard on the subject of jobs. The political class would be wise to pay as much attention to these voters' sense of reality *on the jobs issue* as they do to their understanding of the financial crisis.

The fitful and protracted recovery of the last three years has led the Obama administration to talk about "recovery summer" and "green shoots of recovery" and rush to the pressroom each time there appears to be sustained or newsworthy job creation.[13] The president has become more cautious about heralding progress after so many false starts, but in his 2012 State of the Union address and his speech to congressional Democrats, he began to roll out his narrative about the pace of job creation and said explicitly, "We're moving in the right direction" and more: "America is back."[14]

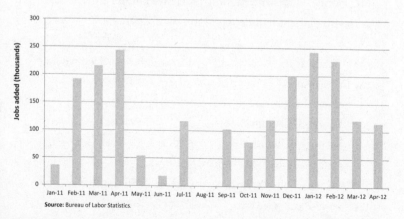

Jobs added, January 2011 to April 2012

Source: Bureau of Labor Statistics.

Well, few things have enraged our focus groups more over the last few years. In one group, participants almost attacked our moderator when he simply read a news report on the 240,000 jobs gained in a month during the recovery. The people rushed to dispute or qualify it, talking over each other as they tried to explain how wrong the conventional wisdom on the economy really is. Listen to these voters in Ohio playing off one another:[15]

"The way people have kicked off the chart and they keep saying they created 225,000 jobs and what is the job doing? I mean, you can work for McDonald's for 9 bucks an hour to 11 bucks an hour."

"Yeah, you can always sway numbers."

"What kind of jobs are they?"

"Exactly, and who got those jobs? I mean, who got those jobs?"

Many people begin talking at once.

"Like he said, McDonald's or . . ."

Another moderator, in Columbus, Ohio, put out the 240,000 figure, noting it was the highest monthly number in five years and that unemployment had dropped to about 9 percent.[16]

"What was the average salary of those jobs? . . . That would be my first question."

"Where are these jobs?"

"What types of jobs?"

"Are they part-time?"

"Yeah, fast-food jobs?"

"Are these jobs that people can live on? Or are they jobs you take because you have to?"

"What kind of jobs?"

"Or there's two million applying for the 240,000."

"Right."

And yet another brave moderator tried asking, "What is your reaction to that report?"

"What office do they get those stats out of?"

"We had three of our largest pharma clients: one laid off 5 thousand people right away. So all of a sudden you have all these highly educated people . . ."

"My Chicago law firm was laying off three partners. That was unheard of."[17] The moderator asked: "Isn't that a step in the right direction though, even though they might not be the higher-paying jobs people need?" "I don't know if you want to know what I think, but I have a forty-two-year-old daughter that graduated from Cornell University and she did that when she was thirty-nine years old. And so she got this fancy degree and she thought she had the world by a string, because that is what they told her when she was going to school. She is in Santa Fe, New Mexico, working for . . . what is considered minimum wage by Santa Fe standards, and that is what she has done for the last two and a half years. And I have had to help her, because she needs medications and she needs things that she can't have. And my Social Security and my retirement is not going up."[18]

Even after this year's (2012) State of the Union address, when we gathered people in Denver to talk about reactions to the president's speech, we found that their understanding of a very difficult job market had not changed: "Just pouring sugar on the thing to create a few temporary jobs is going to get us no place"; "All those jobs he talks about, all the rebound they talk about and all that—personally, I don't see that just from my circle of acquaintances." One person summed up the problem: "I mean, we are still in a deficit in terms of jobs and he didn't say anything about the shrinking middle class and I was disappointed . . . I haven't had a raise in three years."[19]

Apparently the voters are the last to know the good news. According to conventional economic wisdom, if the recovery carries on for enough months, and if political and economic leaders provide an interpretation, eventually the voter will get it—and likely reward the leaders responsible for the economic gains. But it turns out that the ordinary citizen may understand this unique crisis and our current economy much better than the elites. In our economic tracking surveys for Democracy Corps, we found that people's families stubbornly continued to report reduced wages and benefits, whatever was happening on the macro jobs front.[20] And we now know from reports by the Hamilton Project that workers who became unemployed in this crisis and then took a new job took an average $610 cut in monthly salary and benefits, 17 percent below where they started.[21]

A report in the *Wall Street Journal* explored those two million jobs created over the last two and a half years. The biggest gains

Unemployment rate, January 2011 to April 2012

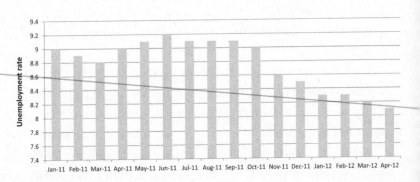

Source: Bureau of Labor Statistics.

have come in health care jobs and leisure and hospitality jobs, mostly in restaurants—not the highest-paying places. In business services, the gains have come with secretaries and temp workers, not architects and lawyers. And while manufacturing has notched gains, it regained only 400,000 of the 2.3 million shed since the crisis. Construction gains are grudging, while better-paying public sector jobs are still being lost.[22]

Let's say it flat out: They're right and we're wrong. They were right and still are—and have good reason to be angry when the macro, elite conversation talks past them on what has really happened in the real economy. Our advice: Listen and pay attention. A lot depends on that.

8.

SMARTER THAN YOU THINK? THEN WHAT ABOUT KEYNES?

James Well, we're not winning the GD argument.

Stan The voters just think getting in debt and spending down makes more sense than spending.

James What are the numbers?

Stan It's not even close.

James Let me hear that again.

Stan They think spending hurts the economy; it doesn't help it. They think more debt makes us weaker as a country. The Chinese have us by the balls, so to speak.

James That may be true, but they clearly aren't reading Krugman.

Stan No, but they are paying a lot of attention to Greece, a country down the toilet: wages cut, state workers laid off, pensions gone. They think our Social Security is next.

James The United States of America ain't Greece. Anybody with money anywhere in the world wants to put their money here. We've got the lowest interest rates. There is nobody more credit-worthy.

Stan Get down to basics, James—and I keep trying to ask it in a way that clashes with what we know to be true. People think spending means fewer jobs and reducing deficits will mean more jobs.

James Well, they're wrong.

Stan That's what they think.

James That's not good enough.

Stan They think spending is just throwing money at the problem—and corrupt to boot. A bunch of corrupt politicians jamming the budget with pork-barrel projects, with big payoffs, bailouts, and tax breaks for their special-interest buddies. The voter thinks they are just trying to up their vote by makin' it smell pretty. But the last thing they think is that this spending is going to help the country.

James They're not total fools. Still wrong.

Stan When they hear the word "stimulus," their ears burn. They just hear a cash register filled with taxpayers' dollars or expect the government to put it all on a credit card. They really just see politicians throwing their money at the problem—pissing it away at a high cost, particularly for their kids, who they think will end up paying the bills.

James Of course, the stimulus worked. Incontestable. It was clumsy, but it still worked. A better-designed and bigger stimulus would have worked better. Maybe it avoided a depression.

Stan They don't think it worked. Where are the jobs? Where are the jobs that pay what they used to? Where is the evidence that we have a better economy?

James   When Obama came in, we were losing 750,000 jobs a month. There was a $2 trillion hole in the economy.[1] They filled at least a bit of it. It is incontestable. Every conservative and liberal economist will tell you. Without the stimulus, we would have had three million less jobs and the economy would have been in worse shape. Flat out. Spending worked and works.

Stan   They don't see it yet—and they don't believe it when they see it, because they know more debt is bad. At least not yet. They are starting to see the need for things that grow the economy, but it doesn't change their view of spending.

James   Keynes would turn over in his grave. But as Nicholas Kristof put it, Europe declared war on Keynes, and Keynes is winning. He's referring to the aforementioned Greece where taking austerity measures in a recession has been disastrous.[2] Everything the Keynesians have said—about interest rates, inflation—they have been right. Keynes would come back and say, "I told you so." But you can't walk into a focus group and say, "People don't believe this." You have to find a way to make it more palatable to them.

Stan   Maybe we need to get Keynes to talk to people in focus groups.

James   Well, I'm not convinced. Maybe Thomas Frank is right: they don't know their own self-interest. They're the ones who'll be hurt when those crazies start cutting their Social Security and Medicare. They are being spooked by the Tea Party and Fox. All that Koch brothers money being used to promote their cause. I don't want to go there, but I'm not convinced we settle for this popular wisdom.

A year after Congress passed the American Recovery and Reinvestment Act of 2009, we began reading to people two simple statements:

The best way to improve our economy and create jobs is to invest more.
The best way to improve our economy is to cut spending and taxes.

Then we asked them which was closer to their own thinking. At no point during that year did even half the voters choose the first statement—for John Maynard Keynes, the most efficient way to get growth. It started with 47 percent for Keynes, while 48 percent sided with the Republican brew of spending and tax cuts but it only got worse each time. In the summer before the 2010 election debacle, 41 percent were with Keynes, but a clear majority of 52 percent was against him.[3] When we asked simply, "Will *reducing the deficit* mean higher or lower unemployment?" a plurality of 48 percent said *"Lower"*—and only a third of the country agreed with the demonstrably correct statement that it would suck demand out of the economy and produce higher unemployment.

We partnered with the liberal organization Campaign for America's Future to examine why we were losing the argument and to develop an argument that could win. We embellished the arguments, getting more elaborate each time.[4] At that point in the crisis, we asked people to identify the greater concern for the national economy:

1. *The danger of throwing more people out of work and extending the recession by focusing too much on deficit reduction; OR*
2. *The danger of putting the burden of debt on future generations by not focusing enough on deficit reduction.*

A plurality of 47 percent said they worried more about passing on debt, and only 43 percent feared an obsession with deficits would throw people out of work. We weren't getting slaughtered, but we weren't winning, either, on something we knew to be true. We faced

the genuine risk that purveyors of the politics of austerity were winning their way. Going further, we asked them to choose:

1. *We need to reduce the deficit over time while making investments vital
   to our future by spending on education, training, research, and a modern infrastructure for the twenty-first century. OR*
2. *We need to catch up with a changing world, but government spending
   is out of control and we need to reduce the deficit boldly so that America can compete in a very challenging twenty-first century.*

By acknowledging the need to reduce the deficit over the long term,
we battled to a draw with the deficit cutters.

Getting people to recall their U.S. history didn't work, either. We
asked them to remember that right after World War II, the country
was even deeper in debt than it is now, but we opted to embark on
large-scale public investments, like highways and the G.I. Bill, and
the subsequent growth wiped out our deficits. Interesting, they
thought, but not more persuasive than cutting the deficit now.

We finally got a majority to support our argument only when we
committed in capital letters to BOTH investment and reduced deficits "over time." The public could be rallied to our cause, but only if
voters thought we were very serious about addressing the deficits
over time. Maybe it was time to take that seriously.

We can't say that our liberal clients were very happy with us. Head
of Campaign for America's Future, Bob Borosage, a longtime friend
and compatriot through many battles, stuck with Greenberg, despite
our repeated inability to defeat the deficit hawks. On survey after
survey, unless we listed deficit reduction as one of our goals, voters
consistently rejected our message. Many of our allies believed we
had surrendered.

———

Bob   Everyone at CAF rolled their eyes each time you showed us losing. Everyone wanted to fire you. After all, what good is a pollster if he or she can't give us the answers we want?

Stan   We got to a draw.

Bob   Sure, by giving away the store. We have to win the intellectual argument. In a deep recession like this one, austerity—as Europe is teaching us—is ruinous. They are preaching ideology, not economics. Why couldn't voters see that? Our job is to find a way to win the argument without conceding it. It's easier, of course, to co-opt their argument, as both Clinton and Obama have shown—but it then abuses the bully pulpit to add to the public miseducation and delusions.

We stayed with you because we wanted an argument that pierced their concerns, not a pollster who hid them to get us the answer we wanted.

Stan   I tried to get myself into their heads. And they weren't foolish. They thought the deficit was produced by two wars, bailouts, and special-interest spending. They thought the deficits threatened more layoffs and the government's ability to make Social Security payments. They were watching California and Greece.

Bob   Okay, assume that's where they are—although I suspect that's only one snapshot of conflicting views. The challenge remains: How do we get them to support what needs to be done despite what is in their heads?

This, we realized, was particularly difficult because the inside-the-Beltway elite consensus was very much about deficit reduction too.

So it wasn't just Fox peddling tripe, it was the *Washington Post* and CNN. So, we needed a compelling populist argument that could hold up not only against the right but against the august conventional foolishness of the center.

Might be easier to find another pollster. Or we could accept the bleak data and work through it.

Stan   Hear them out.

First, they just think a country weighed down by debt is weaker, can't grow, and will have a bleaker future. America will be a weaker nation, its fate controlled by the big creditor countries, like China. As a non-college-educated California man told us, voters see the debt as "so monumental, and it's going to get worse over the next few years that, you know, what are we going to do, print more money?" More and more of the government budget will go to paying the interest and then paying down debt, squeezing out other needs, as we resort to more and more gimmicks that undermine us. They fear we're not going to pull ourselves out of it. When we ask people the main reason they worry about the deficit, that's the starting point: they reply that we keep spending and spending and China keeps loaning and loaning. In the end, they think, we'll be owned by China.[5]

"But I feel concerned because the debt concerns me, looking at where China is as a rising economic power that concerns me. We owe a great deal and we keep spending and spending." —Woman, white, college graduate

"[I'm concerned] that we are in a lot of debt and pretty soon we are going to own absolutely nothing. Everything we make, we're going to have to cut a check to [China], and I know it comes with interest. It is just like I give you a dollar, you give it back to me as a dollar. But I know a dollar is going to equal ten dollars by the time we give it back. I already know how that works."—Man, black, age 30, non-college-educated

"Well, we owe them so much money, if they ever called [in the] debt, we'd be speaking Chinese and eating rice. There's going to be a huge challenge. . . . We owe them a lot of money now; they lent us a lot of money to go to war over in Iraq, a useless war, and all we're doing is killing the future generation off for no reason, and I say this as an honorably discharged veteran."—Man, white, age 45, non-college-educated

"We're getting our ass kicked by China."—Man, white, college graduate

They think their children will never get out of debt and have to learn Chinese. "I want my children to have [it] better than I had," a college-educated Denver man observed. "I don't want my children to take a step backwards in their climb."

Second, people came to this crisis the hard way, via a credit and real estate bubble that took them down along with the country and the global economy when it burst. That is their window into the larger economic problems facing the country, and it is hard to convince them that the metaphor and parallels don't apply. They took on too much debt, magnified by leverage and greed, and that debt right now is holding them down financially: they don't have any discretionary money to spend at stores, they're unable to invest in education for themselves and their children, and their retirement is at risk. It is not surprising that they think you have to pay down debt if you are going to break free of this crisis, and that the same rule should apply to government.

> "I think that part of the problem is that they're spending money that's not there and we as people, as Americans . . . on an individual basis, we cannot do that. We did that for a long time, and that's why a lot of Americans are in such debt—because of credit cards, because they lived beyond their means—and the government should not be able to do that, either."—Woman, Latino, age 50, non-college-educated

> "The government has a lot more bills and responsibilities [than I do]. . . . But you got to learn. I mean, I know [in my family] we don't make [a lot of] money: I'm not buying plane tickets around the world. [So the government has] got to figure out a different way to do it." —Woman, white, non-college-educated

> "My husband and I always paid for what we bought and I see a debt that I'm concerned about for our children and grandchildren." —Woman, white, college graduate

Third, let's talk about the word "spending." When we hear that word, we see images of bridges and roads, high-speed rail, a smart grid of green energy, eager pupils in new school buildings and a teacher still teaching there. We see fast and universal broadband reaching into rural areas, a woman gaining access to new health benefits or a senior not having to pay more for health care bills. It is exhilarating just thinking about it, and we wonder why these voters don't have the same epiphany. Their minds must be polluted by Fox News and manipulative politicians.

But when voters hear "spending," they have to get past the real world of government spending, not this idealization. In our surveys in the summer of 2010, we asked what caused the growing deficits, and voters focused above all on the wars in Iraq and Afghanistan; then they cited the three big areas that they see as special-interest spending: the bailouts of the big banks and the auto industry, the lobbyists and special interests putting unneeded spending in the budget, and President Bush's tax cuts for corporations and top earners. President Obama's recovery or stimulus plan is in the mix, but above all, they see government spending as largely for and by the powerful and connected, not the people, and not in the public interest.[6] When voters say "Cut government spending," they are not talking about entitlements or even "waste, fraud, and abuse" but the guts of the spending increases that really did contribute in a big way to the rising deficits.

Fourth, when the public says "Prioritize the deficits," they do not accept the elite's 2nd ACT taking the axe to rising entitlement spending. That totally misreads why voters think we have the debt problem, what the consequences will be, and what should be done. The average citizen wants to reduce the debt, first so the economy can grow, and second, to make sure Social Security will be able to pay future benefits. They think rising debt threatens their pensions, just as it has in Greece and Wisconsin, and their fears are very close to the surface.

"I just feel like this country is really, I mean, the national debt, all the unemployment, I just feel like it's bound to crash some time. I just feel like the Social Security, eventually, I mean, the government's just going to run out of money. They can only print so much money, and they're going to have to answer to it some time." —Man, Latino

"The bottom is going to fall out. What you see happening in Greece and what you see, you know, the people that are unhappy and this concept about the unions and their rights being taken away, this is just a fraction of what we're going to see on a bigger scale."—Man, white, college graduate

They think the political and economic class chose to fight two wars and run up special-interest spending and tax breaks, and now it wants to use Social Security to solve the problem it created. Sorry. Well over 60 percent of voters oppose increasing the Medicare age from 65 to 67, raising the retirement age for Social Security to 70, or adopting the Ryan plan to turn Medicare into a voucher program.[7]

Voters do prioritize addressing the deficit, but the public's plan starts and ends with the wealthiest and special interests paying more and losing their special breaks. Over 60 percent of the public support eliminating tax breaks for corporations that outsource jobs, lifting the Social Security payroll cap on incomes higher than $170,000, taxing excessive Wall Street bank profits, and letting the Bush tax cuts expire for those earning over $250,000.

Fifth, voters are deeply skeptical about "stimulus spending"— as far as they can tell, it means politicians throwing money at problems—but they are almost desperate to see and support that same spending if they think it is a long-term investment in the country. They are looking for leaders who can make the country successful. Remember, they think greed, short-termism, and special-interest dominance produced the financial and debt crises that pulled the country down. And they also watched Congress pass a new trillion-dollar health care law, but only after a prolonged yearlong, ugly battle that seemed to reaffirm everything they believed about government spending: drug and insurance companies, stakeholders, politicians, and special-interest lobbies at the trough, cutting deals that keep health costs high and at the expense of the middle class. They might be wrong, but not entirely.

Given everything that has happened to them and the country, ordinary people now see themselves as trying to restore responsibility and as guardians of the country's long-term interests. So you have to leap over a high hurdle if you are to convince them that this Congress passing out money will be a good thing. We know that Keynes thought that government employing and paying people to dig ditches and fill them back up was just fine if it also filled the hole in aggregate spending left by the recession. But the voter today does not believe our country is in a position to support such things. The government would end up borrowing that money from abroad, making the situation worse, and they wouldn't help the middle class anyway. Where are the jobs? Where is the accountability? That's the way it works.

"President Obama] has been trying to extend government stimulus packages to people to try to stimulate the economy. Again, where is that money coming from? It's coming from other countries back into ours. But yet, we are going further into debt to try to keep our economy afloat. I don't think it's going to work on a long term." — Man, white, age 30, non-college-educated

"I don't know, maybe [we need] more control over it somehow. Just slow it down a bit, make sure it's going to the right places and not just being thrown around." — White suburban voter

"Once again accountability, it just kind of goes back to that: the government needs to be held accountable for what's going on and it goes back to the spending once again. . . . You know, [you] mentioned spending to help the middle class, but the excessive spending things that they just don't need to do, and programs—I think that's the most important thing."—Man, white, age 45, non-college-educated

"That we bail out, we help people, that we come up with money that is not even there to stop things from totally collapsing, but it puts the economy, it puts us further in debt, so in the end is it really [helping]?"—Woman, Latino, age 50, non-college-educated

"The mortgage bailout—how much did we spend and people still lost their homes? It's the greed factor and corrupt government. Corrupt."—Man, white, non-college-educated

"So, yeah, I think it's pretty reckless all the way around, because they're just throwing money out there, thinking it's going to recover like that, and it's just not happening at all."—Man, white, age 45, non-college-educated

But these voters will embrace this spending if it is a means to an end and not an end in itself. That is, if the workers don't dig a ditch just to backfill it at the end of the day, and instead make it part of an effort to improve the city's water runoff, voters will support it. That's just the sentiment we heard from one woman in Tennessee: "Even though the stimulus packages and stuff like that help out temporarily, to me, especially in our local area, it didn't make much of a difference for long-term." These ordinary citizens know we have serious problems and are impatient for spending and leadership that will address serious issues and offer long-term solutions. "If there truly would be something like a space race for this energy thing, that would be fabulous," one college-educated man said, then qualified his enthusiasm: "But I'm not sure if they really . . . if the government politicians are going to do that."

Despite the whole pall of the spending and deficit debate, you can sense people's eagerness to bring about real change. Finally, leaders are getting serious.

"I agreed with a lot of [the stimulus plan], but, really, looking at our future . . . I think often times we are quick to put a Band-Aid on things, but that doesn't really fix the problem. We really need to get to the root of the problem. And by investing in our future, whether it is education, job training, and so on, is going to be key to keeping us ahead of China and India and the other countries." —Woman, white, college graduate

"[I support spending] because we need to get back on to being economically successful. At least I think we know that China is going to be the largest economy, and obviously we are in debt to them. And I think that we need to invest our education in growing jobs within America to a point." —Woman, white, college graduate

"I'm totally for spending, as long as it's being put in the right areas, like education, environment, stuff like that." —Woman, white, non-college-educated

"[The president is] looking at a long-term picture, which at this point is kind of what we're going to have to do. We're going to have to cut and look long term and there's no easy fix to this at this point." —Man, white, college graduate

"I thought the one thing that came out of this speech is there's conversation about the fact that Kennedy went in and did so much investment and research and development . . . he actually drove telecommunications advances and so many things. . . . [President Obama is] talking about investing now in education to drive the future technology."—Man, white, college graduate

"Well, I think what they should do is solve a couple problems at one time and they should actually reinvest that money in wind and solar energy . . . because that way you can lessen the oil crisis or the deepwater drilling and, at the same time, that particular segment of the economy. It's going to be good for a long, long time."—White suburban voter

"Infrastructure is really the key, because that will generate a lot of jobs here. Not anywhere else. And the manufacturing will be here, because they're not going to be building towers somewhere else and bringing them here."—Suburban voter

"I said we should work to reduce the deficit, increase education spending in the long-term."—Suburban voter

"I think you get what you pay for. I think if you really put the money into jobs and teaching people and getting the training that they need, that it will produce more in the future."—White suburban voter

This does not mean voters suddenly support Keynesian short-term spending: why would they, given everything they believe about how government works and the problems the country faces? But this does encourage them to embrace leaders with ideas that focus on the long term—the deficit, for sure, but even more important, investments that will get our country back on track.

Voters have always had a sense of proportion about the economic problems facing the country. They put a high priority on addressing government spending, the budget deficit, and taxes, but just as many think the main problem entails the rising costs and declining incomes that the middle class and working people now face. Nearly as many believe the real issue boils down to the loss of American jobs to China and the United States' not being competitive.

That was true when we first asked this question in the summer of 2010 and it is still true, although there is growing evidence that voters are now much more interested in *a plan to invest in new industries*

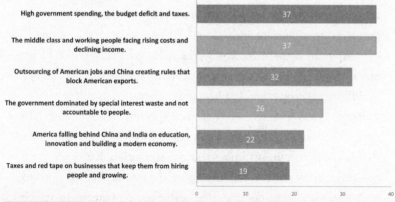

Spending and debt comparable in importance to middle class struggle as top economic problem

Which ONE of the following problems do you think is the most important to be addressed when it comes to the economy?

Problem	Value
High government spending, the budget deficit and taxes.	37
The middle class and working people facing rising costs and declining income.	37
Outsourcing of American jobs and China creating rules that block American exports.	32
The government dominated by special interest waste and not accountable to people.	26
America falling behind China and India on education, innovation and building a modern economy.	22
Taxes and red tape on businesses that keep them from hiring people and growing.	19

Note: Graph depicts combined two most important problems. From Democracy Corps and Center for American Progress National Survey, May 21 to 25, 2011.

and rebuild the country over the next five years" than *"a plan to dramatically reduce the deficit over the next five years."*[8] Voters think we have real long-term problems, including public and private debt, and they are desperate for leaders who get it.

Stan So, James, are they still smarter than you think?

James I think it's unreasonable to expect every voter to understand the economy in terms of collapses in aggregate demand or multiplier factors, i.e., in Keynesian terms. It's hard to explain to me and, I'd imagine, hard to explain to everybody else. But it's not necessary to understand it exactly like this. Break it down and it's much easier: the basic premise that savings are good as long as not everybody is saving is easy enough to grasp. If no one's buying, the government needs to step in.

We're clearly not advocating a stimulus just because we like Keynes, but because it works; let's not forget that. There's some who say you can just spend the money any way you want—dig holes, or bust rocks, or wait to be invaded by Martians and spend money defending ourselves, or drop money out of helicopters—which, to some extent, is what Bernanke was doing. We're not saying any of that.

And we're doing it to rebuild the middle class; we need to press home the point that we want to spend money to help build a better middle class. People get that because it's true.

Stan I wavered on whether to respect their judgments about debt and spending, but not in the end. They are pretty smart about the problem and pretty smart about the solution. They get it when you make a real connection to helping the middle class long-term.

James It also would have helped if we had put it in relatable terms. We need to sell the idea—there's nothing wrong with that. If you can build a highway when there's a zero interest rate, you should.

It's no different from fixing a hole in your roof. Do it now when the rate is zero as opposed to six years from now when, who knows? If the economy has come back, your road costs more, and you're increasing demand when the economy is at full capacity, so you're increasing inflation and interest rates. It's nonsense to say it doesn't make sense on the back of an envelope, but this crap actually works.

In the future, the country should have at its disposal trillions of dollars' worth of shovel-ready public works so when this event happens again, we'll be prepared. And it will, because Warren Buffett has said what we learn from history is that people don't learn from history.

We needn't become slaves to focus groups when we have a whole body of macroeconomic work that tells us something. We ought to get smart people in and figure out how to explain it to people.

Voters will understand why we are doing these things when we explain that we're trying to help build the middle class. If the Democratic Party was branded as the party of the middle class and the middle class needs better roads, rails, schools, and broadband, they would go for it. It's not politicians throwing money away; it's investing in their future.

9.

SMARTER THAN YOU THINK? CORRUPTED GOVERNMENT

Stan James, look at that income graph with the one line for the top 1 percent shooting to the top and the other lines for nearly everybody else just flat, flat, flat for years as far as you can see. I look at this pie chart with the very wealthiest devouring the lion's share of the pie. It makes me think, damn, if people could just see the sheer scale of the problem in a colorful, vivid graphic form, they would be stopped by it first, then angry, but then say no, this is not acceptable in the U.S.A. That could be the start of the middle class's pushing back. The inescapable and worsening reality and our graphs would be the game changer.

So, with the support of our good friends at the Center for American Progress and Eric Liu and Nick Hanauer from Seattle, authors of *The True Patriot* and *The Gardens of Democracy: A New American Story of Citizenship, the Economy, and the Role of Government*, who were think-

Average household income
before taxes

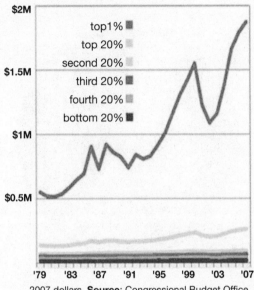

2007 dollars. **Source**: Congressional Budget Office.

ing along the same lines, we gathered groups of swing voters from different class positions and racial backgrounds in different parts of the country to stare at those graphs and talk about them.[1]

James When I look at these graphs I have the same reaction as everyone else. I see flat lines at the bottom of the income graph and a 7 percent sliver of pie for 80 percent of the people on the wealth chart.

I really don't think anyone's going to be very surprised looking at these. I think the charts confirm what they know. The gains are so skewed and concentrated on such a small number of people. They're skewed in a way they've never been before. Looking at it, I see why you put it out there: skewed beyond anything this country has seen.

Stan Well, we had the discussions, and the voters didn't go to the pie chart about wealth, at least not at first, and not because they

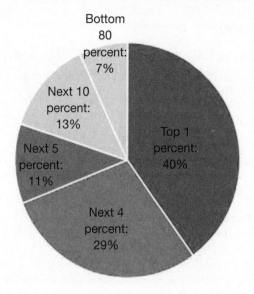

Distribution of financial wealth in the U.S.

Bottom 80 percent: 7%

Next 10 percent: 13%

Next 5 percent: 11%

Top 1 percent: 40%

Next 4 percent: 29%

don't think it is true and important. This is the first time I saw how determined they were to get everybody to focus on the middle class.

While the two of us are focused on inequality, fairness, and the growing gap between the middle class and the wealthy, the voter is focused first on the middle class and what's happened to them. Everything else pales in importance. That's the starting point for everything. This may seem like semantics, but it is a signal that we are focused on the right problem in a period when life is very tough and the middle class is at risk.

They are damn clear about this and we need to take them seriously. At the outset of the focus groups, we asked people to pick three items from a long list of twelve economic problems we face, ranging from middle-class wages, longer working hours and rising costs, unemployment and lost manufacturing jobs, deficits, and home foreclosures to a whole range of items about inequality, including these stunning developments:

- On average, CEOs now earn 531 times the pay of average hourly workers, up from 42 times the average hourly worker's pay in 1980.
- Between 1979 and 2007, after-tax wages for the top 1 percent of income earners nearly tripled, while the bottom 20 percent saw an increase that has barely kept up with inflation.
- The wealthiest 1 percent of American families own as much as the bottom 90 percent.
- The richest 400 people have more wealth than the bottom 155 million people combined.

To the stunned reactions behind the focus group's one-way viewing glass, people virtually ignored these items—each marked by no more than one person per group on average—and quickly marked up all the developments and trends we would expect, based on this whole book.

They went first on the list to the 14 million out of work and the loss of good-paying manufacturing jobs, accounting for about one in three of their marked-up sheets. About one in five marked stagnant wages, longer hours and rising costs for medical care, housing, and college. About one in seven marked the trillions added to the deficit and a comparable number marked the four million foreclosures.

Only one in seven rushed to mark up the whole list of extraordinary facts about inequality over the past decade. Their focus was, first and foremost, lost jobs and lost income in the face of rising financial burdens.[2]

That is what prompted them to declare that "the middle class is disappearing" or "being left behind," "the middle class are becoming the poor," and "it's heading in the direction of the Third World." They know the winners are the CEOs and the wealthy, and "the bad guy that pays less in taxes than his driver," a man in suburban Philadelphia said, then added: "That makes me hate the guy." And they identify the losers as "the middle class," "working people," and "all of us."[3] They describe the game as "rigged."

So they are very clearheaded about the income disparities, which make them angry, but their entry point and perspective on the growing imbalance is the middle class, stupid.

James It's also a pretty goddamn big failure of the market and market fundamentalism. They've been in charge, deregulating, letting the market have its way.

Economists call them externalities, the negative consequences of actions, like pollution following industrialization. The main externality of recent government policy, especially under Bush, has been massive income inequality. We're staring at it.

There's no chance of changing the outcome without government. Who else has the authority to do that? The entity in the United States that has the power to do something about this is the United States government.

It's the government that can make sure people have equal access to education; government can fix health care to save people from the catastrophic events that toss them out of the middle class; government can rewrite the tax code so that a fair share of burden falls on the people who are best able to shoulder it; and government can ensure that federal revenue is distributed so it assists families and individuals who need help.

Stan They don't go to government instinctively, I now understand, for pretty smart reasons. You'll see. They think government is part of the problem. You'll see: they see government as the problem.

James Why are they not that exercised about the even greater inequality of wealth, which is arguably more important than income inequality? It's the institutionalization over generations of income inequality. It means that the kids of the people at the top all start at the top themselves. The club is closing its doors.

Stan I don't doubt you are right, but it is in the income chart that they see the battle over their values—and our values. They have been working harder and harder over those three decades, working a lot more hours, to keep up with health care and college costs. Their pensions are in trouble and so are their families. And when they see CEOs rewarded with gigantic and growing bonuses—even if they bankrupted their companies or because they outsourced jobs or took on big debts—that really violates their gut convictions about right and wrong, which is grounded in their daily and ongoing struggle.

When it gets to the big wealth inequalities, people are a little uncertain what to make of it. It is not that they hanker to preserve an American dream that includes a Horatio Alger race to the top. Almost nobody talked about such things. When we put these facts and graphs out there, they really asked probing questions of the data:

"How did they get their wealth?"

"Did they inherit it? I mean, wealth is accumulated over time, and if they have family money from a hundred years ago, I don't begrudge them."

"How do they use it now? Do they give it away? I don't have any problem with Bill Gates."

"How did they earn it? You have wealthy people that earned it and you have wealthy people that didn't earn it—versus taking it from his employees or whatever and stripping every last dollar out of his own company just to fund his own greed, like that's, it all depends on the particular case. . . ."

There was a real reluctance to take away the lifetime earnings of somebody who played by the established rules, even if they view the game as rigged.

So they cheer any proposal to tax incomes over $250,000 or over a million dollars or to tax executive bonuses. They are really intrigued by proposals that allow workers to gain a larger share of productivity gains or gains from corporate profits, but they have to be convinced to support an inheritance tax. All of that underscores

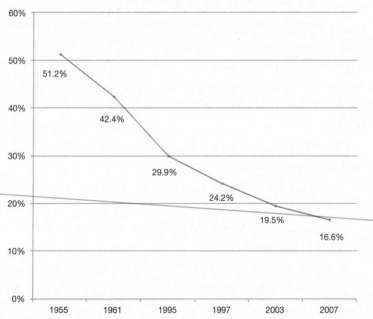

**Effective federal tax rate on the richest
400 families in America, 1955–2007**

their brutal consistency in focusing on what is happening to the middle class, on their view of what is right and wrong and what to do about it.

The discussion changed, however, when they looked at a simple graph of the trend line on the effective tax rate of the richest four hundred families—40 to 50 percent up to the 1960s, but falling steadily to just 16.6 percent in 2007—about what Mitt Romney pays in taxes today. When looking at the graphs, you could see the brains churning as people were really using the focus group information and discussion to educate themselves.

But what they focused on was not the unequal outcomes but the politics of it: the nexus of power and money—Washington and Wall Street—that they think produced all this. "The wealthy people have a lot more access and influence on power," a suburban woman in Philadelphia concluded. "Yeah, he who has the money makes the rules," a man in Milwaukee agreed. When asked "What does wealth mean to you?" the people in Milwaukee were straightforward: "Power."

"The rich are getting richer and they're not stopping. They use their money to gain power by influencing Washington or internationally. They're offshoring American jobs, systematically reducing the standard of living in this country; it's by plan."—Man, white, non-college-educated

"They had the money to get things like that passed and they had the influence to get their tax base lowered."—Latino voter

"Absolutely I think there's an absolute relationship between wealth and power and access. Somebody else mentioned access to the political and what drives what the politicians are doing. Nobody's speaking for the little guy." — Man, white, college graduate

"I think there's just such a control of government by the wealthy that whatever happens, it's not working for all the people; it's working for a few of the people." — Man, white, college graduate

"Well, to me it's that big business has a lot of control over the government, more now than it did in the fifties. Like, big business funds your race so you can get elected, so when you get elected, [they then say] 'I want you to lower my taxes.'" — Latino voter, age 25

They see the politicians increasingly dependent on big donors and influenced by lobbyists. "Power corrupts," one of the men in our suburban groups concluded. "These guys have the power to make the system work for somebody, and the people with money said, 'Make it work for me.'"

And they draw pretty elevated conclusions about our representative democracy and American government. They believe in accountable government but fear that elected officials are now accountable to those they call on for money, not to the individual voter. The few, not the many, are on now in control: "The whole system is corrupt."

"We don't have a representative government anymore. Whoever you vote for, if they're in [somebody's] pocket, if they receive the funds that put them in office, like the Koch brothers gave a lot of money to [Governor Scott] Walker . . . now he basically works for the Koch brothers. He doesn't work for the citizens of Wisconsin anymore, and

Obama works for Goldman Sachs, and half of his staff is from Goldman Sachs."—Man, white, non-college-educated

"I mean, let's face it, everybody's there, you vote, you do whatever people tell you to do, whoever's paying your bills. You know you have a job basically for life: What do they call it? The lecture circuit. It doesn't matter what they do. They're going to get paid huge sums of money. . . . [People] pay them [and then] tell them I want you to vote this way. I mean, the whole system is corrupt."—Man, white, college graduate

"I think there's just such a control of government by the wealthy that whatever happens, it's not working for all the people; it's working for a few of the people."—Man, white, college graduate

James Wow. That gets my attention. Government is part of the problem and in no position to address externalities. That's a new thought for liberals. My thought was, of course, it is the government that has to change it.

Stan So I thought at least then they would be so offended by what's happened to government that they could be mobilized. Damn, let's do something about it.

James They know Republicans aren't going to help because they're fatally implicated in the inequities of the system. That's why there's a real political opportunity here for Democrats to come in and say, "Let's put this issue front and center: What's happened to the middle class?" They can turn to Democrats if we give them a reason to believe we're for the middle class. They can utilize politics and government. There are other actors—even Occupy Wall Street may be the instrument for change.

Stan No. The opposite. They see the political and economic elites so intertwined and the consequences so serious and overwhelming that they feel powerless to change the course of events. When one of the Milwaukee women talked about CEO advantage rising from 42 to 531 times and said, "It's, like, excessive," another woman pushed back, saying, "Don't even go there, because there is nothing we can do about it."[4]

> "Well, with that statistic, how's this country ever going to change if only four hundred people have all the resources? It's never going to change."—Man, white, non-college-educated
>
> "Well, it's hard to say what can be done, because it's, you know, they're piggybacking off each other, so you would think politicians could help, but they're helping the politicians, so you know."—Latino voter, age 25
>
> "I think they upset me, some of them, but, like, what can I do about it?"—Man, white, non-college-educated
>
> "Somebody lobbies for something and I can't afford to go up there and lobby, but somebody with a lot of money can do the lobbying, so they influence the decision, which is not my decision."—Man, white, non-college-educated

There was little push-back in the groups when a non-college-educated white man in Milwaukee observed, "They own Washington, they own it." That leads some to wonder: Why get up in arms, why get involved, and why vote? If you "identify as being in one of these lower bands, you know, no matter what you do, you see their tax rates are coming down. Nothing's changing for you," a man in suburban Philadelphia said, and then went further: "It's frustrating, so maybe you don't vote; maybe you don't, you know, go out and get involved. Maybe you just don't care anymore." A Latino voter in Houston said: "Our voice should be speaking out, but it's not. We're silenced, see."[5]

The spiral downward to withdrawal was pretty powerful, driven by the belief that Washington and Wall Street have worked hand in glove to produce and protect their fortunes. Why would you think the ordinary voter would be strong enough to change this symbiotic relationship? And why would you turn to government, which is part of the problem?

To try to arrest their complete sense of impotence I added material in our groups in Philadelphia that recalled the period before the 1929 crash, when America faced similar concentrations of wealth and income. I reminded them that in the 1930s "government stepped in, regulated the banks that created the problem, raised income taxes on the very wealthy, started programs like Social Security, and protected labor unions. After World War II, taxes remained high on the very wealthy, and the nation passed the G.I. Bill, which helped create the middle class in this country." That got some attention. They listened, but they had also learned. One of the women said, "This worked. It created the middle class, but the middle class is disappearing. If you go to your figures here, there is really not much of a middle class."

Then I introduced a list of new public policies to show that there are things government can do to impact middle-class living standards and imbalances at the top. I wasn't really interested in which of the policies they embraced; I wanted to see if the discussion left them feeling less impotent and less hostile to engaging with government.

They liked policies that gave workers the same kind of performance pay as executives and policies to rebuild manufacturing. But they were no more inclined to trust government on these big economic problems. If anything, it made them more ornery.

James   The voter is just right here. People have lost all faith in government, and for good reason. It's the corruption, stupid. Look, we are two pro-government Democrats who witnessed the U.S. government win the Cold War, educate the masses, and secure civil rights. But now people just don't trust the government anymore, and who can blame them? They're right: government is corrupt and bought. And most of all, they get causality: the rich and connected control the government, and that contributes to the decline of the middle class. It's what we've been saying, but the goal was not to become powerless. We do this to do shit.

Stan   Their conclusions about democracy and democratic accountability, and what they imply about the country, are pretty daunting and troublesome.

James   Well, just because it operates that way today doesn't mean it has to tomorrow. Don't assume it's bought forever; I don't buy that. It can be fixed. Do you know how long it took to get 18-year-olds the right to vote? About six months. People say you can't amend the Constitution, but it's been amended 27 times.

Look at the regulatory changes in Dodd-Frank. A lot of people say that it's flawed, but I would contend that it's a step in the right direction. Where you want to be, that may be a long way off, but it's a step.

Still, even when we take a step in the right direction, we take about three back with the *Citizens United* decision that paved the way for super PACs. Again, people are mad and approval of the Supreme Court is way down. The court probably took a bigger hit from *Citizens United* than from *Bush v. Gore.*

But what do they expect? What is a pissed-off voter supposed to think?

You woke up in the morning and you heard about *Citizens United*, you thought that big business had too much influence over government and there was too much money in campaigns. Then when you went to bed that night, you read that the Supreme Court thinks there isn't enough corporate money in politics. The way you address the inordinate amount of influence that powerful people have in Washington is to give them more!

What are you going to think?

It goes along with campaigns that are being waged to stop people from exercising their constitutional right to vote. The people who want to buy the government have realized that they can't win an election under the 2008 rules. So they're just changing the rules. They're making it harder for ordinary people to vote and they're making it easier for rich people to contribute. Voilà! We've got new rules.

Stan In the past, when it got out of control, the voters had a way of dialing it back. The Nixon impeachment brought the Watergate reforms and a new class of reformers into Congress. But now, with the full support of the U.S. Supreme Court, it's all legal. Where's the scandal? The scandal is that government has been blocked from helping the middle class.

The cost of winning a House race in 2010 was $1.4 million—up 71 percent in the last decade. A Senate seat win was up "only" 37 percent but would cost you $9.7 million. With that kind of price tag, the members know what they have to do. Just last year, the House campaigns raised $421 million, with much more in store this election year.

But understand what small a number of Americans are part of

this game. In the 2010 cycle, a quarter of all campaign contributions came from just 26,783 individuals, or 0.01 percent of the population (that's 1 percent of 1 percent). Members of this elite club gave at least $10,000 each and on average contributed $28,913—that's about $2,000 more than the median individual income.

When President Obama's campaign announced that they intended to raise $1 billion, no one blinked. We shall see what the Republican presidential campaign spends—but we know the outside super PACs have committed to raising almost as much.

And that's the crux of the problem. Since *Citizens United*, a surge of money has poured into the super PACs, those outside pressure groups that work on behalf of the campaigns but are unaccountable to the public. Last year, super PACs raised nearly $100 million, with an average donation of $47,718—nearly ten times what an individual can donate to a candidate's primary and general election campaigns combined. Make no mistake, there are no laws to control how much money these groups raise and spend, and we have no recourse. And yet, when asked about the ads run by his affiliated super PAC, Restore Our Future, Mitt Romney casually noted, "Of course it's former staff of mine." And as he launched his general election campaign, Romney pulled double duty at twin afternoon and evening fund-raisers among high-rollers in Florida—both of which were hosted by donors who had hit the maximum limit for official campaign contributions and had given handsomely to Restore Our Future. (Afternoon host Francis Rooney's holding company reportedly gave $1 million to Restore Our Future, and evening hosts Gerald and Darlene Jordan contributed a combined $400,000 to Restore Our Future.) Like their hosts, guests wrote checks to both the campaign and its associated super PAC. The line between the official campaign and so-called independent advocacy group is more than a little blurry—it hardly exists at all.[6]

The oil industry's subsidies are on the line, and they spent $31.9 million on the 2010 election, and they aren't slowing down. In January 2012, billionaire oil CEOs David and Charles Koch pledged a combined $60 million to defeat President Obama.

With discontent high over the new financial regulations and proposals to repeal hedge fund managers' special tax treatment, Wall Street has given more money than any other sector in this cycle. Just three months into 2012, those in the financial sector have already donated $207.2 million to candidates.

We guess they know the rules and what they get for their money.

James   Again, the only entity in the country that has any power to stand up to these people is the government. In some fantasy world, community organizers rise up against the big bad special interests. I kind of doubt that is going to happen.

Stan   That's the paradox. The liberals and both of us turn instinctively to the government to undo what we are witnessing here, but if government is corrupted and has actively helped create the problem, why the hell would you say, "Of course, government is the solution"? I remember when a Latino woman in Houston observed, "There should be more regulation and stuff," but then posed the question to the group, "Who's going to do it?" And then she answered her own question: *"Our government, who's allowed it to get this way in the first place and gives tax breaks to the richest and these corporations. Yeah, it should be taken care of, but they're not going to do it."* That's the paradox.

James   You had it right in your *New York Times* Sunday op-ed piece "Why Voters Tune Out Democrats." We can't back off that; we have to face it head-on.

This is the most important thing we have established here, and it's the key to everything. If you can't radically reform government, the Democrats are lost. And if the Democrats are lost, the middle class is lost.

If you convince people that there's nothing you can do in the face of all this might, in the face of all this power, then ultimately we're all doomed. People become so cynical or resigned or apathetic. And that's exactly what people in power want us to do. They want to convince us that this is the way it is, that there's nothing that can be done about it. It's like a cop at a car wreck: Nothing to see here, you just go back and lead your life. Take your miserable paycheck and shut your mouth.

They have every reason to promote that point of view. It's a done deal.

Well, actually, no it isn't.

Lost Republic

James   Lawrence Lessig's brilliant book *Republic, Lost: How Money Corrupts Congress—and a Plan to Stop It* details the corrupting influence of money in our political system. Lessig's thesis is that our republic is being undermined by money—that our government is bought and paid for by special interests, lobbyists, think tanks, banks, and corporations. The people involved are not evil; they're acting rationally and in their own interests, and they have rigged the system to facilitate their influence. The result: the system doesn't favor one party over another. Lessig contends that "we have created an engine of influence that seeks not some particular strand of political or economic ideology, whether Marx or Hayek. We have created instead an engine of influence that seeks simply to make those most connected rich."[7]

When Lessig gets to the financial crisis, he shows that we were not brought to our knees by crazy or evil people but by self-interested parties like banks enriching themselves with fatally flawed and risky behavior because no one stopped them. The regulators had been castrated.

Lessig quotes the work of Harvard's David Moss, who notes we had regular financial panics in this country: 1792, 1797, 1819, 1837, 1857, 1873, 1907, 1929–33. Then New Deal regulations were put in place, especially Glass-Steagall in 1933, and they worked. From June 1933 to March 1980 we had financial stability. Then the banks invented derivatives, a whole new way to make money that became massive: by the mid-1990s the volume of derivatives was $13 trillion, much larger than the entire U.S. GDP. The banks escaped regulation and took huge risks to maximize returns, backed by the implicit government promise of support in case of failure.

The deregulation insanity was promoted and protected by massive lobbying expenditures. According to Simon Johnson and James Kwak's *13 Bankers*, financial services firms spent $1.7 billion in campaign contributions from 1998 to 2008 and $3.4 billion on lobbying. After 1989, the one hundred biggest financial industry contributors spent more than energy, health care, defense, and telecom firms combined.[8] And the money didn't just go to Republicans; Democrats were in on it too.[9]

The result? Bank failures peaked in 1933 and then settled down, only to peak again in 2008. What changed? Deregulation.

10.

THE ELITES DEPLORE CLASS WARFARE, BUT WHAT ABOUT THE VOTERS?

James We didn't start class warfare. It's important to make that point right up front. Never, ever let it be said that we did. Warren Buffett was right when he said, "There's been class warfare going on for the last 20 years, and my class has won." (I know Buffett was on our side on this.) That side's been waging it; we haven't.

But the fact that we haven't doesn't mean we shouldn't. Am I right in saying that there is no more popular policy with the public than raising taxes on rich people?

Stan You would be right. That's a fact. That is as close to an absolute truth as you can have in polling. Ask the voters how they want the country to address the deficit, and answers number one and two will be a surtax on millionaires and raising taxes for those earning over $250,000, not to mention a tax on short-term financial transactions. Ask how they want to secure Social Security's future, and answers one and two will be getting rid of the current cap of $107,000 and applying the payroll tax to all salaries no matter how high. Ask about jobs and the economy and they say close corporate tax loopholes to prevent corporations from offshoring profits and shipping jobs overseas, and create new punitive taxes to discourage companies from outsourcing.[1]

When the president gave his State of the Union address in 2011, swing voters who watched it and recorded their responses to his actual words and delivery on dial meters spun them literally off the top of the graph when the president said, "If we truly care about our deficit, we simply can't afford a permanent extension of the tax cuts for the wealthiest 2 percent of Americans." That was the battle cry in the speech for Democrats and independents and even many Republicans. This is a polarized country, but voters are not divided on the issue of raising taxes on rich people.

James So the ordinary voter looks at class warfare waged against them and the state of their economic fortunes and says, "We can wage class warfare too"?

Stan As I said before, they are the only responsible ones at the table. There is a consensus in the country that the citizenry has to pay more taxes to address our challenges and that the rich have to pay the lion's share, because they can afford it and because it is the right thing to do after they reaped the lion's share of the gains over three decades. It is the new common sense.

When the Republican Congress took the country to the brink of default over raising the debt ceiling, public polls explored different ways to address the deficit, and roughly 70 percent of the country agreed that the solution had to include new taxes. The House Republicans and Tea Party members dug in at zero tax increases, even though half of Republican voters said you have to raise taxes to address the long-term deficits. Message to the top earners: Pay your taxes.[2]

James So I was watching my wife on television and Nicolle Wallace, the former communications director for President Bush and adviser to Sarah Palin as the vice presidential candidate, says, "I think Republicans are pleased—every day in the general that we spend debating taxes is a good day for Republicans."[3]

That means Nicolle and I are happy at the same time. I'm very happy when we talk about taxes, but I'm talking about bringing back the 39.6 percent we had under Clinton. I should take Nicolle at her word and say we agree. Let's have that debate. It goes to show there is still room for bipartisanship in Washington.

But actually it's part of the fog machine. They want you to think they're open-minded about it so we won't have a public debate about raising taxes on the rich and won't be electing people and throwing politicians out of office on the basis of whether they have the nerve to tax rich people. I get the deal. "Hey, Democrat, you better be scared: you voted for the biggest tax increase in history. Make my day." And I can see our Democratic friends cowering. If they chicken out, they're missing a great opportunity and making the Republicans look good.

Stan You are not far off, because there are plenty of Democratic consultants and political leaders who have bought the conventional wisdom lock, stock, and barrel.[4] "We just don't need a debate about taxes too close to the election," some of them cried, debating whether to let Bush's tax cut expire for those earning over $250,000 when the Democrats controlled both the House and Senate going into the 2010 off-year elections.

When they had control, Democrats had the chance to force a permanent increase in taxes for those earning over $250,000 but were advised, "Don't chance it." Instead, they deferred to the Republicans' false bravado and the elite's tax presumptions, even though our poll findings were crystal clear: by nearly a 20-point margin (55 to 38 percent) voters wanted to raise taxes on those earning over $250,000 a year—and Democratic candidates *gained* three points when championing this tax rise.[5]

When presenting these findings to members, I had to repeat again and again what I was saying: "This vote not only doesn't hurt you, it helps you. Yes, helps you. Voters long to vote for someone who will ask the top earners to contribute. They will reward you. We want this issue."

Risk-averse Democrats let the status quo stand.

James That's inclined to make someone risk-averse. But just look at the data! If you're a Democrat and you look at the data, how can you say you wouldn't be for raising taxes on the top 1 percent? Someone show me data that says that raising taxes on the top 1 percent is electorally unpopular. There isn't any. Stan, we've seen how much data there is on this—our data, public data, everyone's data—and it all says the same damn thing. It's not arguable.

The classic example people trot out is Fritz Mondale in 1984. He stood up at the Democratic Convention in San Francisco and said, "Mr. Reagan will raise taxes, and so will I. He won't tell you. I just did." They slaughtered him for that, but that was before Reagan and the Republicans created this mad frenzy of cutting taxes for the rich and rolling back business regulation. That's where the disaster that struck the middle class started.

People tend to forget, but Clinton ran on raising taxes. He was really interested in making work pay. Early in his administration, he concentrated on wage earners, but at the lower end, the kind of people who need help right now. Health care, the expansion of the earned income tax credit, tax policy, family and medical leave—all were designed to help make work pay and move people up life's ladder, and it involved tax increases.

So, Democrats, forget about 1984, please. Things change. Maybe Obama needs to go to the convention in Charlotte and say of his opponent, "You know, let's concede, he will not raise taxes on the wealthy and I will. He has not taken any position yet. In fact, he's promised to cut taxes on the wealthy; I will raise taxes on the wealthy. That's a distinction in this election."

Unlike many things that Romney has promised in his life and didn't deliver, this is one that he will try to deliver on. It's central to his campaign and his ideology. If I was running that campaign, I would go right at it. Why wouldn't you stand beside a 55 percent issue? Where else do you have that kind of distinction? As far as I can see, there is no risk—zero; there's only upside. What's the downside?

"Romney wants the Bush policy: I want the Clinton policy. What would you rather have, 2008 or 1998? Take your pick." Consultants, politicians, have some balls and say that.

So, for the faint of heart, it is important to remind ourselves that the Democratic candidates for president since 1992 who ran on raising taxes on the richest won. You would think that would get seen through the fog machine. As a candidate, Bill Clinton proposed raising taxes on families earning over $200,000, closing corporate tax loopholes, and preventing companies from deducting CEO salaries over a million dollars in his economic plan, *Putting People First.* The plan's investment agenda was paid for by *raising tax rates for the wealthiest individuals and corporations.*

On the campaign trail, he put a lot of heat and rhetorical brilliance behind his plans: "I have news for the forces of greed and the defenders of the status quo: your time has come, and gone. It's time for change in America." He reminded people that he "was raised to believe that the American dream was built on rewarding hard work," but "for too long, those who play by the rules and keep the faith have gotten the shaft." The government doesn't get it, because it has been "hijacked by privileged private interests"[6] and the administration in Washington is animated by an economic philosophy that says, "You make the economy grow by putting more and more wealth into the hands of fewer and fewer people at the top."[7]

And if you missed the point, our advertising in the last two months observed pointedly, "only the rich are doing better, because for 12 years we've been dominated by selfishness and greed and a concern for the short run." So "we're going to ask the rich to pay their fair share so the rest of America can finally get a break."[8] Bill Clinton ran on raising taxes on the wealthy—and he won by the way.

James He had a way about him. It sounded like he regretted raising their taxes. When he was out campaigning and I watched the monitor in the war room and I heard him say, "I want to say to them, hey, look, I want to make millionaires too. I just want to make millionaires the old-fashioned way, by putting the people to work."

When you look back at that time and at that policy, it was a great policy. And if it was true in '92, imagine how much more true it is today, when the gains of the Clinton years have been reversed, and then some. The rich got richer, the poor got poorer, and the middle class got screwed. I think Clinton's precise phrase was the middle class got the shaft.

And again, if we bring it back to today, what's wrong with saying that?

Stan We will talk later about Al Gore's campaign, but he actually did not run on raising taxes, as the Clinton administration had already raised taxes and achieved budget surpluses. But Gore was relentless in pointing out the risk posed by Governor Bush's plan to cut taxes for the top 1 percent and millionaires: "The biggest threat to the economy and the continued prosperity would be a giant tax cut mainly for the wealthy that would put us back into deficits again." By contrast, he explained, "my tax cut targets the benefits to middle-class families."[9]

And in case you missed it, Al Gore won a plurality of the national vote and, of course, Florida.

James And through *Bush v. Gore*, the Supreme Court was protecting those interests. And now we have *Citizens United*. Jeffrey Toobin has said that the Roberts Court has never ruled against corporate interests. They say that a broken clock is right twice a day; how is it that corporate interests are always right? The law of averages suggests that can't be the case.

But look at when they were discussing the individual mandate and you get the idea. They talked about the mandate and about how it would hurt the insurance companies. Well, yes, it would have an adverse effect on the insurance companies, but the Court is supposed to debate the virtues of the case, not zero in on how an issue might disturb corporate interests.

What about the 30 million people who wouldn't have health insurance? What about them? They don't count?

I was on TV right after Toobin made that point and I said you have to hand it to old Toobs, he's mentioning the 30 million people, how quaint of him. What a throwback!

My point is, the Court is going to do everything it can to slow or stop the inevitable demographic changes that are coming in the country. They feel that corporate interests can't play on a level playing field, so they're going to make sure there's an uphill and a downhill and you know which is which.

Stan Barack Obama ran for president proposing famously to let President Bush's tax cuts expire for those earning over $250,000 and pledged no tax increases for those earning under that. Our surveys at the time showed that posture to be exceedingly popular.[10]

You may have noticed that Obama won that election in 2008, but you may not have noticed that he won an even bigger win on taxes. On Election Day, 53 percent of voters thought Obama would do a better job on taxes—13 points more than the 40 percent who preferred McCain's approach. Note this: Obama won the tax issue by twice the margin that he won in the actual election. The tax issue helped him in the election, as it did President Clinton before him.

James Grassroots Democrats want this issue; they do. I always say that in campaigns. When you think you want that pitch, you hit the sucker. Come on. Come on. Gimme that pitch. I want the tax pitch.

Stan So my question is: Why isn't the battle for the middle class the default fight for Democrats? Why isn't this where we always start? If, for three decades, people are losing ground in their pursuit of the dream, and the economic and political game is rigged for the most privileged, why aren't opportunistic leaders and their campaign consultants all over this issue and getting a leg up on everybody else? This is a competitive, bloody sport where the most ambitious get to the top and win the ring and all the glory.

James Because the moment President Obama in Osawatomie, Kansas, points to the "breathtaking greed of a few with irresponsibility all across the system," he gets slammed. When he points out, "The typical CEO who used to earn about 30 times more than his or her worker now earns 110 times more. And yet over the last decade, the incomes of most Americans have actually fallen by about 6 percent," he gets slammed. When he says, irrefutably, "We know it doesn't result in a prosperity that trickles down. It results in a prosperity that's enjoyed by fewer and fewer of our citizens," he gets slammed. And he rightly says, "Now, this kind of inequality—at a level that we haven't seen since the Great Depression—hurts us all," and he gets slammed again.[11] But that ain't half of what Bill Clinton said about rich people and inequality.

The fog machine comes in with "No. No. No. Not class warfare! We can't have class warfare."

The point is, we all want the president to do this, but you have to fight the money and the fog machine. And it takes more than one speech. One speech is not going to do this, because one speech can be drowned out by the deniers and the fog machine. And it's not just one speech: I'd say one campaign isn't going to do it either.

The Republicans have built their brand over a long period—since 1981. I'd say they've built it and destroyed it at this point, but everyone knows what they stand for: cutting taxes at the top, less regulation, smaller government. Their rhetoric and bombast has become extreme and counterproductive today, but they established that position over time, not over one campaign and certainly not over one speech.

I'd love to think that 20 years from now they're going to be saying, "Man, I wish the Democrats would get off this middle-class drag." That would be a dream.

Stan Well, let's just say there is a fog machine on our side, too, and it works overtime to make sure this is not the default issue. The moment a candidate says what President Obama said, count on an array of pollsters, consultants, and advisers to leap up and announce, "Class warfare never works." "You have just written off independents." "You have lost the vital center." "This is why Democrats lose elections." "Out of desperation, he's cynically playing the populist card." "I think treating the middle class like they're victims is an enormous mistake." "He should be bringing the country together rather than dividing it through class warfare."[12]

James   I'm sorry. Given everything, the country's divided, not united. The Republicans have divided it and waged class warfare.

I can't say I'm overjoyed at the response of some of my consulting colleagues on this issue, or the politicians, either, mind you. But there's been a change in what some Democratic consultants do. When I started doing this, you worked for a campaign, period. Now some people work for campaigns, and also for banks and insurance companies and God knows who else. The distinction between clients has become blurred in a few cases: Is the consultant advocating for the client or the candidate?

I'd say to these dumbasses, "What you would do is reunite the country"—which is no small feat.

Stan   Put aside the shrillness of the reaction and scrutinize what they are saying.

First, they are saying class warfare doesn't work because you drive away independents and moderates. It is all well and good to throw red meat to our angry base voters, but any gains will be more than outweighed by your losses with the less angry middle, and thus you will fail. But second, they say the opposite: populist appeals do work, but you are cynical to use them, as you are allowing short-term, divisive campaign tactics to trump the need for unity. And third and most important, they are saying the issues of inequality, irresponsibility, and the future of the middle class are not legitimate issues, because they are divisive.

James   And duhhhh. Why is that?

The bottom line is that you'd unite 80 percent of Americans behind this issue. Isn't that enough unifying? Find me another issue that has that level of support. If you talk about the 80 percent as opposed to the 1 percent, you're a divider, but if you talk about the 1 percent, you're a uniter? That makes no sense. You're holding the graph upside down.

If they keep using the language, let 'em say it. Like we said before, we can't hide 'cause they say boo. Whatever we say, they're going to talk about division. We want a government that works for the 80 percent, not the 1 percent. That is not divisive.

Stan We have two big presidential campaigns—Gore versus Bush in 2000 and Obama versus McCain in 2008—which were multimillion-dollar national tests of the thesis whether class warfare drives voters away or attracts them. That's the big question to be answered. I recall these because I promise you, the chattering class will warn Democrats of the dangers of class warfare before and after this election.

In July 2000, just before I was recruited to conduct polling for the campaign, Gore unveiled the theme of his campaign, "The People Versus the Powerful," something he took on the stump—the handiwork of Bob Shrum but happily delivered by the vice president. Gore intoned in Chicago, "I'm on your side and I want to fight for the people. The other side fights for the powerful. That's why the big pharmaceutical companies are supporting Governor Bush. That's why the big oil companies are supporting Governor Bush. That's why the big polluters are supporting Governor Bush."[13] Pundits like David Gergen were contemptuous: "This business about being for the working class against everybody else, against the powerful, is divisive."[14]

I did not love the phrase, as I preferred a more inclusive populism centered on the middle class. What's new? The strongest testing message in our polling for the Gore campaign right before the convention stated:

With the current prosperity and surplus, this is a time to make sure that our prosperity enriches not just the few but all working fami-

lies. We should invest in education, middle-class tax cuts, and a secure retirement.[15]

And in his acceptance speech at the convention, Al Gore embraced that and extended it:

"I'm not asking you to vote for me on the basis of the economy
we have. Tonight, I ask for your support on the basis of the better,
fairer, more prosperous America we can build together.

"Together, let's make sure that our prosperity enriches not just
the few but all working families. Let's invest in health care, education, a secure retirement, and middle-class tax cuts."

And then he added: "So often powerful forces and powerful
interests stand in your way, and the odds seemed stacked against
you—even as you do what's right for you and your family."[16]

I had worked to contain that theme, as I did not think that ordinary people thought the powerful were the main blockage in their
lives. Nevertheless, the day after the convention, Gore and Joe
Lieberman stood under the backdrop—"The People Versus the
Powerful"—a slogan I tried valiantly and unsuccessfully to paint
over. But this is the truth. Al Gore insisted on it, because that's the
formulation he thought best captured the moment—and because
the phrase continued to test as strongly as anything I came up with.
He's the decider.

As for the idea that class warfare will fail, Gore had trailed Bush
badly for most of the year, but the convention wiped out a 16-point
deficit in the *USA Today*–Gallup–CNN poll, producing an immediate dead heat, and then Gore led until late in September. In the campaign's polls, we led from Labor Day to the first debate—the period
that the Gore campaign waged so-called class warfare. His lead was
wiped out by Gore's disastrous performances in the debates, but

that's another story. None of that detracts from the fact that voters rallied to his cause under his banner, "The People Versus the Powerful."

The 2008 election is an even stronger case. I never liked Gore's battle cry and I liked even less Obama's inelegant phrasing, "Spread the Wealth Around," in an impromptu exchange with Joe Wurzelbacher, "Joe the Plumber." I'm sure his campaign advisers groaned, as this was not his organizing theme, unlike Gore. Nonetheless, he owned it and John McCain mentioned Joe the Plumber nine times in the third debate, took Joe Wurzelbacher to his campaign rallies, and elevated him in the campaign's advertising—the total topic of the campaign's final paid advertising.

An important academic study by Kate Kenski, Bruce W. Hardy, and Kathleen Hall Jamieson, *The Obama Victory: How Media, Money, and Message Shaped the 2008 Election,*[17] unfortunately gets this piece of their groundbreaking work wrong. They label the period after McCain joined the issue in the debates as the "McCain Surge" (October 15–28). Just to be clear, there was no McCain surge. Obama's vote did not drop after the third debate; in fact it went up over the coming days. Confidence in Obama to handle the economy remained unaffected, dropping not even a point. Indeed, Obama's small advantage on handling "taxes"—the subject of the debate—surged to 10 points and Obama's lead on taxes grew further on election day to 13 points.[18]

During this exchange, McCain's vote went up 2 points and confidence in him to handle the economy went up 5—both to 38 percent—well short of an even normal consolidation of the Republican vote at the close of a presidential election.[19] He was clawing his way back into the campaign after saying "The fundamentals of the economy are strong" on the same day as the Lehman Brothers' collapse and after his disastrous trip to save the day in Washington. Claiming Obama would raise your taxes and give the money to the undeserving did help in this incomplete consolidation of the normal Republican vote. That is what the authors mean by "a turning point for McCain on the tax issue."[20]

Their analysis reminds us that when you join the tax-the-rich debate, no matter how innocently, the Republicans will throw in the kitchen sink and every sleazy, sometimes patently false assertion about Democratic plans. That's a fair characterization, because that is the reality.

While Paul Ryan and Mitt Romney actually defend trickle-down economics with a straight face, Republicans generally prefer just to charge that Democrats are going to kill you and every small business in the country with higher taxes. It sometimes works. "The whole premise behind Senator Obama's plans are class warfare, let's spread the wealth around," McCain pointed out in the third debate. "[And] by the way, the small businesses that we're talking about would receive an increase in their taxes right now." McCain and his team fanned out and appeared on all the Fox shows to sound the alarm that Obama was quietly lowering the threshold for paying higher taxes: "Obama voted to raise taxes on individuals making $42,000."

That's par for the course, but then McCain, energized by his rallies, took it a step further. "His plan gives away your tax dollars to those that don't pay taxes." The crowds booed, and McCain fed the beast: "That's not a tax cut. That's welfare!" I wonder, why that inference? McCain then took up the charge that Obama was secretly planning a socialist agenda. "At least in Europe, the socialist leaders who so admire my opponent are up front about their objectives." McCain would call out "Share the wealth!" and the crowds chanted, "Socialist!"

Obama advantage on taxes produced by "Joe the Plumber" debate

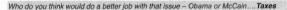

Who do you think would do a better job with that issue – Obama or McCain.... **Taxes**

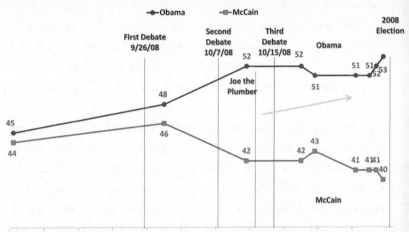

Source: From ABC/Washington Post surveys leading up to the 2008 election.

And we should remember the closing argument from the McCain campaign. They put $5.7 million behind their "Joe the Plumber" ad, airing it 12,750 times. It began with the Obama exchange. "Spread the wealth?" asks the announcer, followed by a series of individuals facing the camera and saying things like "I'm supposed to work harder just to pay more taxes. Obama wants my sweat to pay for his trillion dollars in new spending." The announcer brings the ad and campaign to a close: "Barack Obama: higher taxes, more spending, not ready."

The "Joe the Plumber" debate reminds us how misplaced was our admiration for John McCain.

Yet for all that effort, McCain lost the tax issue and the election.[21]

We tested in real time the argument and words that McCain and

Obama were using, and it could not have been clearer. Obama was slaughtering McCain on the "Joe the Plumber" exchange:

> *John McCain says, "Senator Obama has made it clear that he wants to raise your taxes so he can, quote, 'spread the wealth around.' Now is not the time for Obama's socialist policies and now, more than ever, small businesses should be reinvesting their earnings to create more jobs rather than sending that money to the tax-and-spend liberals in Washington. Senator Obama is more interested in controlling who gets your piece of the pie than he is [in] growing the pie, but I'll support policies that keep your taxes low, stimulate growth, and get our economy back on track."*
>
> *Barack Obama says, "John McCain is attacking my plan to cut taxes for the middle class and working Americans, but I think it is just common sense and so do Colin Powell and Warren Buffett, who have endorsed my campaign. Under my plan, no one making under a quarter of a million dollars, including 98 percent of business owners, will see their taxes increase a single dime and 95 percent of Americans will get a tax cut. But Senator McCain wants to give corporate executives more tax breaks with no relief for the struggling middle class."*

When we asked this after the third debate, a large majority of 54 percent said they agreed with Obama, while only 40 percent agreed with the McCain depiction of what was at stake in the "Joe the Plumber" debate. We got identical results when we gave people the same choice in the final week of the election.[22] Had the election been waged only on this issue, Obama's landslide would have been even greater.

James So what are we waiting for?

11.

THE DISASTER OF 2010

James So they told us to go screw ourselves in 2010. Right? We got smashed—lost 63 House seats and suffered the biggest wipeout since 1948 and hung on to the Senate by the skin of our teeth. In state after state, they gave Republicans supermajorities in the legislature and governors. Crazy governors like Scott Walker in Wisconsin, John Kasich in Ohio, Paul LePage in Maine, Rick Scott in Florida. They weren't subtle about it at all.

Stan Well, it is a little more complex than that, but, yes, they dissed us. Our impressive national majority, built up since 2004, crashed. Swing blocs fled us, particularly independents, seniors, and white non-college-educated and working-class voters. Among white non-college-educated men, the Democrats' congressional vote dropped from 41 to a pathetic 29 percent. But Democrats also lost a lot of support among groups that had emerged as our new base of loyalists, young people and unmarried women in particular.[1] So it was a mess. A lot of those voters viewed themselves as the hardworking and middle-class that we have tried to work for.

Why they left us is a little more complex.

James Don't you find it curious that they gave us the boot after just two years and after what those guys did to the country? I think there was some kind of collective amnesia about the state the country was in at the end of the Bush presidency. That's not to say we didn't bring a lot of it on ourselves in 2010, but we were not in good shape. When his honeymoon was over, Obama had to remind us where we had just been. A year after he won, he made a speech and talked about "the worst [financial crisis] that we've seen in generations," "record deficits, two wars, frayed alliances around the world," and an economy saved from "imminent collapse."[2] All that was true, but it didn't help much.

My feeling about 2010 is that the electorate got very energized and electrified. And they also thought they were seeing the same old, same old. I didn't agree, but it was a fairly common feeling: that nothing had really changed. As was their right, they went to the polls and shook things up again.

Stan Part of 2010 was a reaction against government spending and "big government." But understand what they meant by "government": they revolted against the bailout of the big banks and those responsible for the crisis. They revolted against the new health care law, seen then as a big giveaway to special interests, shaped by special deals in the Congress to win passage, and all paid for with $500 billion stolen from seniors from their Medicare. So they see this government spending as corrupted.

James Look, I am in a new place when you say "government."

Until I'm persuaded otherwise, I think the voters are right about government. It's going to come down on the side of big money and big lobbyists every time unless something changes.

Stan That gave the Tea Party its opportunity to exploit this moment and mobilize. This was a heyday for Fox and Glenn Beck. But they were damn effective: 47 percent of the voters in the 2010 election called themselves conservative—up from about 40 percent in 2008 and right now.

James These guys all played a big part in agitating their base. 2010 was about the unbelievable energy and anger of their base. They drove it and we're living with it.

Stan But Democrats will still not get 2012 right if they blame the Tea Party, and once again those poor voters who keep getting manipulated by the conservative media machine vote against their own interests. Democrats got a lot wrong. First, voters were frustrated by the lack of progress on unemployment and the seeming ineffectiveness of the president's policies—totally understandable at that point in the economic crisis.

But what really angered them was the perplexing and sustained lack of focus on economic issues as people themselves struggled to survive the "Great Recession." While voters were looking for FDR-like passion for moving the economy forward, the Democrats and the president focused on it only sporadically. People were desperately listening but heard no economic vision or story showing where the president and the Democrats wanted to take the country. And despite the great hope for change after 2008, people could not see that anybody was battling for the middle class and American jobs; yet for Wall Street and the lobbyists, it was business as usual.[3]

James I'm getting crazy now. I remember shouting, "What's the story? What chapter are we in? Where are we going?" My biggest complaint with this president is that there's a narrative in front of him and he refuses to drive it.

He's very effective at catching a knife here, catching a knife there. I even give him a whole lot of credit on health care, but the health care bill was never sold as part of a plan to secure people's status in the middle class, which it should be. Or to give people a chance to move up to the middle class if they weren't one expense away from being thrown out of it. And I think that would have been a much better set of formulations.

I badgered you to test a simple narrative: This is what we did and why. Here is where we are. This is where we are going. They need to see the whole story.

Stan I think you are right: day by day, voters did not hear a story. When we asked people, year after year through the crisis, what the Democrats' and the president's economic approach is, they hadn't a clue, other than spending.

But the White House did have a metaphor that it carried all the way into the 2010 elections—and I heard him personally deliver it in the Arena at Harbor Yard in Bridgeport, Connecticut, in the final weekend of the election:

"Imagine that the economy is a car and the Republicans drove it into a ditch. And it's a very steep ditch. So somehow the Republicans walked away from the scene of the accident. And we had to go in.

"And we put our boots on, us Democrats. We started pushing and shoving on that car, trying to get it out. And it's hot and dusty down there. And every once in a while we'd look up, and there are the Republicans standing up there, sipping on a Slurpee—fanning themselves.

"And we'd say, 'Why don't you come down and help?'

"And they'd say, 'No, no, no, no, thank you.' And they'd kick some dirt down into the ditch—make it a little harder for us. But we kept on pushing. We kept on pushing until finally we get this car up on level ground.

"Finally we have this car pointing in the right direction. And suddenly we feel this tap on our shoulders, and we look back, and lo and behold, who is it? It's the Republicans. And they say, 'Excuse me, can we have the keys back?'"

Regrettably, I have to tell you that metaphor was an insult to the middle-class voters. "I'm still in the ditch," they would shout at us in focus groups.

There is an underlying story in the metaphor, which was even more problematic at the time: Bush and the Republicans got you into this mess and we are making progress. As we saw earlier, voters totally get who is responsible for the crisis but don't want you blaming others and whining when you should be rolling up your sleeves, doing everything possible to make things better. They will listen to that message when we get to the election choice in 2012, but not when you are supposed to be working for them to make things better.

"Who wouldn't want to go back to six or eight years ago? There was less unemployment back then. I'd rather go back. I'd go back to eight years ago. I would rather go backwards than forwards right now." —Woman, white, non-college-educated

"Bush has been out of office for a long time. Anytime I hear his name, I get pissed off. He is gone. This incites me." —Man, white, college graduate

"Looking back and blaming isn't taking responsibility."—Man, white, college graduate

"You always hear about Bush, but who really cares? You can't keep looking back. We have to look ahead."—Man, white, college graduate

"I'm still living paycheck to paycheck."—Woman, white, non-college-educated

"Obama hasn't done anything for the economy. . . . He's trying to say things are turning around, but the numbers are still bad."—Man, white, college graduate

"Refusing to take ownership for the economy . . . is not funny." —Woman, white, non-college-educated

Much more problematic was the emerging happy ending in the metaphor: we tackled the financial crisis and its abuses and the economy is coming back and creating jobs again. The White House kept coming back to that touchstone, heralding the "green shoots" of recovery and "recovery summer" and declaring "We are poised for progress" in the State of the Union even after the 2010 defeat: "Two years after the worst recession most of us have ever known, the stock market has come roaring back. Corporate profits are up. The economy is growing again."⁴ But as we saw earlier, people's personal economy had not remotely come back, the new jobs were downsized, and the U.S. was a very long way from having an economy where the middle class prospers.

The more voters heard our economic message going into the

tough 2010 elections, the less likely they were to vote for a Democrat. These were going to be tough elections in any case, but we were making it that much harder. In our own poll that began on election night, we presented the president's economic message, but barely a third said it made them more likely to vote for a Democratic candidate—more than 20 points weaker than a Democratic message focused on changing Washington for the middle class and 44 points weaker than a Republican one on big spending and big government.

The Democrats' Economic Message

Republicans hope you forget. It was their policies that hurt middle-class incomes, lost eight million jobs, and put us in the hole. They obstructed every effort to help get us out. The Recovery Act has started to bring the economy back and we've curbed Wall Street abuse. And now they want to go back to the same policies that caused the mess in the first place. America has to move forward.

The 2010 debacle took place at a time when big majorities in the country strongly agreed that America was in decline, that our problems had been building for years, and that special-interest money and lobbyists had government by the throat, catering to CEOs and Wall Street while the rule-abiding middle class was sinking. Even more, they strongly believed America needed a "clear strategy" and a government that "works for the middle class."[5] Yet the Democrats did not make the election about any of that—only a metaphor about blame and progress. It was bloody.

After the election and for a good part of the next year, the president was much more cautious about trumpeting good economic news and telling people that things were getting better for them. Still, the economic story remained rooted in the crisis. It was an administration that acted to keep the country from facing a deep depression and to prepare Americans for the "tough, long journey" ahead, with people "understandably impatient." There were "strong headwinds" that lengthened the journey and required we do more.[6] The assumption, articulated by the president himself, was that at some point on the journey, people would see results, look back, and credit him for getting them through the crisis:

> Well, what I would say is that for the last two and a half to three years, we have been working tirelessly and nonstop to deal with the worst economic crisis of our lifetimes, and ultimately, I'm going to be judged by, you know, whether we have stayed focused on making sure that this economy is moving in the right direction. . . . [M]y hope is that when we're on the other side of it, folks will look back and say, you know, he wasn't a bad captain of the ship. . . . [T]his country always gets through these storms.

But that was a tall order for voters living with downsized jobs, diminishing incomes, and rising costs for health care and gasoline. It invited them to shout back, "What kind of job?" And it required the president to jump on each sign of progress, making the White House look out of touch along the way. It left us all captive to events. We were asking voters to look back at events of more than four years ago and vote for continuity in what will certainly be another change election.

We came to the counterintuitive conclusion that Democrats must forget about the past and the financial crisis and recognize that "the story is not the recovery, but a set of powerful on-going realities: a middle class smashed and struggling, American jobs being lost, the country and people in debt, and the nexus of big money and power that leaves the common people excluded."[7] The story *was* the middle class.

Faced with a Republican-controlled House and a reduced majority in the Senate after the midterm elections, the president was determined to reach a bipartisan deal that would advance the interests of the country. He made a big offer to reduce the deficit by $4 trillion and even put Medicare cuts into the mix. He appealed for an end to the blame game in Washington and acknowledged "neither party is blameless for the decisions that led to this problem, [and] both parties have a responsibility to solve it." He identified with Americans who are "fed up with a town where compromise has become a dirty word." While people are struggling to "put food on the table," they turn on the TV and "all they see is the same partisan three-ring circus here in Washington."[8]

This appeal was grounded authentically in the president's personal project to bring people together, seek pragmatic solutions, and overcome partisan and ideological polarization. That was the horse that got him here, and voters for sure were angry about the partisan bickering that made Washington dysfunctional. That was one of the biggest reasons people said they punished Democrats in 2010, and maybe it is one of the biggest reasons they will punish Republicans at the next opportunity, in 2012.[9]

And that's a story: a president reaching out his hand and offering to compromise the programs dearest to his heart, including help for the poor, in pursuit of a bold bipartisan deal to make progress on the out-of-control deficit and the country's biggest problems. In his private negotiations with the Speaker, he accepted significant changes to Medicare and Medicaid, including raising the eligibility age to 69, and to Social Security cost-of-living changes that would reduce monthly benefits. He chided Washington, the Congress, and even his own party to do the right thing for the country. With the nation on the brink of defaulting on its debts in the summer of 2011, the president had a story to tell about a dysfunctional Washington and how he offered a better future.

James The road to hell truly is paved with good intentions. This is not our grandmothers' Republican Party. They are swearing faith in absolutes and any wavering or dealing with the devil is treated as heresy. The Republicans were never going to cut any kind of deal that made Obama look good, or capable, and certainly not statesmanlike. Obama was chasing a grand bargain on the Republicans' terms. They were trying to deal with the deficit that had largely been caused by Republican tax cuts by cutting Medicare and Social Security.

According to Matt Bai, John Boehner was prepared to accept revenue increases in return for cuts in entitlement programs, but there was no way he could get this past Eric Cantor, who represented the majority of the party, which would never accede to anything that looked or smelled like a tax increase. If the grand bargain had been struck between Boehner and Obama, both men would have had trouble in their parties, but the Republicans walked away.[10]

The battle with the House Republicans over raising the debt ceiling ended in tears: both the president and the Republicans were hurt dramatically. The latter took most of the blame, but with the president not blaming them for this downgrading of the American economy, he looked "overwhelmed" and "not strong enough" to help people.

But that has totally changed. The president points out Republican intransigence and madness every day, and Republicans are on the defensive and paying a big political price. That sets the stage for a very different story.

When All Is Said and Done, There's a Lot Better Chance the Middle Class Will See Better Times When a Democrat Is President

James In my last, prescient book *40 More Years*, I was proud to say that I had been praised by eminent academic Larry Bartels for stating that the American economy does better under a Democrat in the White House than it does when there is a Republican president. Professor Bartels is now at Vanderbilt University; he was at Princeton then, but from whatever vantage point he sees me, I'm still right. And so was Harry Truman when he said, "If you want to live like a Republican, you have to vote like a Democrat."

Information in Larry's 2008 book *Unequal Democracy* shows how much better the economy has performed under Democrats. For our purposes, it's stunning how much better the lower-middle and middle class has done in income growth. Unemployment and economic growth are better too. Between 1948 and 2001, the great middle—stretching from the 20th to the 80th percentile—saw annual real income grow between 2.37 and 2.63 percent when a Democrat was president. It looked much different under Republican presidents: in the bottom 20th percentile it grew 0.6 percent; in the 40th it grew 0.93 percent; in the 60th it grew 1.32 percent; and at the top, from the 80th percentile up, annual real income grew 1.6 percent. All lower. Under Democratic presidents, unemployment was about one-third lower, and GDP growth about one-third higher, than under Republicans. And inflation is a wash . . . but aren't Democrats supposed to let spending, the money supply, and everything else get out of control?[11]

Think about the job situation. I don't believe George W. Bush created a single private-sector job in his eight years in office. In his first term he lost 913,000 private-sector jobs, whereas Obama was heading into positive territory by March 2012.[12] Obama was hit by public-sector job losses—in state and local government—while Bush oversaw big gains in government jobs, ironically enough.

There's another indicator that shows how much better off we are with a Democrat as president. If you had put $1,000 in a fund that followed the S&P index when Democrats were in power since Kennedy, you'd have had $10,920 in early 2012. For Republicans from Nixon through Bush, the figure was $2,087.[13] With the Democratic fund, you'd have done *nine* times better! Fellow Democrats, I urge you to tear out this page and keep it on your person, so if you run into Larry Kudlow in a social situation somewhere, you can take this page and stick it in his—uh, you can show it to him to politely.

Let's say you have a Democrat fund and your capital gain is $9,920. In a well-ordered society, you would pay 35 percent capital gains tax on that money, leaving you with $6,448 and the U.S. Treasury with $3,472. With a Republican fund, the gain is $1,087, but you pay no tax in your trickle-down world. You get $1,087 and Uncle Sam gets zip. It's easy to see that both the investor and the country are better off with a Democrat; under a Republican, the investor is poorer and the country is poorer. What is there to think about?

12.

WHY DO YOU FEEL BETTER ABOUT 2012? BECAUSE WE HAVE A STORY TO TELL

Looking ahead to the November election, we feel really good that President Obama and the Democrats are focused on the economy and the fate of the middle class. We mean, really good. It was painful getting here and we still have some big choices to make, but we really do have a story to tell, and that makes all the difference.

At the low point for the president in the summer and fall of last year, the White House and the Obama campaign took a fresh look at their story about the state of the country and economy; we know for certain that they listened to a lot of outside folks to get their views. We got heard and are proud to have played some role in deciding where the president staked his banner.

James The main reason I feel better is I feel the country is evolving into a coalition that is increasingly favoring the Democrats. I'm also feeling more positive because the Republican contenders for the nomination made such fools of themselves.

If we look back at 2010, if I'm right, 2012 is going to show that the vote in 2010 was very transitory. I certainly hope I'm right about that.

I don't think there's any doubt that Fox will play less of a role in 2012, just as they didn't have so much influence in 2008. I think they don't have the same power they used to. They're certainly still a factor, as it were, and it's not all about ratings, but I don't think they have the same power. And look at Limbaugh: he doesn't have the same power anymore.

I'm not saying that 2010 was their last gasp, but they have been absolutely relentless on Obama. They wouldn't even give him credit for getting Bin Laden. But if you had said that the unemployment rate was going to be over 8 percent, the growth rate under 3 percent, and the "right track" number (i.e., those who believe he's on the right track) under 35, you'd never guess the president would have an approval rating of 47 percent. So, as of this writing, the president's numbers are better than you might expect, given the right-wing media bias against him.

We just have to make sure we're getting the right message out on the positive side.

Stan We did a wild experiment in a September 2011 survey where we took the president's policies in his jobs bill and surrounded it by his own language about the long-term problems facing the middle class and getting back to a country "where hard work and responsibility pay off." The goal was to embed his actions in a new story.

Simulated Long-term Middle-Class Message

We need to *rebuild the economy for the middle class that has been under attack for decades.* We should cut payroll taxes by $1,500 for families and small businesses and give incentives to companies that hire returning veterans and the long-term unemployed. Get Americans back to work rebuilding our schools and installing new technology. *Let's get back to an America where hard work and responsibility pays off.*

That combination was much more powerful than a Democratic message with the same policies, bracketed this time by language about overcoming bipartisan differences and acting for the country. The middle-class message decisively defeated a Republican message that said, "We can't spend our way to prosperity. America needs jobs, not more government spending, which will leave our children saddled with a mountain of debt." There is a powerful story here.

In December 2011, President Obama traveled to Osawatomie, Kansas, to give a major speech in the same small town where Teddy Roosevelt gave his 1910 "New Nationalism" speech setting out his progressive critique and vision.[1] Obama rushed almost immediately to his entry point, which was a similar statement on our times. America still has great industries and workers, he observed, "but for most Americans, the basic bargain that made this country great has eroded.

Long before the recession hit, hard work stopped paying off for too many people. Fewer and fewer of the folks who contributed to the success of our economy actually benefited from that success. Those at the very top grew wealthier from their incomes and their investments—wealthier than ever before. But everybody else struggled with costs that were growing and paychecks that weren't—and too many families found themselves racking up more and more debt just to keep up.

He could not have been clearer in his embrace of the fundamental critique expressed by the real people throughout this book. And he got their sense of grievance: the "breathtaking greed of a few with irresponsibility all across the system" took us all down. "It was wrong."

He let it be known that this is the starting point for the public political battle ahead:

> This is the defining issue of our time. This is a make-or-break moment for the middle class, and for all those who are fighting to get into the middle class. Because what's at stake is whether this will be a country where working people can earn enough to raise a family, build a modest savings, own a home, secure their retirement.

He has set out what is at stake—what kind of country we *will* be in the future—and the choice voters will have in the election. This is about the future, not the past.

It is also about inequality. We have not seen this level of inequality since the Great Depression, he observed, and that threatens "our democracy." Ordinary citizens think the "system in Washington is rigged against" them, giving "an outsized voice to the few who can afford high-priced lobbyists and unlimited campaign contributions." But "this kind of gaping inequality," the president pointed out, also "gives lie to the promise that's at the very heart of America: that this is a place where you can make it if you try. We tell people— we tell our kids—that in this country, even if you're born with nothing, work hard and you can get into the middle class."

That was the dream that so many of the people we interviewed refused to give up on—and now the president was with them in that.

The greater the scale of the problems we face and the greater your passion for the fate of the middle class, the greater the urgency for change and solutions that can get America back on the right path. For the president, "it starts by making education a national mission." You work for an "innovation economy." You rebuild our infrastructure. You "rethink our tax system more fundamentally."

If your goal is to restore the middle class, then "we simply cannot return to the current conservative brand of 'you're on your own' economics" or "survival of the fittest." Instead, we have to build a nation "where we're all better off. We pull together. We pitch in. We do our part"—as Teddy Roosevelt would have urged. "We believe that hard work will pay off, that responsibility will be rewarded, and that our children will inherit a nation where those values live on."

The speech elicited great applause.

James Wow. That was seriously good. I called Stan. You know, I can pick at some words or some things, but I have to tell you, he got this pretty right. That was a powerful statement. That is a powerful story. It really sets up a choice for the election. I wouldn't want to be on the Republican side of that choice.

I just hope we're able to tell the story consistently. Events are constantly changing the way the debate is framed, but we have to make sure we stick to the story. The other side wants to take us back to the twenties, it seems like. Our narrative has to be that the middle class is taking it on the chin. It was only for one brief moment under the Democrats, when Republicans as well as Democrats were asked to pay their fair share, that we had any kind of real growth. Republican policies haven't helped the middle class at all. Their policies have been brutal in the past and they continue to be brutal. I'm not sure we're getting the word out on this.

Stan I had the same reaction to the speech: wow. He did it. He really did it. I immediately sent an e-mail to David Axelrod congratulating him. And reporters like Ron Brownstein of the *National Journal* and Dan Balz of the *Washington Post* who have been around since the Macomb County work on Reagan Democrats called and said, "You must have really liked that a lot."

And then in his remarks before the Associated Press in early April, he made all this even clearer: "I can't remember a time when the choice between competing visions of our future has been so unambiguously clear."[2] The Republicans have tried their approach "on a massive scale" and only the wealthier got wealthier. That led him to a powerful insight to take to the election. "In this country, broad-based prosperity has never trickled down from the success of the wealthy few." In this country, opportunity "grows outward from the heart of the middle class."

We really do feel good about our chances, because Democrats do have a story to tell. What story they tell may decide what happens in November—and what is the mandate for action at the end of this year and in 2013.

We do not know yet what story and choice Democrats will be taking to voters in November. Because of the improved job numbers and unexpected growth in the last two quarters of 2011, some will make the case for going back to the crisis-recovery story. With each jobs report, the president is out there: "Now, here's the good news. The good news is that we are moving in the right direction. . . . And over the last 22 months, we have seen 3 million jobs created, the most jobs last year since 2005, more jobs in manufacturing than we've seen since the '90s."[3]

When the April jobs report showed only 120,000 jobs, he qualified the enthusiasm: "It's clear to every American that there will still be ups and downs along the way, and that we've still got a lot to do." That allowed Mitt Romney to respond, "This is a weak and very troubling jobs report that shows the employment remains stagnant"—as they contest whether the glass is half full or half empty.[4]

Whether or not the president needs to be the voice of the recovery, it is a hell of a lot better for Democrats when the president's approval rating is nearing 50 percent rather than 40 and the number saying "We're seriously off track" is down 20 points. And at least Democratic voters feel a lot better.

We totally understand the mind-set of leaders who pushed big economic policies for the good of the nation and want to get credit for them. Under the same set of circumstances, President Obama could never have beaten Bill Clinton to get in front of the cameras to hold up the monthly job results for the last four years.

Stan   With real job gains over a year, this is at least a more plausible story than the one offered by the president and Democrats up until now, though that story is still hard to get heard. That chart could offer a platform to contrast not just the economic records of Bush and Obama but also their differing future approaches to the economy, taxes, and Medicare and how you pay for deficit reduction. And then you contrast the two people, Barack Obama and Mitt Romney.

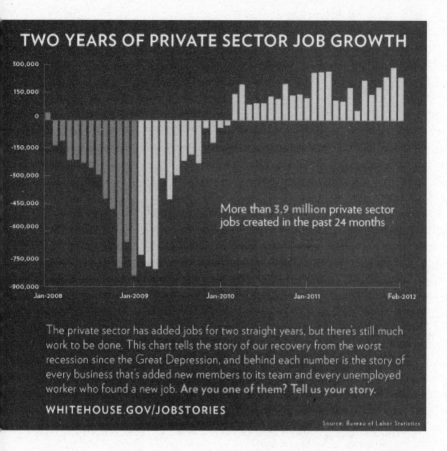

TWO YEARS OF PRIVATE SECTOR JOB GROWTH

More than 3.9 million private sector jobs created in the past 24 months

The private sector has added jobs for two straight years, but there's still much work to be done. This chart tells the story of our recovery from the worst recession since the Great Depression, and behind each number is the story of every business that's added new members to its team and every unemployed worker who found a new job. **Are you one of them? Tell us your story.**

WHITEHOUSE.GOV/JOBSTORIES

Source: Bureau of Labor Statistics

James This is how I would do it: I'd tell people the basic truth that there are two things going on here at the same time. Sure, the economy is getting better and some people are beginning to feel the benefits of that. But for every one person who's feeling it, there are ten who don't. You have to address the needs and fears of those people.

If you run only on the first part—that there are people who are feeling better about their situation—you're telling the other ten that you don't understand their lives.

I understand the temptation for the president: it's human nature for anyone in a leadership position, whether it's a businessperson or a politician, to take credit for something positive. The tendency, then, is to say, "Look—the economy's getting better!" It's true, it really is. But it wasn't in a very good place to start with.

Let's say you're fifty and out of work right now and feeling like you're a long way from finding anything. Or you're lucky enough to be working but you're feeling the effects of the lower wages that are on offer in this economy. People who are working are just happy to have a job, and it's going to be tough for lot of them to reconcile their own situations with a message of economic rebound from the president.

Stan   We accept that there is a story there building on what Bush did to the country and what Obama did and the budget choices ahead, but in the end, it is a weak economic message, at odds with the long-term economic problems, full of serious economic and political risks, as Romney contests whether America is really back. The story also reduces the need for a serious policy agenda.

James   It's a problem that voters have with politicians. They see the person come in and shuffle a lot of stuff around and there's a modest change and it gets blown up out of proportion to the issues that remain. If I were the president, I'd acknowledge the 220,000 people who got jobs one month but then I'd focus entirely on the 13 million who didn't. I know we differ on that. He wants to talk about the areas where we're doing okay, and not the many who are still struggling.

Stan   We tested the two key parts of this story, the jobs record and the optimistic assertion that America is back. They do not move the needle: just 44 percent said the crisis-recovery message and progress on jobs made them more likely to support the president—well below his vote and no stronger than the Republican messages on the economy. Our monthly economic tracking measures on unemployment, salaries and benefits, health care insurance, and reentering the labor market have still not improved even a point, despite voter recognition of the macro gains.

Remember, voters are very discerning about the economy, and they know the difference between macro and micro. So, despite the steady progress on jobs, a large majority as late as February believe that "the economy is not moving in the right direction and we need a change." Almost half of voters believe that "strongly."[5] This is still a change election on the economy.

Much more problematic was the more satisfied and idealistic statement from the State of the Union address that "America is back." The swing voters in Denver responded unenthusiastically to that part of the president's speech: in the survey, just a third of them said it made them more supportive of the president. We have no doubt voters will embrace an optimistic view of the American character and what Americans can achieve, as the president declared before the UAW: "[No] matter how tough times get, Americans are tougher. No matter how many punches we take, we don't give up. We get up. We fight back. We move forward."[6] But the country is not ready for a Reagan-like "Morning in America." In any case, a story that concludes with "America is back" contradicts the idea that "this is a make-or-break moment for the middle class."

We believe that the second story and choice centered on the middle class is the much more powerful way to win this election and govern afterward. Above all, it is situated in the deep problems people believe will control whether they and the country succeed. Those were reflected in the president's speech at Osawatomie, Kansas, and used word for word in the two middle-class messages below. A large majority of 54 percent says it makes them more likely to support Barack Obama and Democratic leaders—10 points above the Republican vote and equal to Obama's 2008 vote for president. Intensity of support in a middle-class narrative is 8 points higher than any other narrative, Democratic or Republican.

When progressives offer this story, they do not need to argue with voters about their economic condition or whether we face uncertain headwinds in the period ahead. It is incontestably an election about the middle class and about America's future. Within that story, voters will take the measure of Mitt Romney and Barack Obama and decide who has the right priorities on how to rescue the middle class, build a strong American economy, and address our long-term deficits.

James We want this election because we need to smash this aberration of a Republican Party. That's the main reason we want it so badly. This story gives the Democrats the best chance of winning in

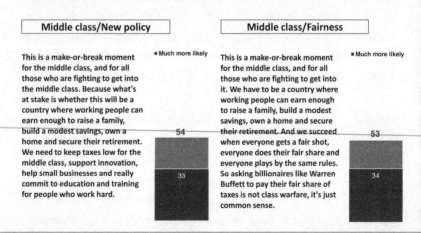

Middle class messages very strong

Now, please imagine that Barack Obama or a Democratic leader in Congress made the following statements about the economy. After hearing each statement, are you much more likely to support this Democrat, somewhat more likely, just a little more likely, no more likely or less likely to support them?

Middle class/New policy

This is a make-or-break moment for the middle class, and for all those who are fighting to get into the middle class. Because what's at stake is whether this will be a country where working people can earn enough to raise a family, build a modest savings, own a home and secure their retirement. We need to keep taxes low for the middle class, support innovation, help small businesses and really commit to education and training for people who work hard.

■ Much more likely

54

33

Middle class/Fairness

This is a make-or-break moment for the middle class, and for all those who are fighting to get into it. We have to be a country where working people can earn enough to raise a family, build a modest savings, own a home and secure their retirement. And we succeed when everyone gets a fair shot, everyone does their fair share and everyone plays by the same rules. So asking billionaires like Warren Buffett to pay their fair share of taxes is not class warfare, it's just common sense.

■ Much more likely

53

34

Source: Democracy Corps National Survey with the Voter Participation Center, February 11 to 14, 2012.

November. And it's not just about winning—winning is always good, but it also means President Obama and the Democrats have a chance of governing and fixing this mess.

But we're only going to get there if we raise the stakes and address the actual character of America. If we do that we can redefine the Republicans into obscurity for a generation, like FDR did in his campaign speech in 1932 when he championed the "forgotten man at the bottom of the economic pyramid," and in the 1936 State of the Union when he aligned the Republicans with the "resplendent economic autocracy" that fights to control government in order to achieve the "power for themselves, enslavement for the public." FDR defined his opponents, then he consigned them to the margins where they belonged.

This is just such a time, we believe. Everything is on the line for the ordinary, hardworking people who have fallen victim to another resplendent economic autocracy that flushes their dreams away while incomes surge at the very top of that same pyramid as corporate lobbyists and their money dominate politics. It's time to bring down this house of cards. If the election is not "just a matter of math" on how we pay for critical national goals but a referendum on whether we will be a middle-class country, the Republican Party can become an anachronism. They will own all of their inexplicable efforts to block affordable and universal education, to undermine our systems of retirement and health care for the middle class, and they'll sit out there on the golden margins complaining with the richest people just how unfair life is.

Stan But we'll be honest with you: only if Obama and the Democrats run on the principle that "it's the middle class, stupid!" do we have any chance as a country to address the state of the middle class and their dreams, expressed with some anguish and hope by people in this book. We owe it to them. The deep problems at the heart of this book have to be at the heart of our politics. The other crisis-recovery story does not mandate big changes or policies to rescue the middle class. It requires only that we address our problems in a balanced way. That story does not require that you wake up the day after the election, and every day thereafter, and put the fate of the middle class at the heart of your work. It doesn't require you to offer different opportunities from what we have seen over the last three decades.

We think Democrats are ready to tell the middle class story. That's why we feel better. Democrats do indeed have a story to tell.

Honoring Stay-at-Home Moms

James While I don't think it was well said, I do think Hilary Rosen was essentially correct when she said Ann Romney had never dealt with "the kinds of economic issues" faced by most American women. Because of what has happened to the middle class, most women with families don't have a choice about working or staying home. Sure, for the 1 percent, you have a choice, you can stay home. Even the husband can stay home. The realities for the middle class are that the family is facing unbelievable higher-education costs and they just had a health care disaster somewhere in the family or a job loss. It is difficult for the mom to stay home and raise children in those circumstances. Some of my sisters made that choice and it is noble and important, but someone needs to check in and remind people that it's becoming increasingly rare because it's not possible when all of the income growth for this country is taking place for 1 percent of the people who live in it.

I have more issues with what a Romney administration would do to poorer stay-at-home moms. If he put forward the Ryan budget he endorsed, programs like Head Start and the Supplemental Nutrition Assistance Program (SNAP) would be gutted. Even fewer mothers would be able to afford to stay home even if they wanted to. There are just few mothers who can afford to stay at home now, given what's happening with incomes. Of course, we want to honor stay-at-home moms, but Republican policies make it almost impossible for middle-class families to afford to do it. Come to think of it, *everything* they do makes it harder, so we ought not be surprised.

As the furor over what Hilary Rosen said played out, evidence emerged of Mitt Romney's hypocrisy. Campaigning in New Hampshire in January, Romney said this:

"I wanted to increase the work requirement. I said, for instance, that even if you have a child two years of age, you need to go to work. And people said, 'Well that's heartless.' And I said, 'No, no, I'm willing to spend more giving day care to allow those parents to go back to work. It'll cost the state more providing that day care, but I want the individuals to have the dignity of work.'"

Romney talked about how hard his wife worked, and how she was advising him on women's issues. He's certainly honoring the stay-at-home mom of their five children. That's all fine, but he needed to acknowledge that his family made a choice not open to everyone, a choice that would be much harder to make if his own policies are implemented. He might also explain why his wife wasn't expected to experience "the dignity of work" when her economic circumstances, far different from most people's, didn't demand that she do so.

13.

PAUL RYAN HAS THE ANSWER

James On March 20, 2012, the House Budget Committee chairman, Representative Paul Ryan, and the House Republicans unveiled their budget resolution for fiscal year 2013. Make a note of that date, because March 20, 2012, goes down as a special day in class warfare the Republicans are waging: it's the day they decided they were going to start shooting prisoners. We've agreed with Warren Buffett that class warfare has been won by the rich, but the Ryan budget marks the point at which they threw the Geneva Convention out the window and started lining the middle class up against the wall.

Among its provisions, Ryan's budget would cut the top tax rate from 35 to 25 percent, slashing taxes for the wealthiest Americans. My question is: When are rich people in this country going to say, "Okay, I have enough now"? They've won this war in a rout and still

they want more. They got the Bush tax cuts and that wasn't enough. Then they said, "We can't pay anything on capital gains. We can't have an inheritance tax. We have to subsidize our oil companies." And the Republicans said, "Okay, we can do all that." But at what point do you declare victory? When you have all the money rather than just most of the money? None of the new gilded nabobs or plutocrats are saying, "My cup is full of gold." They can't be, because Representative Ryan is rolling out his class warriors again and mounting a new campaign. And this budget isn't out there floating past Jupiter on the lunatic fringes of the far right: it's Republican Party policy endorsed and supported by congressional Republicans.

Now, let's be fair to Paul Ryan. Here is how he framed his budget on *Face the Nation* the weekend after he released his plan:

> We have a moral and legal obligation to stop this debt crisis from happening. We have the most predictable economic crisis coming, and to ignore it is wrong. We think we owe the country solutions. We think we owe the country a path to prosperity, to get the Amer-

ican Idea back, to get people back to work, to get this debt under
control. . . . We have an obligation to put solutions on the table.
People in America are ready to be talked to like adults. They don't
want to be pandered to like children. We owe the country a sharp,
clear difference—a choice of two futures—so they can decide what
kind of country we want to be, what kind of people we want to be
in the 21st century. The president has us on a path to debt and decline. We owe the country an alternative path.[1]

Among other things, the Republicans say their plan:

- cuts spending by $5.3 trillion relative to the president's
  budget;
- prevents the president's tax increases and reforms the broken tax code;
- reduces the debt as a share of the economy over the next
  decade;
- reduces the size of the federal government to under 20
  percent of the economy by 2015;
- repeals the president's health care law.

Sounds good. Right?

What would Paul Ryan's "alternative path" do to the American
people?

Jeff Zients, acting head of the Office of Management and Budget, gave a cogent rejoinder to Ryan's March madness a day after it
was released:

[T]he GOP plan gives those making over $1 million per year an
average tax cut of at least $150,000 and preserves tax breaks for oil

and gas companies and hedge fund managers. These tax breaks are then paid for by ending Medicare as we know it and implementing deep cuts in what we need to grow our economy and create jobs in years to come.[2]

As the Office of Management of Budget says, the proposals cut muscle, not fat. So much muscle that the Center for Budget and Policy Priorities says that by 2050, other than Social Security, health care, and defense, the federal government would "cease to exist."[3] Robert Greenstein has looked at a lot of budgets, but he called this one "Robin Hood in reverse—on steroids":

> It would likely produce the largest redistribution of income from the bottom to the top in modern U.S. history and likely increase poverty and inequality more than any other budget in recent times (and possibly in the nation's history)."[4]

Stan The Ryan budget is now their defining choice, as Ryan told *Face the Nation*. So we tested it in our Democracy Corps battleground survey of 1,500 likely voters in 56 Republican seats and in the 23 most endangered Democratic seats. It is the only poll we know of that is conducted just in the congressional seats that matter—the front line of who controls the majority after November. Every Democrat voted against the Ryan budget and every Republican, save for one, voted for the Ryan budget. A pretty stark choice.

When people heard a straight (not Carville-esque) description— simply, "a budget for the next 10 years that cuts an additional $5.3 trillion from the federal budget"—they were taken aback. Just a third supported the plan; almost 60 percent opposed it, 44 percent strongly.

But we wanted to go further and test the palatability of different elements of this budget just as Democratic candidates across the country would: by asking the voters to throw the bums out and go in a different direction. The Ryan budget is the battleground and the mandate for change.

These were the attacks we tested, setting up the 2012 election to be the barometer of this view of government and how we help the middle class. Almost two-thirds said they opposed each of these proposed cuts.

Raises taxes on middle class, but cuts for top (The member) voted to raise taxes on middle-class and working families in order to pay for tax cuts for CEOs, big corporations that outsource jobs, big oil companies that are more profitable than ever, and millionaires and billionaires, giving them a tax break of $265,000 on top of the Bush tax cuts.	**Total opposed: 64%** **Strongly opposed: 35%**
Cuts Medicaid, hurts seniors and poor (The member) voted to cut Medicaid by almost half—$1.7 trillion over the next ten years—including coverage for seniors, the disabled, and the poor, leaving 19 million people without guaranteed health care and shifting the costs to states already strapped for cash.	**Total opposed: 63%** **Strongly opposed: 33%**

Ends Medicare as we know it	Total opposed: 62%
(The member) voted to end Medicare as we know it and instead give seniors a voucher to pay for traditional Medicare or a private plan that is not guaranteed to keep pace with the rising costs of health insurance and inflation, forcing seniors to pay thousands of dollars out of pocket.	**Strongly opposed: 34%**
People lose health insurance and companies can deny preexisting	**Total opposed: 61%**
(The member) voted to eliminate health insurance coverage for 33 million people who lack coverage now, allowing health insurance companies to deny coverage to people with preexisting conditions, charge women higher rates than men, and eliminate coverage for millions of young people who can currently join their parents' plan.	**Strongly opposed: 34%**

James We could dismiss the Ryan budget as the crazed fiscal musings of an ultra-ambitious conservative were it not for the fact that Republicans are lined up lockstep behind it. It is their economic manifesto. They've signed up for it with a blood oath. The Ryan budget is unironically entitled "The Path to Prosperity" and it was passed with all Republican votes, only four voting no (and you don't want to know why). Half the House Republicans voted for an amendment that would achieve this strangling of the government in just five years. Just so you know how crazy they are. Every Democrat voted no and the proposal was mercifully put to sleep in the

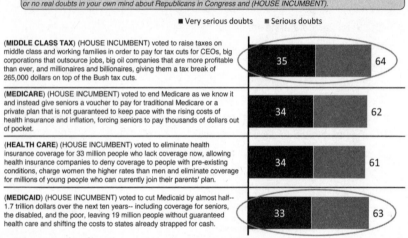

Weakest points in Ryan plan: middle class tax hike, Medicare, Medicaid, eliminating popular provisions of the health care law

Now I am going to read you some of the things critics are saying about (HOUSE INCUMBENT) and the Republican Congress. After I read each one, please tell me whether this raises very serious doubts, serious doubts, minor doubts, or no real doubts in your own mind about Republicans in Congress and (HOUSE INCUMBENT).

■ Very serious doubts   ■ Serious doubts

(MIDDLE CLASS TAX) (HOUSE INCUMBENT) voted to raise taxes on middle class and working families in order to pay for tax cuts for CEOs, big corporations that outsource jobs, big oil companies that are more profitable than ever, and millionaires and billionaires, giving them a tax break of 265,000 dollars on top of the Bush tax cuts.   35   64

(MEDICARE) (HOUSE INCUMBENT) voted to end Medicare as we know it and instead give seniors a voucher to pay for traditional Medicare or a private plan that is not guaranteed to keep pace with the rising costs of health insurance and inflation, forcing seniors to pay thousands of dollars out of pocket.   34   62

(HEALTH CARE) (HOUSE INCUMBENT) voted to eliminate health insurance coverage for 33 million people who lack coverage now, allowing health insurance companies to deny coverage to people with pre-existing conditions, charge women the higher rates than men and eliminate coverage for millions of young people who can currently join their parents' plan.   34   61

(MEDICAID) (HOUSE INCUMBENT) voted to cut Medicaid by almost half-- 1.7 trillion dollars over the next ten years-- including coverage for seniors, the disabled, and the poor, leaving 19 million people without guaranteed health care and shifting the costs to states already strapped for cash.   33   63

Source: Democracy Corps Congressional Battleground Survey with Women's Voices. Women Vote Action Fund, March 29 to April 4, 2012.

Senate, but we imagine only after nearly every Republican senator supported it. This thing is fast becoming a sacred text of the Republican Party.

It's a measure of how much Ryan has tapped into the Republican mainstream when he is criticized for his plan from the right. Eagerly, Rick Santorum says he would cut $5 trillion in five years— twice as fast as Ryan. "[It's] a great blueprint . . . ,"[5] he said. "We need to move forward quicker."[6] The plan squeaked through the Budget Committee 19–18, with two Tea Party–backed conservatives voting against. Tim Huelskamp of Kansas said, "It's good—but it's not good enough or the type of bold statement Republicans need to make." Amazing.

Mitt Romney has spoken warmly of the budget, as you'd expect, inasmuch as it's a policy associated with increased prosperity for the wealthy:

> I'm very supportive of the Ryan budget plan. It's a bold and exciting effort on his part and on the part of the Republicans and it's very much consistent with what I put out earlier. I think it's amazing that we have a president who three and a half years in still hasn't put a proposal out that deals with entitlements. This budget deals with entitlement reform, tax policy, which as you know is very similar to the one that I put out and efforts to rein in excessive spending. I applaud it. It's an excellent piece of work and very much needed.[7]

Along with his friends and colleagues, Mitt stands to add to his massive fortune while middle-class Americans fall further behind.

The most egregious thing that Romney has embraced is the strangling of Medicare and the abandonment of seniors. Last year, when the Republicans walked this same plank, they flat out ended Medicare as we know it and said, "How about coughing up $6,400 more each year?"—and it will only get worse each year. This year they supposedly give people a choice, but it is rigged. Their intention is to drive seniors back to the private insurance market (who would benefit then?), freeze the payments below the real inflation of health care costs, and thus shift the rising costs to seniors. It would leave Medicare as a program for the least healthy and poorest seniors. That's no choice. It's ending Medicare as we know it.[8]

Republicans help themselves. The Ryan budget is a perfect manifestation and reflection of what it means to be a modern Republican. And it's who they are. It's a very useful document to peruse if you want to understand what Republicans stand for and the utter contempt they have for people who aren't like them—for example, poor women, infants, and children. The Ryan budget would cut $1.25 billion from the Women, Infants and Children program and "cuts of this magnitude would require kicking about 1.8 million pregnant or postpartum women, infants, and children off of WIC and denying another 100,000 from receiving critical foods necessary for healthy child development."[9] Who *are* these people?

In lieu of "healthy child development," the Ryan plan offers instead an unhealthy dose of old-fashioned Dickensian moralizing:

> The federal government can help provide a strong safety net for Americans who, through no fault of their own, have fallen on hard times. But government can never replace the core institutions of a vibrant civil society—families, neighbors, churches and charities. Aimed first and foremost at buttressing these institutions, government reforms should promote upward mobility and security opportunity, especially for society's most vulnerable.[10]

EDUCATION

- **Pell grants:** The Ryan bill would cut Pell grants 19% below the 2012 level, and 9.6 million students would see their grants fall by more than $1,000 in 2014. In addition, over the next decade, more than one million students would lose support altogether.
- **Special education:** Approximately 27,000 special education teachers, aides, and other staff serving children with disabilities could lose their jobs.
- **Head Start:** The bill cuts $1.5 billion from the Head Start program and would result in 200,000 low-income children losing access to early childhood education.
- **Work Study:** This bill would reduce the Federal Work Study program's funding almost $185 million below the 2012 level, denying work-study jobs to more than 166,000 needy students.

POVERTY PROGRAMS

- **HUD:** This reduction would result in more than 400,000 very low-income families losing their housing through the Housing Choice Voucher program. A cut of this magnitude would also likely result in the permanent loss of these affordable units that serve 1.1 million of the nation's poorest residents.
- **WIC and SNAP:** The Ryan bill cuts $1.25 billion from the Supplemental Nutrition Assistance Program and the Women, Infants, and Children program. Cuts of this magnitude would require kicking about 1.8 million pregnant or postpartum women, infants, and children off WIC and denying another 100,000 from receiving critical foods necessary for healthy child development.

This is just a glimpse of what the OMB predicts the Ryan budget would mean for those "who through no fault of their own" are trying to make it in Paul Ryan's America. But for those fortunate enough to find themselves on the other end of the economic spectrum, this Republican budget attempts to end what Paul Ryan sees as the "punishment" of the successful. On the day the budget was released, Paul Ryan told the American Enterprise Institute that the problem with the current tax code is not that the middle class are squeezed but that "as you become successful, you're going to pay a much, much, much higher tax rate."[11] To remedy this, he closed the gap between the bottom and top rates, creating a "flatter tax code" that would "lower tax rates and broaden the base."[12] And as if we didn't know that this was trickle-down redux, House Majority Leader Eric Cantor said it would allow businesses to "keep more of their own hard-earned money and use it to invest and create more jobs in the private sector."

Republicans are unapologetic and frank about it: they propose tax cuts for corporations and for rich people, and they're saying, "It's a good thing, that's what we are for." They call it "pro-growth." It's an open assault on entitlements when in the past they tried to sneak those attacks through. I suppose we need to give Republicans credit for being open about it.

James This has got me as steamed as I've been in a long time. Remember, the bottom 10 percent has gained about 10 percent in real wages in 30 years, while the top 1 percent has gained more than 250 percent. Hotel maids, ditch diggers, and dishwashers are being crushed by high health care costs, high energy costs, high education costs, you name it. The squeeze hits graduates and retirees alike. The policy response from Mr. Ryan is more "Let's crush them and keep giving more to the top 1 percent." How asinine can we be as a society that we take the most vulnerable people—who have suffered the most, who are working the hardest—and say, "*You're* the problem with this world. We'll give your money to the top 1 percent, who have the lion's share of the growth."

Every cockamamie, goofball, jackass, stupid idea that has come up in the last 30 years has come from Representative Ryan and his ilk. I'll be glad to enumerate: (1) Tax cuts pay for themselves. Simple answer: Bullshit. (2) We go to Iraq because there are WMDs and we must establish a model democracy. Don't even get me started. (3) We don't go after Bin Laden and we have an open-ended commitment in Afghanistan. (4) We deny the federal government the right to negotiate with prescription drug companies for prescription drug benefits. And (5) We dismantle the right of firefighters and police officers to collectively bargain and we give out more tax cuts, as they did in Wisconsin, resulting in the worst job growth of any state. They're 0–5 on this list.

How much victory does this product of inherited wealth need

before he stops? It's not enough that the working poor have been crushed and he and his kind have gotten every kind of break; they have to have more. They have to eliminate the inheritance tax; they have to keep all their subsidies. And none of this is going to help balance the budget. Ryan doesn't care about deficits; he doesn't care what happens to these people; all he cares about is that he and his ilk keep winning more and more and more. Look at these provisions we've highlighted and tell me the Ryan budget isn't utterly immoral. It is necessary for every Democrat to do everything he or she can to expose this for what it is, as we have in this chapter.

James   For we can see now that they don't just want to win the war for themselves, they want to win the war for the generations to come: for their children, their children's children, all of whom will inherit great wealth. Anything they can buy but the middle class can't afford has to go. Pell grants, medical research, national parks— it all has to go.

Only when rich people own Yellowstone will they be happy. Then when they buy Yellowstone they will want an exemption so they don't have to pay property tax on it. When every beach in the country is a private beach, when every road is a toll road, when every school charges, then they might declare they've won their class war. We shouldn't forget that. In the end, that's how they think and that's who they are.

Ayn Rand and Paul Ryan

James   Paul Ryan is described as a "devout" Catholic who requires his staffers to read the turgid works of novelist and philosopher Ayn Rand.[13] Ryan also said Ayn Rand was "the reason I got involved in public service,"[14] and that, "Ayn Rand, more than anyone else, did a fantastic job explaining the morality of capitalism, the morality of individualism. . . ."[15] Paul Ryan was very much a fan of Ayn Rand, until he started getting some heat from it.

Let's be clear about what Ayn Rand advocated. The central tenet of Judeo-Christian religion—love your neighbor as yourself—is thought of by Rand as evil. According to Jonathan Chait, she thought, "The central struggle of politics is to free the successful from having the fruits of their superiority redistributed by looters and moochers."[16] What's more, she vehemently denied the existence of God, was arguably one of the most pro-abortion people who ever lived, and said that embryos don't have rights.[17] For the longest time, this seemed to bother the hierarchy of the Catholic Church not one whit. (Meanwhile, the second the government took a somewhat clumsy stand on contraception [church teachings on which 98% of Catholic women in the U.S. disregard], the Catholic Church threw itself a collective conniption.)

As I understand it—and I had some help on this from my friend, the ethicist and president of Loyola University, Reverend Kevin Wildes—the obligation to help others is at the core of everything in Church teachings. In Matthew 25, Jesus blesses the "sheep" among men because when he was hungry, they gave him something to eat, they gave him clothes, they sheltered strangers, they cared for the sick. Jesus says, "Whatever you did for the least of these brothers of mine, you did for me." (It's come to something in the discourse when James Carville is quoting scripture.) Last time I looked, the Church did believe in God, did not advocate abortion, and promoted helping others.

I can't attest to Representative Ryan's personal religion. I'm not a right-winger, so I don't profess to know who's going to heaven or hell, but I do know that his public positions are almost diametrically opposed to what the Church teaches. If Ryan is a devout

Catholic, as he says, then it can truly be said that he does not allow his religious beliefs to affect his public policy. One has to give him credit for that.

I ask a question: What would Catholics say if a devout Catholic required his employees to read the works of Margaret Sanger, the founder of Planned Parenthood? Many people have a problem with her, including me, but she's not in the same league as Ayn Rand. She's not on the same planet. I would love to see the reaction of the hierarchy to that. I find the whole thing to be somewhere between absurd and sickening.

In his inimitable way, Matt Taibbi pillories Rand as "a bloviating, arbitrary, self-important pseudo-intellectual. . . ." Taibbi says Rand was a "great career rabbi" for Alan Greenspan and her "lunatic religion" was the intellectual context for Greenspan's fiscal policy.[18]

Where it fits with Republican thinking is that Objectivism essentially means that self-interest is good and capitalism should be unrestrained. The state has no role (no taxes, no regulation) and poor people are just lazy. Thalidomide, dioxin dumping, Madoff, insider trading? Ignore them—the market will take care of it. It's the Ryan budget taken to its logical extreme.

There are interviews with Ayn Rand on YouTube, including a famous one with Mike Wallace from 1959. You can hear her say that antiabortionists calling themselves "pro-life" is a "disgusting fraud." You can see for yourself that what she is saying is diametrically opposed to the social teachings of the Church. You don't have to read *Atlas Shrugged* for that. The book has a speech given by the hero that goes on for seventy-five pages. If someone worked for me and I made them read that, I should be sued for mental cruelty. The interviews might serve one purpose: as a cheap form of birth control. Watch one of them and you won't want to have sex for a week.

A year after Ryan unveiled his budget, Catholics too prominent to ignore spoke out against it. On the eve of a visit to Georgetown

University, 90 faculty members and administrators wrote a letter of protest. "I am afraid that Chairman Ryan's budget reflects the values of his favorite philosopher Ayn Rand rather than the gospel of Jesus Christ," said Father Thomas J. Reese, who helped put the letter together.[19]

Ryan went into full fog machine mode. He said the story about him making staffers read Ayn Rand was an "urban legend" that showed he'd arrived in politics. Yes, he had read Rand but, "I reject her philosophy." He told the *National Review*, "Give me Thomas Aquinas . . . Don't give me Ayn Rand."[20] He turned his philosophy into so many pretzels trying to make it sound like he's following Church teachings. Then the Randian Atlas Society released audio of Paul Ryan talking in 2005, sounding like "a total Ayn Rand fanboy."[21] So it's not just me saying this.

Frankly I don't believe his Damascene moment. I don't believe him at all. Again I ask, am I able to know what is in another man's heart? When a person apologizes or says that he has changed his view, am I able to determine his true motives, intentions, or feelings? I can't. But I don't believe him because the budget that he continues to propose is an almost perfect mirror of Ayn Rand's philosophy, no matter how much he disavows it. The budget is the proof. QED.

If Representative Ryan truly believed Ayn Rand was such a horrible person, he would not have proposed this most Randian of budgets. In terms of public policy, the real Paul Ryan and the real Ayn Rand are inseparable. Representative Ryan says that he is a believer in the Gospels—I really doubt that anyone who has read the Gospels could have produced that budget.

The Strange Story of Food Stamps

Stan In his most consistent and provocative attack on the president, Newt Gingrich declared, "Barack Obama is the most successful food stamp president in American history," sometimes adding that black Americans in particular should take note: "We need a president who is a paycheck president, not a food stamp president."

How did this benign program to use our agricultural surplus to keep our poorest from being hungry, supported by iconic senators and presidents of both parties, become the red-meat attack of the Republican primary and come to deserve a full chapter in the Ryan budget? That story will tell you a lot about our country and the current state of the Republican Party.

Born in 1939, the food stamp plan began as a farm recovery program that permitted the unemployed to purchase agricultural surpluses, particularly from local farmers. Vacationing in Maine in 1941, first lady Eleanor Roosevelt wrote in her column that the whole state would participate and "125,000 needy people in Maine will have the opportunity to increase their food consumption." World War II brought the unemployment, agricultural surpluses, and this program to an end, but John F. Kennedy, in his first official act, issued an executive order "providing for an expanded program of food distribution to needy families." The first pilot program began in Paynesville, West Virginia, in 1961. He expanded the test to 43 areas in 22 states and Lyndon Johnson got Congress to pass the Food Stamp Act of 1964, but in 1969, Richard Nixon still felt the need to call for more: "The moment is at hand to put an end to hunger in America."[22]

Senators George McGovern and Bob Dole worked together on the Senate Hunger Committee in the early 1970s and together worked to pass the Food Stamp Act of 1977. For the first time, recipients did not have to make a cash contribution and could buy any kind of food, not just agricultural surpluses. That allowed the program to pass with the enthusiastic support of both parties and all interests across the food sector, but possibly at the expense of people's nutrition. This program was popular in the Congress and with voters, too, two-thirds of whom supported it, including a majority in both parties.[23] Senators Paul Douglas and Bob Dole both tried to amend the law to get it more focused on farm products, but there were big interests shaping the character of the emerging food stamp program.

Newt Gingrich got his first shot at food stamps when he and the House Republicans negotiated with President Clinton to pass the new welfare reform law. What he succeeded in achieving in 1996 was changing eligibility rules that reduced participation and ending key indexing to inflation, which means food stamps lost value over more than a decade. In 2006, the Department of Agriculture reported that on average SNAP participants used half of their benefits in the first week of the month and three quarters by the end of the second week.[24]

Then you should ask yourself if it matters whether you elect Democrats or Republicans and whether you should even bother to vote. My wife, Congresswoman Rosa DeLauro, became chairman of the Agriculture Appropriations Subcommittee when the Democrats took control of the Congress in 2006. She had worked for some time on the committee on food safety issues, pushing to get beyond incremental change to a single food agency, but as chairman she decided to devote her work to reducing hunger and impacting the nutrition programs. From New England and not from a historically agricultural state, she was not constrained by the traditional interests that shape agricultural policy. Her allies were Congressman Jim McGovern and Congresswoman Jo Ann Emerson, co-chairs of the Hunger Caucus, and a boatload of outside advocacy groups.

You soon learn in the Congress that there are "legislators" and "appropriators," and food stamp policy and benefit levels are mostly established in the farm bill that is renewed every five years. Speaker

Nancy Pelosi appointed Rosa to serve on the conference to negotiate with the senators on the nutrition provisions of the final bill. What? An appropriator as part of the conference? This had not happened before, and "some of my colleagues saw me as an invasive species," Rosa commented in a speech. When the Democratic and Republican senators, all from farm states, turned to Collin Peterson, chair of the House Agriculture Committee, he stood with her: the Speaker says Rosa speaks for us on nutrition.

The new law increased the minimum benefit, which had been frozen for three decades; increased the standard deduction for assets to allow more participation; indexed it to inflation; and excluded all retirement and education savings for eligibility. Amazingly, 35 Republican senators and 100 House Republicans joined the Democrats to pass the bill, overriding a Bush veto that did not mention food stamps.

Then Rosa got to use her role as appropriator. After Obama's election, both the Congress and the Obama economic team moved to fashion the American Recovery and Reinvestment Act, which would be signed into law on February 17, 2009. Rosa inquired whether food stamps would be included in the plan, and she was told she could get $4 billion, maybe $8 billion, for nutrition. Not one to accept that response, Rosa asked economist Mark Zandi at a hearing which policies are most stimulative. He responded with three things: unemployment benefits, refundable tax credits, and food stamps. Well, that was all she needed to hear. She went to the chairman of the Appropriations Committee, Dave Obey, who was fashioning the House bill, and, with Speaker Pelosi's support, got a temporary increase in the monthly benefits, as people were being hit both by the recession and higher food prices, adding more than $20 billion for nutrition. Eventually, 14 million additional households would be able to get food stamps.

After just a year, the increased number of people able to get food stamps brought the poverty rate down 8 percent, despite the surging unemployment, according to Sabrina Tavernise, writing in the *New York Times*, making it "one of the largest antipoverty efforts in the country."[25] In 2010, food stamp aid lifted 5.2 million people out of poverty, including 2.2 million children.[26]

We should not lose track of the fact that we are talking about $4.45 per person per day.[27] For many Americans, access to food stamps in this struggling economy is the only form of steady cash they can get, as welfare support has disappeared. Jason DeParle writes poignantly about the poor in Arizona—"mostly single mothers, [who] talk with surprising openness about the desperate, and sometimes illegal, ways they make ends meet—all with children in tow."[28]

The Republican Party is now determined as a matter of high policy to rip away this bit of support. Candidates like Newt Gingrich set the stage, but the Ryan budget devotes a whole chapter to "repairing the social safety net," which he says is at risk of becoming "a hammock." It slashes the food stamp program by at least $134 billion or 17 percent over the next ten years; a family of four would lose about $1,000 a year in food support.[29] And they think there is no time to lose: the Agriculture Appropriations Committee has been instructed to cut $33 billion next year, nearly all from nutrition. If Chairman Ryan gets his way, the average family of four would face an 11 percent cut in monthly benefits after September 1 this year.[30]

Seeing food stamp participation rise even before the crash, the Ryan budget report argues that this could only be caused by a culture of dependency, certain to produce "relentless and unsustainable growth." For the readers of this book, why participation rose after 2007 is no mystery, although ignoring the changes Democrats crafted allows Ryan to assert, "Centralized bureaucracy is no substitute for a vibrant civil society in which citizens help each other on a personal basis." The Ryan plan: cut the budget, shift the funds to the states, and make food aid contingent on work and training. According to Ryan, these cuts will free states to "come up with innovative approaches to delivering aid to those who truly need it."[31]

And the Farm Bill, where this story began, is supposed to be renewed in 2012, and guess where the Republicans say they want to achieve the bulk of their budget savings?

Fortunately, the American voter still gets the final say on how this story ends.

14.

AND DO YOU THINK YOU CAN REALLY DO SOMETHING ABOUT IT? SURE DO

Shared There are some who want to be "quiet" about the impolite topic of the fate of the middle class. There are others who want to distort the problem, or deny there even is a problem. Still others— and they might be on our side—acknowledge the problem but fumble the narrative. We're here to tell you that none of these positions is going to work. We're pushing back and saying no. If you aren't discussing the problem and looking for real solutions, then you're irrelevant and should be out of office.

That's the biggest change we have to offer. If you take this perspective, you have the best chance of getting to the big policies and actually doing something about it.

We're going to have a big discussion. And the predicament of the middle class is the only thing we're going to talk about. Basically the biggest change we can bring to the issue of the future of the middle class is to be assholes about it. We are not going away.

There are too many forces at work in the country that don't want to discuss it. Many of them, you know exactly why they want to be quiet. Aside from the Clinton years, three decades of public policy has created a new generation of rich Americans who have millions of reasons to protect the new status quo. Others have legitimate issues that they think are more important, primarily the deficit but also maintaining the armed forces or energy policy or whatever. We're sure those issues are important, but we say there's *nothing* more important than the middle class. Not anymore.

There's a lot of inertia. It's hard to drag this front and center when there's too much pressure and too much money trying to bury policy discussions in the backrooms, leaving out the middle class. Change the topic; be quiet; don't be divisive.

And there is the massive fog machine that distorts and denies the whole problem. We'll get to that. The whole middle class—the whole shrinking, beleaguered, shafted, and squeezed middle class— must get on the agenda no matter what Fox News and right-wing talk radio and the congressional foggers and the phony economists are saying.

If we are going to seriously address the problem of the decline of the middle class, the country in general and the Democrats in particular have to debate the issue incessantly. It has to be central to every conversation, every strategy, and every piece of public policy. When we consider an issue and a solution, we have to stop and think, *How does this protect America's middle class?* That is the filter through which everything must pass. This should be the number-one priority of the country.

The Republicans are so far out in the weeds on this that Democrats have a great opportunity to seize hold of the entire issue. As Democrats, we have to get to the position where Americans look to us as the party of the middle class. Our strategy, our advertising, our policy, must have the perspective that we are the party of the middle class. "What is the effect of this policy idea on the middle class?" "How does this rebuild the middle class?" It doesn't matter if it's tax policy, foreign policy, or energy policy. What policies are best for the middle class?

We apply the same filter, then, to identify the big policy changes that we want to discuss. What policy ideas we decide to highlight follow from that same principle and only come from that perspective.

If our goal is to restore the middle class, what policies would seem to make the most difference? And why hasn't that been the primary problem people have been trying to solve? Right now, we don't care about anything else.

People do not read James Carville and Stan Greenberg because they think we are policy experts. They think we know politics and how to impact the agenda. Remember "It's the economy, stupid"? Well, now it's the middle class, stupid. After the 1992 election, Bill Clinton gave his first joint session address to the Congress—in effect, the State of the Union—but he cleared the tables right at the beginning by saying, "We are only talking about the economy."

Well, we are only talking about the middle class.

James   Why is there not an Institute for the Expansion and Protection of the Middle Class at Princeton (or LSU or OSU or anywhere else you care to mention)? There should be. There should be NGOs in Washington and interest groups and think tanks solely promoting the expansion and protection of the middle class. Where is the presidential commission on this? Or the Congressional Select Committee on the Expansion and Restoration of the Middle Class? Or the Bureau of Middle Class Protection? Why aren't there any of these things? When are we going to acknowledge that this is crisis number one in this country?

When there is a crisis in this country, we get somber-faced, credentialed people in gray suits to talk about it. We need to get to the point so that when two other guys decide they want to write this book in 2016, they should have 60 ideas to choose from. Or 100. The political culture will have ginned up on the debate already: the facts in our book will be part of the popular political lexicon, and it will be accepted fact that the middle class has been undermined since the late seventies and poleaxed under Bush.

It sounds blindingly obvious, and I can hear people saying, "We have to talk about it." But we aren't. And without that level of debate, we're going to be short of ideas. Make it part of the conversation and things are going to happen. Of course, a few sharp minds are trained on this, but not enough. Why? Because you can't make money out of thinking about the middle class.

Where you make money is on expanding drilling. You make a lot of money protecting expensive drugs. You make a lot of money on for-profit colleges. There's a lot of national creativity and brainpower that goes into these areas. But there is an incentive to get involved in this, and the incentive is that the public rewards those who help them with two pretty precious commodities: their votes and their trust.

We need to go back to Mitt Romney's statement in January when he advised that questions about the distribution of wealth ought to be confined to "quiet rooms." If you like the status quo, that's the best way to proceed. If you don't want to help the middle class, confine talk about income inequality to your quiet room where you can look at pictures of each other's yachts and count how many Cadillacs you're running. Then you'll legitimately be able to claim, "If it's a problem at all, there aren't any solutions."

What we are offering are some solutions, or suggestions as to where we might look for solutions. Books like this are always criticized for outlining the problem but not offering any concrete solutions. But above and beyond the specifics—before we get to that point—we have to learn to talk about the problem, to insert the middle class into every policy discussion from health care costs to foreign policy to environmental policy to tax policy to immigration, so that each revolves around one simple question: How does this help restore and rebuild America's middle class?

Our philosophy is to investigate anything that can help the middle class. We can worry later how it will get done. That's not our job; our job is to suggest bold initiatives.

Stan What passed first through that filter is the money that dominates politics and drives the middle class off the agenda. As we saw earlier, there is a reason why rich donors, think tanks, and lobbyists are flooding our politics and corrupting the entire decision-making process.

We would certainly make the case with all our conviction that as long as campaigns are financed as they are—and the addition of super PACs has just made this worse—the middle class is doomed to get stomped. So look at campaign finance reform from the perspective of helping the middle class. Do that and you'll help the country.

If we don't find a way to stop the flood of money, or at least slow it down and regulate it, we can't save the middle class. We will never be able to say, "This problem and agenda is number one." Unfettered political money ensures that health care reform is compromised, that the tax code is loaded in favor of the rich, that wealth

inequality is set in stone over generations. The folks who have benefited have done just fine, while the middle class has sunk over the
past three decades. They know the stakes. That's why they ponied
up massively in this election. That's why they have funded the fog
machine that wants us all to keep quiet.

We have to fix it. Politics and campaigns and government are
broken. That's the starting point.

We asked David Donnelly, executive director of the Public Campaign Action Fund, what he would do to tackle the money that is
corrupting politics and government. We wanted five big things—
but not things to get through this Congress. Let's assume that it
is all too corrupted to really enact serious reforms over the short
term—but that if we refuse to discuss any other subject apart from
what is happening to the middle class and how government has been
hijacked by big money, we may tilt the balance.

We may yet have an election that is about a Supreme Court that
votes five to four to turn elections over to unlimited corporate contributions and that votes five to four to overturn key parts of the
new health care law. The Supreme Court and the conservative principles it is promoting will be on the ballot then. Let's assume there is
an opening for change—that the next president (we hope it's the
same as this one) and the new Congress (we hope it's not the same as
this one) feel they have to clean up this cesspool. Where do we start?

We want to confess that we borrowed shamelessly from David's
memo, "Ten Ways to Reduce the Impact of Big Money and Corporate Influence in Washington and Give Middle Class Voters a Fair
Shake":

1. **Amend the U.S. Constitution, or change the Supreme
   Court, so that money is no longer speech and corporations are no longer people.** These astonishing princi-

ples have somehow been pulled out of the Constitution, and as we have seen, that translates directly into the richest Americans and special interests getting what they want from government. (What era are we in?) So we think there is no choice but to make this agenda item number one. We won't worry about which amendment or Court decision to overturn. Others can sort that out. But it is vitally important that the principle be challenged at the highest level by taking a constitutional amendment to the Congress and into the elections.

Mobilizing for a constitutional amendment is critical, because this election may indeed be about the appalling record of the U.S. Supreme Court and the need to establish new governing principles that respect the ordinary voter, not corporations.

2. **Establish independent funding of campaigns.** All federal candidates would gain access to campaign funding appropriate to their race if they raised a threshold number of donations of under $100 in their home district. The donor should get a tax credit to encourage participation. And if a candidate accepts those funds, they would not raise funds from private contributors or PACs. That is a game changer.

The Public Campaign Action Fund proposes a small fee on government contracts to pay for the fund, though we are intrigued with the idea of taxing campaign advertising. Since the money circulates back to the broadcasters, there is no reason why they should oppose the change.

This form of independent funding has worked at the state level—in Connecticut, for example—and has been introduced in Congress in the form of the Fair Elections Now Act. (Sign us up!)

3. **Disclose every dollar spent on ads to influence elections; do it immediately, and on the Internet.** As David points out, corporations and wealthy donors are hiding behind trade associations and front groups—and the Republicans are doing everything possible to block voters from knowing what is really happening. Well, voters are not fools, and they will soon demand it. These donors should be called out and, once identified, become part of the public debate. It used to be that Democrats were for regulation and Republicans for transparency—and it used to be that Republicans like Romney were for the individual mandate—but now it is just a conspiracy of national Republican leaders to buy elections with as little transparency as possible.

What are you afraid of? we ask.

And while we are at it, shareholders should get a say in whether publicly traded corporations are spending money to influence elections.

4. **Require broadcast and cable operators to discount campaign ads and advertising to influence elections to reduce the amount of campaign spending.** We think it will be hard to control the money unless you limit what campaigns spend, which we know from experience can be insatiable. Understand, the broadcasters and cable operators will hate this proposal, but it is worth the fight.

5. **Put a wall between elected officials and lobbyists.** We recognize that this is the toughest area to get anything substantial done—and those we know well in Washington and

in state capitals are incredibly inventive. But let's do three things:

- Require that all meetings with elected officials and lobbyists be transparent, i.e., published on the Internet the day they take place.
- Do not allow registered lobbyists who are trying to influence the members to raise money and bundle contributions for their campaigns. That is where the worst instances and appearances of corruption occur. We know that there are numerous ways around this rule, but at least stand by the principle.
- Stop the revolving door between Congress and K Street lobbying firms by creating a two-year cooling-off period for all staff and former members involved in lobbying and advising.

We are convinced that only by attacking the big money in politics can we change any of the things that we are writing about. If government is corrupted and officials aren't accountable to the people, nothing will happen.

If we want to reclaim the country for the middle class, this is where we should start.

Getting Real: Unplug the Climate-Change Fog Machine

James The fog machine's denials are always agenda driven: Just follow the money and see who benefits. Steaming ahead without taking full account of man-made climate change is worth trillions of dollars to fossil-fuel companies. In 2012, BP made a profit of $5.9 billion—in the first quarter. For 2011, ExxonMobil announced they'd distributed $29 billion to shareholders through dividends and share repurchases. This is money that is bypassing the middle class on its way up to the top, exacerbating all the inequality trends we've identified.

The earth is getting warmer. We know conclusively that the worldwide emission of greenhouse gases like methane and carbon dioxide trap heat and prevent it from escaping the atmosphere, causing the earth to heat up. Science is as close to unanimous as science can ever get in believing that global warming is real and that humans contribute to it.

That still does not deter the fog machine from continuing to put out information sufficient to cause doubt in the public's mind that would prohibit any real action on the part of Congress or the president to do anything about it. Climate-change denial is a major industry. If it can be shown that we're not screwing up the planet with greenhouse gases, then we're absolutely free to keep polluting.

Texas governor and former Republican presidential candidate Rick Perry wrote a book called *Fed Up!* in 2010. He railed against "doctored data" on global warming and laid down some fog:

"[Democrats] know that we have been experiencing a cooling trend, that the complexities of the global atmosphere have often eluded the most sophisticated scientists. . . ."[1]

Perry ranted about Al Gore, saying he was stoking up his ego, dented by the 2000 election, by becoming a global climate prophet "raising concerns about melting icebergs and undersized polar bears." "It's all one contrived phony mess," wrote Perry, and Al Gore is "a false prophet of a secular carbon cult."

Never mind evidence: What doctored data? What atmospheric complexities? Which sophisticated scientists? Who cares? Just fog.

And what cooling trend? Brad Johnson on ThinkProgress.org

points out that Perry served as Texas agriculture commissioner during killer droughts and record heat in the state in 1996 and 1998. When Perry was governor, the state recorded droughts in 2002, 2003, 2005, 2006, 2008, 2009, 2010, and 2011 when Texas had its hottest July in history. In fact, it was the hottest month in Texas history, period. ThinkProgress talked to Dr. Andrew Dressler, professor of atmospheric sciences at Texas A&M, who said:

> There are dozens of credible atmospheric scientists in Texas at institutions like Rice, UT, and Texas A&M, and I can confidently say that none agree with Gov. Perry's views on the science of climate change. This is a particularly unfortunate situation given the hellish drought that Texas is now experiencing, and which climate change is almost certainly making worse.[2]

Texas A&M may be one of the more conservative large research universities in the country and it has twenty-three members in its faculty of the Department of Atmospheric Sciences. All twenty-three endorsed a statement saying the climate warming was caused by human hands and could have seriously bad consequences.[3] And Professor Dressler is not some special-interests-driven zealot: he's a scientist who deals in data. He used to work on Wall Street as an investment banker, a job he left in 1988 to go to graduate school in chemistry. "I certainly didn't make that choice to get rich, and I didn't do it to exert influence in the international arena, either."[4]

Berkeley physicist Richard Muller used to be a leading global warming skeptic. I am no physicist, but I'm told that, in the scientific world, physicists think they're smarter than everybody else. He decided to do some research and shut the climate change geeks up, and a quarter of the $600,000 he spent came from the Charles G.

Koch Foundation. The Koch brothers, David and Charles, aren't skeptics; they're deniers who've spent, Greenpeace says, close to $60 million on climate-denial groups since 1997.[5]

Well, guess what? After two years, Muller found that indeed the land is 1.6 degrees warmer than it was in the 1950s. He went back and studied Benjamin Franklin and Thomas Jefferson and found that the talk of a warming world "is no different from what mainstream climate scientists have been saying for decades."[6] If Richard Muller had found conclusively that the whole climate change thing was a hoax, you couldn't have kept him off Fox News; in fact, he'd have been given his own channel.

The vast majority of scientists believe that the humans on the planet are altering the climate, and not in a good way. In a study quoted in the *New York Times*, a Stanford PhD student headed a survey of climate researchers that found 908 scientists who had published at least 20 papers on climate change, meaning they were well-published and peer-respected. Of the top 200, ranked by the number of papers published, 97.5% accepted the evidence that we're changing our climate. There are skeptics out there, of course, but they publish less and have less influence in the field.[7]

Or they write op-eds for the *Wall Street Journal.* In January 2012, sixteen scientists put their names at the end of an op-ed entitled "No Need to Panic About Global Warming." They claimed there was a lack of warming over ten years; that climate "alarmism" is driven by researchers and bureaucracies eager for funding; and that it is "an excuse for governments to raise taxes." "There is no compelling scientific argument for drastic action to 'decarbonize' the world's economy," the sixteen conclude.

The op-ed was embarrassingly easy to debunk since the last decade was the warmest on record. What about the *WSJ* Sixteen? Who is laying down this fog? A letter to the editors of the *WSJ* written by scientist Kevin Trenberth said the authors of the op-ed may be distinguished but not as climate scientists. It was "the climate-science equivalent of dentists practicing cardiology."[8] What's more, six had links to think tanks funded by fossil-fuel interests, and two were former employees of Exxon.[9]

What do companies like ExxonMobil have at stake if we put 565 gigatons (a gigaton is a billion tons) more carbon in the atmosphere? "We'll quite possibly go right past that reddest of red lines," according to author Bill McKibben. "The oil companies, private and state-owned, have current reserves on the books equivalent to 2,795 gigatons—five times more than we can ever safely burn. It has to stay in the ground." These are $20 trillion of reserves that McKibben says the companies should write off. Otherwise, in scientific jargon, we may be screwed. But $20 trillion means a lot of profit, and it will pay for a lot of fog.[10]

15.

THE ELITE CONSENSUS ON ENTITLEMENTS AND DEFICITS

Stan We have a rule for judging which problems the country should address. Is it good for the middle class or not? Actually, in my family, it was "Is it good for the Jews?"

If it makes it harder for those people on the edge, we don't accept the priority, the economics, the politics, or the morality of it. And so we are likely to begin in a contrarian position to what many think is the biggest problem facing the country: the federal deficit.

We accept that reducing the deficit is extremely important, and both of us have a history with President Clinton of supporting a deficit reduction plan that contributed to the low long-term interest rates and rapid employment and income growth of the late nineties.

James Right. We're the first to acknowledge that high deficits over a long period would have an adverse effect on the middle. We have to pay interest: it crowds out spending when demand returns to the economy. We know this because we come to this argument with a history of having supported the most successful package of deficit reductions that's ever been passed, with an assist to President Bush 41 and his 1990 deal with tax increases, which Democrats helped him pass.

Based on our own surveys and analysis, we have both urged Democrats to acknowledge the need for long-term deficit reduction. For the ordinary citizen, reducing private and public debt is part of getting to a good economy. But that was before we wrote this book and came to our current preoccupation. And by the way, voters, too, have soured on Republican messages focused exclusively on spending cuts, deficits, and big government.[1] That's no longer good enough.

Again, we take the deficit seriously and much of what we propose—from increased tax revenues to reduced health care spending—will indeed reduce the deficit in dramatic ways—but we take the fate of the middle class even more seriously. We just can't live with the prevailing wisdom of the deficit reduction plans on two of its most important recommendations: entitlement spending and reducing government's Medicare spending. These are hardly quibbles, which is why we wanted to get them out up front.

We have our plan for the middle class. As we saw earlier, it begins with getting money out of politics, because that turns what's possible upside down. But after that, our biggest accomplishment would be to fundamentally challenge the rush to cut middle-class entitlements. Our goal is to defend and maintain Social Security benefits and reduce total health care costs.

Let's start by asking, "What is the problem the country needs to address?"

A pretty big swath of the political class—from *The Moment of Truth,* by the National Commission on Fiscal Responsibility and Reform, chaired by Senator Alan Simpson and Erskine Bowles, to *Restoring America's Future: Reviving the Economy, Cutting Spending and Debt, and Creating a Simple, Pro-Growth Tax System* by the Debt Reduction Task Force, chaired by Senator Pete Domenici and Dr. Alice Rivlin; from the American Enterprise Institute to the Heritage Foundation; from Budget chair Paul Ryan to Republican presidential candidate Mitt Romney; from the *Washington Post* to the *Wall Street Journal* editorial board—says the biggest problem facing the country is the growing deficit, driven above all by unsustainable entitlement spending. All of the reports begin with the urgency and stakes, starting with Simpson-Bowles:

> "Without regard to party, we have a patriotic duty to keep the promise of America to give our children and grandchildren a better life.
>
> "Federal debt this high is unsustainable. It will drive up interest rates for all borrowers—businesses and individuals—and curtail economic growth by crowding out private investment." If the deficit were not tackled boldly, "each American's share of the nation's economy" would be reduced by 15 percent by 2035.[2]

The Domenici and Rivlin report for the Bipartisan Policy Center begins with a like urgency: "The federal deficit is on a dangerous unsustainable path." Failure to act will "push interest rates up, endanger our prosperity, and make us increasingly vulnerable to the dictates of our creditors." They cite Federal Reserve chairman Ben Bernanke's statement on the "real and growing" risk and Joint Chiefs of Staff chairman Mike Mullen, who says this is "the single biggest threat to our national security."[3]

The conservative think tanks embrace the shared conclusion on the primary problem: "We face a staggering fiscal problem that threatens the very future of our nation. Not only will we continue to struggle with huge federal deficits into the near future, but the problem will become ever larger and ever deadlier in the decades to come." That allows them to champion slashing government as the route to saving the middle class. "Unless we act wisely, massive government spending and surging public debt will destroy the foundation of our economy and darken the American dream for our children and grandchildren."[4]

Some of those who have embraced the problem and reports have given equal weight to other problems and national priorities. To be fair, Tom Friedman puts the growing debt alongside global warming and other challenges. And we recognize that the two major bipartisan reports have bravely protected the fragile economic recovery as they have advanced proposals for long-term deficit reduction. With Republican support, they have challenged conservative orthodoxy on imposing a Europe-like austerity. Domenici and Rivlin in particular say, "First, we must recover from the deep recession that has thrown millions out of work, slashed home values, and closed businesses across the country."

These bipartisan reports have been crystal clear on the need to raise taxes *and* revenue. Be sure, this goes against the Republican party line and we do not underestimate the heat they must have taken for proposing any new revenue.[5]

So we are respectful, but respectfully disagree—and strongly. So, let's lay out why.

First, we share the frustration of ordinary Americans who will ask, Where is your plan for growing incomes and jobs? You delay immediate cuts to allow for a recovery from the economic crisis, but how do you address America's long-term growth? This is the very reason why voters were cynical about stimulus spending. They want the political and economic leaders to be focused on the long-term problems that they understand all too well.

Second, we challenge the underlying premise for many of these bipartisan efforts—that all have to "throw some skin in the game." We have all created the problem and we all have to give up something to get to a big solution.

In a valiant but not very successful effort to get the Republicans in Congress to agree to a long-term deficit reduction package, President Obama offered to give up things that he thought important, including aid to the poor in the form of the Community Services Block Grants and the Low-Income Home Energy Assistance Program:

> Simply put, it will take a balanced approach, *shared sacrifice*, and a willingness to make unpopular choices on all our parts. That means spending less on domestic programs. It means spending less on defense programs. It means reforming programs like Medicare to reduce costs and strengthen the program for future generations. And it means taking on the tax code, and cutting out certain tax breaks and deductions for the wealthiest Americans.[6]

Editorial and op-ed writers underscore the premise: "To regain our future, we are going to have to all participate in *shared sacrifice*" (*National Journal*);[7] "Everyone is pointing fingers at each other: Republicans blame Democrats and vice versa. Business people blame politicians. But the reality is that it will take *everyone to sacrifice* and to work together to solve the nation's economic problems" (*Washington Post*).[8]

Senator Alan Simpson, co-chair of the Simpson-Bowles commission, is blunt and to the point: "But you have to—it has to be *self-sacrifice* and know that this country is going broke."[9]

Count us out. The way we see it, the middle class has been sacrificing over these three decades, and they are in trouble. The starting point for any deficit reduction plan is that the top earners in the country have to pay the lion's share of any change in our budgeting, spending and taxing. That is our premise and principle.

James   Let me say something about "shared sacrifice." When I hear that phrase, what I'm really hearing is certain people saying, "This is another opportunity to whack the middle class." Of course there is going to be some sort of sacrifice: the middle class has *always* been willing to do its part for the country; it's absurd to think that they don't. But Paul Ryan's idea of shared sacrifice is that the middle class gets to sacrifice and the rich get to share the money.

Plenty of people have been profiting mightily, benefiting from the rigged system, and ripping off the country: the oil and coal conglomerates with their subsidies; the hedge fund managers with their carried interest; the top 2 percent with their Bush-era tax cut bonanzas; the private contractors in Iraq with their cost overruns and crony contracts; the big farmers with their subsidies. I'm the biggest guy there is for shared sacrifice if it's sacrifice and it's *shared*.

We need to be sure that people who have made more than their share of sacrifices over the past 30 years see those who've made none ahead of them in line. If you tell anyone in the middle class that we have to strengthen Social Security or reduce health care costs and there might be some inconveniences attached, they've been there. They know.

I mean, it's not as if the middle class has been running wild at a huge party for thirty years. Not the case. Just look back at some of the charts we've published here—hourly wages and hours worked and income growth, the middle class versus the one percent—and tell me who's been sacrificing and who's been "sharing."

Stan What the commission heads are really saying is: we will put our special interests on the block if you will do the same. Senator Alan Simpson is at least honest about the necessity of taking on the interests and "sacred cows," as he described it to Fareed Zakaria on his CNN show *GPS*.

> You have to go deal with Medicare, Medicaid, the solvency of Social Security and defense. And if you can't raise the retirement age to 68 by the year 2050 without the AARP losing their marbles and Grover [Norquist] slavering at the mouth on every kind of thing you talk about, calling it a tax increase, we won't make it.

Alan Simpson offers equal bipartisan disdain for the antitax conservative groups and the AARP. "We had the greatest generation," but now "I think this is the greediest generation."[10]

James This is what I would say to Mr. Simpson. If you milk one sacred cow, you'll find it's full of milk, because it's been building up in there for thirty years. The other sacred cow, you may want to milk it, but there ain't much milk left. The notion that more than one sacred cow has as much milk as the first, with all due deference, I'm not buying it.

"Medicare Reform": Shifting Government's Health Care Costs onto Seniors

Stan We object to the broad bipartisan conclusion that "entitlement spending is unsustainable" and the most important goal is to get control of the government's health care spending.

Simpson-Bowles offers the starting point: "Federal health care spending represents our single largest fiscal challenge over the long-run." And note: the focus is on cutting back what the federal government spends on health care, not cutting back the cost of health care. There is a big difference. This starting point sets off a wave of proposed changes to Medicare and Medicaid—including Domenici-Rivlin's proposal to "transition Medicare, starting 2018, to a 'premium support' program that limits growth in per-beneficiary federal support." While preserving the choice of traditional Medicare, this will make Medicare a refuge for the poorest and shift costs to seniors.[11]

That is kind compared to the conservative think tanks that use this debate to abolish the Affordable Care Act and gut federal health programs for seniors—getting rid of "its current defined-benefit philosophy to a defined-contribution system, mostly to serve the poor."[12] The first Paul Ryan budget became the centerpiece of the new House Republicans' agenda for the whole Republican Party. His budget ended Medicare as we know it, turning it into a voucher program where seniors go back into the market to purchase health insurance—but, criminally, have to pay at least $6,400 more a year. This year's Ryan budget shifts to premium support but freezes payments below inflation and thus shifts substantial costs to Medicare beneficiaries while leaving Medicare with the least healthy and poorest seniors. Saving America from its debts requires transferring the bills to seniors, many of whom are retiring after three decades of work.

And we haven't even talked about the impact of their proposed Medicaid cuts, the great majority of which would hit seniors. Most nursing-home patients are there under Medicaid and their care or bills would shift to their families.[13]

The public, to be sure, wants none of this. Democrats paid a price for seeming to take $500 billion from Medicare to finance the new health care reform law. Karl Rove wrote, "The administration would cut $622 billion from Medicare and Medicaid, with a big chunk coming from Medicare Advantage, to pay for overhauling health care."[14] His attack ads featured a beleaguered woman saying, "Instead of fixing health care, my mom's Medicare will be cut, and our health insurance premiums went up."[15]

Well, the Republicans have been on the defensive since the Paul Ryan budget was accurately characterized as a plan to turn Medicare into a voucher program. In our polls, two thirds of voters turned against a House member who voted to *"end Medicare as we know it, forcing seniors to pay $6,400 more out of pocket every year and buy insurance directly from the insurance companies."*

And all hell breaks loose when they learned he pushes those costs onto seniors so they could continue "tax breaks for those earning over $200,000 and special interest subsidies for oil companies." Rarely have we seen a potential campaign attack register so powerfully.[16]

What all these plans share is a health care cost shift from the government to seniors. Could any idea be so mad? That is the responsible position in the elite debate, and again, we side with the middle class. These changes to Medicare would be a crushing blow to the middle class and we flat-out oppose them.

James Why does everyone talk about cutting Medicare and not about cutting the overall cost of health care? It's in the middle class's interests to get the cost of health care down, which is what affects them.

The health care lobby is interested in keeping the costs artificially high, which is the biggest driver of long-term structural deficits, and the government's priority has been to talk about cutting Social Security so they can cut taxes. As usual, the middle class comes last. It seems like the consensus in Washington is that to show strength, you take on the middle class rather than taking on the health care lobby, which is a messed-up sense of priorities. Surely it's smarter to go after the health care costs themselves, not the people bearing the brunt of the costs.

Personally, I have problems with raising the age for Medicare, because, for one, it doesn't reduce health care costs by itself at all. Secondly, it might not even reduce health care costs to the government, because some people will just put off the procedures they need until they become Medicare-eligible. The lower half of the population from an economic standpoint also tends to be much sicker than the upper half, which clobbers them further.

And again I return to my point that reducing costs will have a dramatic effect on the amount the government spends on health care. To illustrate, the government of Canada spends a lower percentage of its GDP on health care than the government of the United States. Think about that for a second. The government of Canada provides 99 percent of the health care in the country where we have every kind of market. Obviously, they have found a way to reduce the overall cost and increase the total coverage.

The most important damn thing in the campaign ahead is to defeat these "Medicare reforms" as Social Security privatization was defeated at the outset of George Bush's second term. The presidential election should center on it—and every Republican incumbent should face the wrath of the voter on the votes they cast. Only then can we get on with the real job of reducing the country's health care costs.

Renegotiating Terms

James It seems at the writing of this book that the consensus among pundits is that President Obama will be reelected in November 2012. If the collective wisdom of the pundits is correct (relying on it is always a risky proposition), then we know what President Obama is going to do. He is going to try to strike a grand bargain that is something along the lines of the Simpson-Bowles commission. It was impossible to read Matt Bai's *New York Times Magazine* piece in April 2012 and not walk away thinking that this is a man who really wants a big deal on the deficit and is willing to give up a lot along the way.

The terms of the surrender that the president was trying to negotiate with Speaker Boehner would have effectively given the Republican Party almost anything that they wanted, but because Boehner refused to accept the terms, we were left without a deal. I fervently hope that we reelect President Obama so he can negotiate a deal much stronger than the one he capitulated on in August 2011.

Social Security: Why Not a Bipartisan Commission to Secure It Again?

Stan Social Security and Medicare are essential elements of middle-class life and survival. After a lifetime of work, we have built up a system that allows most Americans to retire without falling into poverty and have the security of an assured monthly income and coverage for health care. If you get retirement right for middle America, it will reverberate all the way down through the generations. This is the one place where thanks are due to Franklin Roosevelt but also Dwight Eisenhower and Richard Nixon, who repeatedly increased Social Security payments and also indexed it to inflation, making sure Social Security today remains central to what it means to be middle-class in America.

We all know that Social Security can be put on a sustainable path without the drastic changes required for health care and Medicare. Social Security is not in crisis.[17] But the gap between the elite debate and the public debate could not be larger. The former talk about "entitlement spending" (translation: "We can only achieve fiscal stability if we cut Social Security, Medicare and Medicaid"). Well, in my entire life watching focus groups, I have never heard a human being use the word "entitlements." But when the debate mentions the real programs, they say "Hands off." They know these are the final critical pieces that make a middle-class life in America possible.

Elites should get it into their head that two-thirds of the country rejects this statement: "The federal deficit is such a national problem that we have to cut spending broadly, including possible future cuts to Social Security and Medicare spending."[18] In other words, two-thirds just reject the legitimacy of this debate. We conducted a series of polls for the Campaign for America's Future in the summer of 2010 as the Simpson-Bowles commission was moving to its bold recommendations. Near 70 percent said, literally, "Politicians should keep their hands off Social Security and Medicare," adding, "The American people can't afford cuts in these programs."

As Simpson-Bowles and Domenici-Rivlin were recommending raising the retirement age and reducing benefits for some beneficiaries,[19] our polls showed just a quarter of the public accepts that the deficit is such a national threat that we have to make major changes in entitlements. When we describe the recommendations of the bipartisan commission to reduce the deficit by $4 trillion, only a third support it.[20] The problem we face is not gridlock; it is elites not getting how central this issue is to Americans. This is not about the power of the AARP.

Again, the public will not join the elites unless Social Security is addressed on its own terms.

James Why hasn't there been a cry for a commission to secure Social Security? We've done this before in a bipartisan way, so why not again? The public is ready. We're ready as long as everything is devoted to Social Security, not something else the elites want to get done.

We are going to do whatever we need to do with Social Security within the context of Social Security. We don't advocate making changes to Social Security to address the deficit. If you want to make changes in the cost of living or move the retirement age up, do it if it's a good idea on its own merits, not because you're trying to pay for something else.

We actually have no problem touching the third rail in American politics as long as the train is going on the track of Social Security and the last stop is maintaining benefits. We don't want to touch the third rail if people's Social Security taxes are going to pay for rich people's tax cuts or wars that don't work.

I still don't know why Al Gore's lockbox wasn't a great idea. The press pundits picked at it, but voters said, "Sounds like a reasonable idea to me." Lock up that money and make sure it's only to protect Social Security.

Stan The president and Congress should appoint a bipartisan commission as they did under President Ronald Reagan to make recommendations to secure Social Security. It would be charged with securing the system and ensuring that benefit levels are consistent with the challenges facing most Americans today.

The report's preface would conclude, "At no point since the beginning of Social Security has our country faced successive generations of Americans more on their own and dependent on the system." Three decades of slumping incomes and fewer jobs with retirement plans—along with lowered home values and lost savings and wealth as a result of the recent crisis—have made Social Security the primary income for a growing majority in retirement.[21] With growing integration with China and India and advances in information technology, wages will likely be under pressure for a long time. The need to get Social Security right will not diminish.

James Unless the country listened to Carville and Greenberg and acted to restore the middle class. If you can get middle-class incomes up and rewarded work again, this wouldn't be so critical.

Stan In that context, the commission's focus should be on maintaining benefit levels in this new world. This is the one place where America has the legal structures, precedents, ability, and the public support to make a long-term difference for the middle class. We should not fail to act.

Most of the elites' work to "save" Social Security begins with reducing benefits. That is not where the rest of the country begins.

A large majority of the public—often approaching two-thirds—opposes any proposal for reform that reduces the benefits people receive in retirement.[22] For the public, the purpose of "reform" is to maintain if not increase benefits.

When you propose to reduce future benefits for those entering the labor force now—by 17 percent for those whose salaries average $43,000 and by about one-third for those who average over $100,000, as in Simpson-Bowles—60 percent of those under 50 years of age, including those under 30, oppose it. After all, these are policies that would diminish their own retirement prospects.[23] They will casually comment to reporters and our focus group moderators that "Social Security won't be there when I retire," but as we see in practice, they are damn certain to make sure Social Security maintains its benefit levels when they get there.

Critics say that young people don't expect it. They are wrong, but it does not matter. We are opposed to reducing the benefit level—especially given what is happening to wages and retirement plans for the younger generations.

Nearly as large a majority opposes proposals to gradually raise the retirement age from 67 to 69 years, though opposition may have dipped down in public polls.[24]

Stan   I could be convinced to support that shift, as it reflects real-life changes in work and life expectancy, and people have accepted the current slow rise in the retirement age.

James Why do we have to raise the retirement age by a full year? Can't we raise it three months? If you're a hotel maid, three months is a lot less than a year.

Stan One thing the bipartisan commissions and the public agree on is the need to raise the amount of wages subject to the payroll tax, currently capped at $106,800. When the cap was first introduced, 90 percent of all wages were taxed and then indexed to inflation, helping make this all more sustainable. That should be done again, and three in five voters favor this proposal.[25]

If it were up to me, I would advocate an increase in Social Security benefits, given what has happened to incomes and retirement. Senator Tom Harkin's Rebuild America Act would increase retirement plans on average by 15 percent, about $65 a month and $800 a year. I'm pretty confident the public would support it, but amazingly, the elite debate is so dominant that no pollster, including myself, has even asked about support for increased benefits.

James You and I do have slight differences. You'd be willing to somewhat raise benefits and I'd be less enthusiastic about that because we wouldn't be credible. But I'm very enthusiastic about protecting the benefits we already have. Again, as long as we are talking about it, we're moving forward.

So I'm in favor of whatever cost-of-living formula best reflects the rising prices facing seniors.[26] To be honest, you are for whichever formula gives seniors more money.

But what we both care about most is changing the elite presumption on entitlements and Social Security. America should be protecting benefits to reflect what has happened in the labor market and economy over the last three decades. We hope this chapter is a shot across the bow that gets the country thinking about what we really have to do.

Stan's Letter to Tom Friedman

Dear Tom,

You called me about that article you were writing on a few things a presidential candidate will have to stand for to get your vote.[27] First, the candidate "advocates an immediate investment in infrastructure that will create jobs and upgrade America for the 21st century." Second, the candidate supports "a long-term plan to fix our fiscal imbalances at the real scale of the problem." Bowles-Simpson was the only serious offer at the time. It "hashed out a sensible plan of spending cuts, entitlement program reforms, and revenue increases that would shave $4 trillion off the deficit over the next decade. It shares the pain of needed deficit reduction while protecting the most vulnerable and maintaining investments in our future productivity." Third, "I want to vote for a candidate who has an inspirational vision, not just a plan to balance the budget."

We talked about these three things, and after some discussion you agreed to add a fourth conviction: "Finally, I want to vote for a candidate who supports a minimum floor of public financing of presidential, Senate, and House campaigns. Money in politics is out of control today. Our Congress has become a forum for legalized bribery."

We went back and forth on Simpson and Bowles, and I tried to mumble something that would be unintelligible, uninteresting, and unquotable.

My mumbling reflected my ambivalence about the release of the actual report and majority support for it in the commission. I knew the

Medicare and Social Security proposals were a no-go for me, but I also knew the commission was pretty brave on revenue at a time when there were not many heroes, particularly on the Republican side. Their deficit reductions were achieved with both spending cuts and tax increases, including raising the cap on Social Security. When do we get the support for that again? They took on some sacred cows, like the home interest deduction, that saved serious money. At the time of the release, I was working overtime to convince my progressive friends that debt and deficits matter. A whole chapter of my new book with James Carville is devoted to why people think private and public debt brought down the country and weakens us for the future. And I liked the boldness of it, when so much of politics is games and image. So I did not want to react in a knee-jerk way to the release of the report.

That's why I mumbled and you had the good grace to quote me on the American voter's search for bold leaders: "'The people are so far ahead of the politicians,' says Democratic pollster Stan Greenberg. His polling, he adds, shows that many Americans today 'think that China, Germany and Brazil have strategies for success, and that we don't. But they are looking for that. They are looking for a leader who will be really bold.'"[28] That is an important theme in this book.

Now that James and I have written this book, I am no longer ambivalent. So I wanted to put before you the conclusion that compels us now. There is no more important issue for America than saving the country for the middle class, and if the president had appointed a commission to address that great threat, it would have offered different recommendations. Social Security would be treated differently. If you move to health care costs rather than the government's health care expenditures, you go to wholly different policies.

I know you know all this because we've talked about it, and rising health care costs featured in your piece.

So here is what I want to ask you: Would you rethink whether support for Simpson-Bowles is still on your list of the four threshold convictions to win your support? Would you still want President Obama to embrace the proposal? Would you mumble when we talk about this on the phone?

Talk to you soon.

Stan

16.

LET'S GET SERIOUS ABOUT WHAT REALLY MATTERS: HEALTH CARE

Now, let's get serious and focus on what really matters: reducing total health care spending, which has almost doubled as a percentage of our total economy these past three decades.[1]

James I'll tell you my reaction. Raise your hand and repeat after me: Rising health care costs are probably the most significant ongoing contributing force taking down the middle class. Suppose that all of the people that thought up all the derivatives, the CDOs and CDSs and whatever else—at Goldman Sachs, say—suppose all these smart and talented people decided they were going to put their minds together to figure out how to fix health care costs. Imagine what we could do!

America spends most on health, but still has lower life expectancy relative to industrial peers

Life expectancy and health spending per capita, 2007

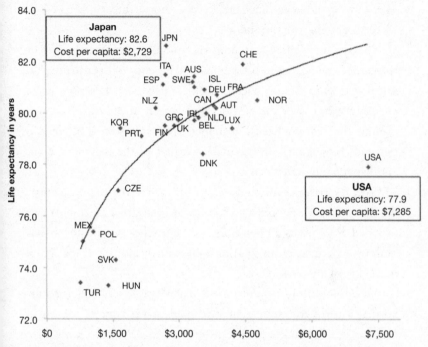

Source: EPI analysis of Organization for Economic Cooperation and Development Health Data.

Stan This graph ought to stop the whole elite, entitlement debate. Our health care system is failing the country and the middle class, and the by-product is rising health care expenditures facing the federal and state governments. Our total focus in this debate should be on how we reduce health care costs and get better results for average people.

Americans are spending an average of about $7,500 a year on health care. That adds up to 15.7 percent of our total economy. That is multiples of what any other country spends; yet virtually every developed country that we respect—and some that we don't—has a longer life expectancy. Canada borders us and spends two-thirds of what we do on health care and they live a lot longer. To the south, Mexicans spend much less but have a shorter life expectancy, so we're sure that is not our model.

The system is flat-out failing the middle class. You have seen the earlier graphs, but to press home the urgency of overturning the status quo, note that production workers have seen a 38 percent increase in wages over the past decade—barely ahead of inflation—even as their family health insurance premiums have gone up 131 percent.[2] Now, that's unsustainable—to adopt the language of the entitlement and deficit debate.

Over the past decade, and well in advance of the financial crash, the percentage of people with job-based health insurance coverage dropped from 69 to 59 percent.[3] For high school graduates, barely more than a quarter are getting jobs with health coverage. Now, that's unsustainable too.

We cannot afford to wait for the day when the country is so fed up that it turns to a Canadian-style single-payer system, i.e., Medicare for all. The stakes for people are too high and too immediate not to double down on the new health care reform law—regardless of what the Supreme Court decides—to reduce health care costs sharply. The transition is going to be pretty messy, with a lot of unintended results, some good and many bad—particularly when it comes to employers, many of whom are contemplating dropping coverage.[4] So with the prospect of political dysfunction in Washington, there is a pretty dangerous period ahead.

The next three years will be a period to consolidate health care reforms as the health exchanges come online. We need to make sure this new system delivers both universality and reduced costs—indeed, even more than the law offers on its own. If the Supreme

Court throws out only the mandate that people have insurance, there are ways to offset that in each state, and we would need to mobilize. If they throw out just the mandate and associated insurance reforms, that, too, becomes both a state and national battle. One could see the president sending to Congress a stand-alone law on insurance reforms and dare the Republicans to block them.

But this totally ideological and political Supreme Court is very capable of throwing out the whole health care reform law. If they do, we will have an election about something vitally important to the middle class.

James If they knock down this law on a five-to-four vote, then we'll be electing Democrats for the next eight years. I've starting saying that, and people say, "You're crazy!" No, I'm not crazy. If they knock this thing down, the Court owns every damn thing that is wrong with the health care system. And it's only getting worse.

There's only trouble ahead for them if they do that. We tried and they just took their ideological majority and said, "We're not changing anything." And do you want to see them play defense every time somebody can't get insurance because of a preexisting condition? They will *own* that.

Stan We think that the new health care reform law has been undersold. The big innovation is the health exchanges: they are the key to the success of the reform law in reducing costs. That is where the consumer will choose between competing plans that provide real insurance and preventive care. The government should be turning its operation over to an Amazon or an eBay and selling the hell out of the exchanges as the future.

James It doesn't just have to be the government selling the exchanges. Politicians would run on the fact that Missouri's plan is better than Michigan's plan; or Michigan's plan is better than Minnesota's plan; or Minnesota's plan is better than Montana's plan. With competition, people will strive to make one better than the other. Republicans should like that.

Stan While some Republican governors are doing everything possible to stop the health insurance exchanges, progressive governors ought to be making them really attractive and expanding their use as much as possible. If the U.S. Supreme Court throws out the individual mandate, that will increase the incentive for states to find effective ways to achieve universal coverage, including state-level mandates.

The key is to use the federal law and create a race to achieve universality, real competition and choice, and attractive insurance options, and to drive down costs for consumers—forcing other state governors to follow or pay a price with voters. Reducing health care costs has to become a national mission.

But Take On the Vested Interests

Stan If we are going to make a difference, we need to build on whatever stands in the current law, use elements that are there, and take them much further. We have to be willing to make a lot of people uncomfortable along the way, because nothing is more important than getting health care costs down and preserving working- and middle-class incomes. If you are serious about the middle class, then you have to get serious about health care. And you have to be serious about the vested interests that keep us from making the right kind of change.

We spent some time talking with Zeke Emanuel, and no one knows the new health care law and the health system better than him. He's a doctor, ethicist, academic, health care expert, and the author of *Healthcare, Guaranteed: A Simple, Secure Solution for America*, and he was adviser to the White House on health care. He's very smart and a good friend. We also spoke at length with John Wilhelm, president of Unite Here, also a friend, leader of the largest union representing restaurant and hotel workers, and intimately involved with the struggle to win health insurance coverage for low-paid and part-time workers.

We talked through all the options, but James and I take responsibility for where we put our money.

Let's not forget that the current health care reform law saves $200 billion in the first decade and more than $1 trillion over the next twenty years. That's not chump change. And as Henry J. Aaron and Austin Frakt point out, the new law includes a whole set of reforms that, if implemented with great seriousness, will result in "accountable care organizations, bundled payments, comparative effectiveness research, a center for innovation, and an independent payment advisory board" whose goal is to "transform the financing and delivery of health care."[5] So this is one time when there may be more savings than expected if we embrace the new law and its levers.

We would start with the low-hanging fruit—things that almost made it into the new health care law but got knocked out by federal bureaucrats or industry lobbyists, or in the ugly deals to win approval in the U.S. Senate. They were opposed by vested interests that had something to lose.

1. **The health insurance companies that blocked the public option.** The insurance companies succeed in killing the public option in the Senate, so we should create a public option to compete with the private insurance plans that will be offered on the new health exchanges. This was the issue that my wife said that Joe Lieberman should be impeached on. The Congressional Budget Office determined that competition from a public option would save

taxpayers $110 billion over a decade, but it is also important to make sure insurance companies do not call all the shots.[6]

2. **Doctor and hospital groups that restricted the new Independent Payment Advisory Board.** The new health care law includes this board, but it is highly restricted because some worried it would produce "rationing" and limit the availability of costly procedures. If the board's powers were expanded to impact coverage decisions by Medicare and Medicaid, it would seriously restrain costs. So pushing back against the vested interests and allowing the board more freedom could result in significant savings—perhaps $100 billion to $200 billion over ten years.

3. **The pharmaceutical companies that have blocked negotiations over what they charge the government.** If the government were able to negotiate Medicare prescription costs similar to the way the Veterans Administration negotiates with pharmaceutical companies, the savings over a decade would exceed $200 billion.[7] Pharma won the last round on the issue, but we can no longer afford the success of their lobbying.

4. **The Medicare bureaucracy that is afraid to identify scale of fraud and abuse.** Democrats should accept that this abuse threatens Medicare and the middle class and should join Republicans to aggressively root out waste. Medicare is part of the problem, so it should allow an outside agency, using predictive modeling like credit card companies and increased penalties to maximize savings. This could save at least $300 billion over a decade.[8] And given that this is a national crisis, penalties should be higher for stealing from Medicare and Medicaid.

5. **The inertia and interests that block IT and continue paperwork and processing.** Administrative simplification and IT cuts paperwork, saving significant money. For example, there should be a central database for credentialing doctors that any institution or agency, including Medicare, can access. A serious effort could save $300 billion.

6. **Lawyers resistant to malpractice reform.** Apparently, the health care law considered creating a safe harbor for doctors—with presumption of innocence when they use electronic health records, with guidelines and decision support. These reforms would reduce doctors' fear of being sued and possibly result in savings.

7. **The doctors and Medicare bureaucracy that are committed to fee for service—the killer cost driver in the system.** The imperative, we are told by everyone, would be getting rid of fee-for-service payments to doctors, which is inefficient, involves massive paperwork and oversight, encourages overuse, and subject to abuse. The alternative is bundling the different practices and services and have Medicare pay doctors on a much simpler per-patient basis.

Bending the cost curve requires all of the above, but the real game changer is putting the spotlight on the bureaucrats and doctors invested in the current system—particularly fee-for-service. We think that Medicare should announce that at some future date, perhaps ten years from now, it will no longer accept fee-for-service arrangements with doctors. That would produce a change in health care delivery that is good for everyone and could save $500 billion over a decade.[9] Private insurers would follow suit and reduce costs across the board.

Employer-Based Health Insurance

We want to go further. It is hard to look at this whole book and not conclude that our entire system of employer-funded health insurance coverage has failed. It may work for those in professional occupations and some in the public sector, but even that is being renegotiated state by state. As we mentioned, just a quarter of high school graduates are getting jobs that provide health insurance. In this recession, employers are shedding and reducing health coverage and there is no rush to reclaim lost ground.[10]

We need health insurance coverage that sticks to the individual rather than the job or the employer and that provides real coverage in the face of rising costs. And we need to do it in a way that recognizes how hard it is to make sure working people win out when you accelerate reforms. Employers over these three decades moved from offering pensions to structuring 401(k)s and transferred much of their cost and risk to employees. The same is happening in health care, so we have to be inventive and serious.

The biggest change we would propose is encouraging the shift to individuals purchasing their own coverage on the health exchanges—allowing them to make that choice—with strong measures to ensure maintenance of total compensation for employees who lose company-based coverage. That will require going way beyond good intentions.

As a start, union health plans that cover about 30 million employees, dependents, part-time workers, and retirees should be offered as an option on the health exchanges. The same may be true for many professions that have special needs and that transcend any particular employer—like teaching, law enforcement and firefighting, and construction trades.

With a much larger portion of the population buying insurance on the exchanges, and choosing among competing plans, it would bring down premiums by a lot, perhaps as much as 10 percent.[11] It would require a new attitude toward purchasing health care as the individual took control from employers and worked to reduce health care costs for the middle class.

It all looks so simple on paper but in the real world, employers are looking at the new health care law and thinking seriously about taking the $2,000 penalty per full-time employee—much below their current costs for insurance—and encouraging them to buy their insurance on the exchange, with a government subsidy. Without the cost controls we talked about earlier, the government could face a surge of payments to cover those turning to the exchanges.

The shift of health care costs from employers to individuals—and to government and society—has taken a huge toll on the middle class up until now. It's continuing and perhaps accelerating under the new law, though with a new safety net and an alternative system for coverage. Economists tell us that employees will get more of their compensation in wages rather than benefits, but we don't believe it. Workers were supposed to get productivity gains, too, but they haven't. Employees have too little leverage to battle for these gains.

That's why we have to think about it differently. Only the president of the United States will be able to elevate the importance of this moment of transition and construct a grand bargain involving employers and business organizations, unions, the health insurance sector, and the public as a whole. This transition and these reforms will benefit businesses that pay less for health care and be more globally competitive. The president will welcome the transition to a new platform where more and more people are choosing among plans in a competitive market.

But this health compact requires serious new measures to make it work:

- a financial transaction tax to fund the rising cost that has been shifted to the government—necessary to maintain this system for a growing population
- a transition to a national or regional health exchange where insurance companies have achieved a local monopoly or oligopoly pricing position
- a significant increase in the minimum wage

The president will make it clear he will use all his capital in this new term and this new period to shine his spotlight on companies that fail in their obligation to their employees and insurance companies that fail in their obligations under this new law. He will say, "This is a new period of personal responsibility and choice, and we have to make it work for the middle class."

We know we have to find a way to make this work—not just to reduce health care costs for the middle class but also to change the way we do health care so that our country gets "sustainable" costs and better health.

These are real changes that help the middle class. They would also be the best way to restrain entitlement spending and reduce the deficit. But by starting with the needs of the middle class, you get to a better policy result for the country.

17.

DOING SOMETHING ABOUT IT: NUMBERS

Everything the two of us have done with our lives and the campaigns we have fought lead us to this concluding and, we hope, pivotal obligation: to talk about no other problem but the state of the middle class and to entertain or embrace any new idea or initiative that can improve the prospects of the middle class or put their values front and center in the country. Anything. Instinctively we embrace ideas aligned with our worldview because we are FDR, Truman, LBJ, Hubert Humphrey, RFK, and Earl Long Democrats. We do think government can be badgered into doing the right thing for average folks, and we have witnessed it in our own lives and the leaders we have worked for. So we are comfortable advocating policies that secure Social Security by protecting benefits and Medicare by boldly tackling health care costs. But remember, we advocated "ending welfare as we know it" and supported NAFTA when not many in our party and even in the war room agreed with us. (They may have been right on NAFTA.) On health care costs, we said there is no bigger threat to the middle class than letting the status quo continue, so we said, "Show us what we got." We are open to radically rethinking how America does health care, and I'm sure we have fewer friends today because of it.

We started with the need to radically change the role of money in politics. Our system of government is corrupt, barely democratic, and cannot get in the game for the middle class unless it is reformed. We don't know whether that is a liberal or conservative idea, but because the Koch brothers, Fox and Murdoch, the oil industry, the NRA, and the Chamber of Commerce are so determined to defend this system and rev up the fog machine, I guess we're with the liberals. But there have got to be conservatives and independents who want to clean the stables—grab their shovels and join the country. Hopefully this coming election will usher in a period of Watergate-type reforms, or maybe that will just have to wait until somebody goes to jail.

We acknowledge that Charles Murray's book *Coming Apart*: *The State of White America, 1960–2010* has helped concentrate the mind of many of the pundits on the problem we are trying to address. He says flat out: the working class and poor, regardless of race, are in increasing trouble. He puts his spotlight on whites whose incomes are going down, whose marriages are in trouble: they are less happy, less committed to work or any church. So if he wants to add his voice to the rising clamor, go for it. Join us.

But we also became much more self-conscious about our own methods and path to solutions when we realized how stumped Murray was on what to do about so urgent a problem. We kept turning the pages, looking for the recommendation, but just found pathetically small ideas and some incantations about small government. He would give people less assistance, but without any evidence that this would end the indolence of the white working class. And as David Frum points out, his "remarkable—and telltale—uncuriosity as to why any of this might be happening" means his doctrine "remains undisturbed and possible solutions locked up in the closet."[1]

We, too, accept that rescuing the institution of marriage and civic engagement would be good things and probably would help to restore the middle class's economic prospects and values. Count us as open to ideas that might move the ball.

And we are damn curious about why and how the middle class was marginalized over these last thirty years, because it tells you at least where to start looking. But it is not the only route to the right changes, because we're also pragmatic: tell us what works.

Why did employees stop receiving productivity gains from the late 1970s onward? We know the erosion of union power and the decline of union jobs, first in manufacturing but now in the public sector, are a factor. How much of that was a result of America becoming more integrated into the global economy at a time when Asian economic powers were bringing millions of workers into the labor market? What role did innovation and information technology play, particularly when joined to globalization? What role was played by Chinese mercantilist policies that supported and subsidized state industries, overvalued their currencies, and rigged the system of trade? How much was due to deregulation, greed at the top, and rigging of the tax system to favor the wealthy? How much is due to our declining investment in education and infrastructure and our failure to modernize?[2]

We do not know the relative importance of each of these developments in marginalizing the middle class, though I promise you, we are damn curious. These working hypotheses are in our minds as we think through and test different solutions. Our filter is still the question "What can make a difference now?"

39.6

James   I can't help but go back to that magic number: to me, it's always going to be the place to start. The golden ratio in nature is 1.618; the golden number in economics is 39.6. It works beautifully. Why rack your brains for anything else? It's the first step, like the one Neil Armstrong took on the moon. It's a giant leap, but still just the first step. And my point is, what the hell was wrong with it? Everyone says, "We've gotta do this," "We've gotta do that." Well, we created 22 million jobs and had a $5 trillion projected budget surplus with 39.6 percent, so why not do that?

39.6 percent was the top tax rate under President Bill Clinton, and before he negotiated with Speaker Gingrich to get a budget deal, that rate applied to everything a worker got paid for a hard day's work and to everyone's investment income. It's important to fight for people who work hard and the revenue that produces. Not only was there a balanced budget, but there were these surpluses in the trillions of dollars as far as the eye could see. Clinton ushered in a pretty prosperous half decade at least. We shouldn't forget that.

And if we look at the evidence of what happened to the country in the Clinton economic period, including the research of the conservative intellectuals, it is only in the Clinton period where those in the middle income range made serious gains, where gains were more broadly shared, and where the bottom quintile and the poor did particularly well.[3]

The lesson's pretty clear: Restore the top rate to 39.6 percent and defend the expanded earned income tax credit and the refundable child tax credit that George W. Bush expanded in his presidency. We need that combination as a starting point for everything else.

This change at the top will happen on January 1, 2013, when the Bush tax cuts expire, unless the president can be persuaded to make a deal for something less. Restoring a 39.6 percent marginal rate should be our highest priority, and we can work out the details from there.

We have support for this position from the most articulate spokesperson in the history of capitalism, Adam Smith. He wrote in *The Wealth of Nations,* "It is not very unreasonable that the rich should contribute to the public expense, not only in proportion to their revenue, but something more than in that proportion." He also wrote, "Every tax, however, is, to the person who pays it, a badge, not of slavery, but of liberty."

In other words, progressive taxes are a badge of liberty.

In June 1985 in a speech in Atlanta, Ronald Reagan talked about closing tax loopholes that allowed millionaires to pay no taxes while a bus driver had to pay his taxes. That was crazy. "Do you think the millionaire ought to pay more in taxes than a bus driver or less?" he asked, and the crowd shouted, "More."[4] In Luke 12:48, Jesus says, "For unto whomsoever much is given, of him shall be much required . . ." With credit to my friend Paul Begala, if it's good enough for the founder of capitalism, the founder of modern conservatism, and the founder of Christianity, it's probably good enough for me.

39.6.

50-50

Stan   It is another simple number.

We just have to change the terms of the debate on taxes. We need a new conventional wisdom and common sense. We know the country is for it—and it is important that the president be adamant that we can only meet our needs, priorities, and obligations if we restore balance to our budget calculations. We need a 50-50 bargain and a new contract with the country.

The public battle is trapped in the arcane language and contortions of Washington: letting or not letting the Bush tax cuts expire, sequestering or not sequestering defense spending. Help! The president has to transcend this and make the case for balance.

The public debate and the president too are trapped by Grover Norquist and the pledge of virtually every Republican candidate to vote against any tax increase. It is clear now from Matt Bai's account in the *New York Times Magazine* that President Obama and Speaker Boehner were poised to reach a $4 trillion budget deal, including some pretty surprising cuts in Medicare and Social Security, in exchange for $800 billion in revenue. What matters is that he was willing to settle for an $800 billion bargain where higher taxes provided only a quarter of the deficit reduction.[5]

We think the president and the Democrats should offer the same deal that President Bill Clinton offered the country in his final Oval Office address before Congress voted on his budget and economic plan. He pointed to a big pie chart labeled "A Fair and Balanced Plan" that showed that every $10 of deficit reduction comes from $5 in spending cuts, $4 in taxes from the wealthy and $1 in taxes from the middle class. Clinton said, "This plan is fair. It's balanced. And it will work."[6] The Congress voted for it—and committed to a 50-50 bargain.

We know the result for our economy. It worked fine.

James   Clinton's plan came in, and in the aftermath of it, we had unprecedented economic growth and income growth across the board. People might say, "Well, there were other forces at work."

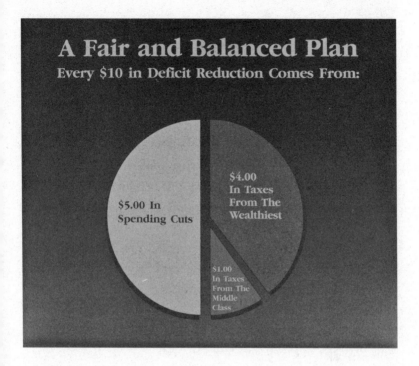

A Fair and Balanced Plan
Every $10 in Deficit Reduction Comes From:

$5.00 In Spending Cuts

$4.00 In Taxes From The Wealthiest

$1.00 In Taxes From The Middle Class

Maybe there were, and maybe they had something to do with it. But this certainly didn't stop the country from growing, and it did balance the budget.

We had a combination of surpluses and jobs and income growth, so why wouldn't you want to go back to some element of that policy? Because under Bush, you went to tax *cuts*—and *big* tax cuts, by the way—and what did we get? A recession, close to a depression. Then we got the only recovery we've had since the Great Depression with no income growth.

And here we are, still arguing over the Bush tax cuts versus the Clinton policy. Why shouldn't we be arguing over the policy that worked, as opposed to the policy that didn't work? I have no idea.

I'm actually happy to call it the Clinton tax increase. Remember Bush senior at the 1992 convention attacking Clinton's tax policy? He asked who to trust: "The candidate who's raised taxes one time and regrets it, or the other candidate who raised taxes and fees 128 times and enjoyed it every time?" I won't say we enjoyed it, but we'll accept credit for what Clinton did.

Stan   That is the deal we favor for our times, and with everything that has happened in these three decades, it is even more urgent that this become a presumption. That formula should carry across the totality of efforts to invest in infrastructure and education, address the deficit, and preserve Social Security. It could encompass restoring the inheritance tax to a defensible level. That 50-50 formula is roughly the formula in the Domenici-Rivlin plan, and it is critical to embrace it and defend it as a principle. Only such a commitment allows us to offset the inequality and use those funds to support a growing middle class.

A Ten-Year Infrastructure Plan to Rebuild America and Our Middle Class

It is time to give as much or more attention to investing for the future as we do to deficit reduction and austerity. Without a robust public debate about where we invest, we will not escape the elite pressure to talk only about deficit reduction and austerity. Only if we think differently about investment can we begin to tackle the central problems raised by Tom Friedman in *That Used to Be Us* and Gideon Rachman in *Zero-Sum Future*.

There is no proposal that makes more sense and that has won more support across both parties, from liberal and conservative economists and key stakeholders, than moving immediately to make long-term investments in our country's infrastructure to overcome our deep deficit in transport, bridges, highways, mass transit, air traffic control, rail, inland waterways and water systems, the electric grid, and broadband and telecommunications. And that investment should be financed by leveraging government funds with private capital—an infrastructure bank—as it is already being done on a large scale in Europe and elsewhere.

This is a no-brainer. Yet the president has not yet stepped up on this issue, while the Republican leaders in Congress are stuck in the stimulus debate and describe this as a big slush fund for Obama's big union pals. In fact, the Ryan budget cuts total spending for transportation and infrastructure by a quarter over the next decade.

But Tom Donahue, head of the Chamber of Commerce—often mistaken for the corporate head of the Republican Party—says we have moved from "first in the world to middle of the pack," requiring long-term investment and an infrastructure bank to make it feasible. So does Simpson-Bowles's bipartisan deficit commission and the bipartisan coalition of officials led by Mayor Michael Bloomberg, Governor Ed Rendell, and Governor Arnold Schwarzenegger. But so do Leo Gerard, president of the United Steelworkers, and his co-chairman on the Task Force on Job Creation, former corporate CEO Leo Hindery. Their number one recommendation: "Create a national infrastructure bank."

What really brings them together is the American Society of Civil Engineers 2009 Report Card for America's Infrastructure: D– for roads, waterways, and levees; D for transit, aviation, and dams; C– for rail; and an overall grade of D.[7] We have outdated passenger and freight systems that are running over capacity and on dirty, costly gas-based platforms and an air traffic control system from the 1950s marshaling the skies.

And while the United States has no national plan to modernize, China has invested $3.3 trillion in transportation since 2000. In 1918, U.S. troops built a rail yard at La Rochelle in France that today makes high-speed trains that will be part of a $220 billion plan over twenty or thirty years in that country.

Citing that D grade and factoring in current investment, the organizations all agree that we need at least $2.2 billion of added investment over ten years just to overcome the deficit from inaction, but we need more if we are to fix the vision deficit in addressing new needs, like high-speed rail and broadband. It would be safe to say we need to spend $2.2 trillion in five years. Each billion of investment creates up to forty thousand jobs and the Chamber says such an effort can create 1.9 million jobs over ten years.[8]

Thankfully, the pioneers in this story include Congresswoman Rosa DeLauro, Stan's wife, who introduced the infrastructure bank legislation fifteen years ago, and the legendary banker and savior of New York City, Felix Rohatyn, who embraced the bank as a much-needed "domestic IMF." DeLauro is the lead sponsor of the legislation that has become a rallying point for those who want to act on the right scale of investment and scope of economic infrastructure and, most important, create independence from Congress. That is the only way you can really leverage private capital, but progress has been hamstrung by the unwillingness of all the players to confront those barriers and interests.[9] Only a president can rally the country to get beyond the transportation lobby and congressional interests to act for the long term and help create the kinds of jobs we need to maintain the middle class.

With Rohatyn's book in hand, DeLauro often reminds us in her speeches that the "chapters of our American success story have always been written in stone and mortar, iron and steel, granite and fiber-optic cable. Jefferson doubled the size of the nation with the Louisiana Purchase; Governor DeWitt Clinton of New York, even during the Panic of 1819, pursued the Erie Canal for his state. When Lincoln invested in the Transcontinental Railroad, Roosevelt the Tennessee Valley Authority and rural electrification, Eisenhower the National Highway System." The wisest leaders made their biggest marks in times of adversity, including the Civil War and Great Depression. This is such an opportunity.

The model to emulate is the European Investment Bank, which is currently spending about $100 billion a year on almost five hundred large projects, DeLauro points out. Like the EIB, $25 billion of U.S. government investment can be leveraged with the sale of bonds to reach $455 billion, though it would have to operate on twice that scale.[10]

Michael Stewart, partner and global director of communication at McKinsey & Company, reports that investments in pension funds, asset managers, sovereign wealth funds, private groups, and companies are particularly interested in infrastructure in the advanced economies. He focuses on an infrastructure bank as the most practical vehicle, particularly if process reforms can speed up the modernizing of the power infrastructure, wireless broadband, air transport, and ports.[11]

We realize how big a break this would be for business as usual in Washington. They can't even pass a long-term transportation bill; the gas tax, at 18.4 cents, has not been raised since 1993. When the economy is growing again that should be doubled and locked up for transportation spending.[12]

But committing to invest at least two trillion new dollars over the next five years, developing a plan for doing it right over the next ten, and using innovative financing would allow us to get started on the job of modernizing the American economy and creating middle-class jobs again.

James You can argue that infrastructure spending isn't really spending. If you fix a hole in your roof, is it really spending or is it something you will have to pay for anyway? And pay much more for down the line as the damage deepens. So, why wouldn't you accelerate infrastructure spending because eventually you're going to have to repair the highway or the bridge or the rails anyway? Why not do it when interest rates are nonexistent, the damage is less extensive, and there's plenty of people that are willing and ready to go to work?

So if you spend $100 million today repairing a highway, that's $100 million you don't have to spend five years from now or ten or twenty. You almost could argue there really is no net increase in overall spending.

Obviously you just can't go and do everything at once, so you have a ten-year plan to rebuild the country, which in effect rebuilds the middle class, because all of these projects are going to make the country more competitive, are going to create more jobs, and it's really debatable how much they cost, if they even cost anything.

Education, Research, and Innovation: 10 Percent

That's the percent of GDP we should be spending on education, research, and innovation. After conceding unacceptable ground to other countries and a Republican Party now determined to cut federal support for education and science, it's time to stake our ground. We have no idea whether 10 percent is the right number, but in this critical area we are with Samuel Gompers, the first head of the American Federation of Labor. When asked what the goals of the American labor movement should be, he said, "We do want more, and when it becomes more, we shall still want more. And we shall never cease to demand more until we have received the results of our labor." So our answer is "More."

The president has consistently promoted and defended investment in education, research, and innovation and made a persuasive case that this is critical to the country and to the future of the middle class. "But we need to meet the moment," he declared in Osawatomie, Kansas. "It starts by making education a national mission—a national mission." We are with him when he says, "In this economy, a higher education is the surest route to the middle class."

Yes, we studied the evidence that a college education no longer pays off in the same way, but we also know that the more education, the less likely you are to be unemployed and the higher your earnings. Today's aspirant middle class believes that for America to be exceptional, everyone has to have a chance to go "to college and you don't rack up $100,000 of debt."[13] Rick Santorum thought that it was a misplaced goal, but we think it is central to being a middle-class country again.

"In today's innovation economy," the president made very clear, "we also need a world-class commitment to science and research," and that requires "giving people the chance to get new skills and training at community colleges" and more young people choosing careers in science and engineering. Here the president applauds Democratic and Republican presidents Franklin Roosevelt and Dwight Eisenhower, who gave veterans of World War II "the chance to go to college on the G.I. Bill" and "who started the Interstate Highway System, and doubled down on science and research."

The Republican Party in this election has decided to fundamentally reduce support for education, research, and technology. Amazingly, the Ryan budget cuts education funding by half over the next decade. It cuts science and technology by a quarter.[14] And just as employers are starting to rehire, many of the retraining and skills programs are being cut, leaving companies unable to fill long-haul truck driver positions, for example, because trainees can't afford the $4,000 it costs to train for a license.[15]

James   Who *are* these people? How can you look at our country and say, "The biggest problem we face is we have too many teachers, too much science, too many NIHs?" I grew up with my parents telling me that an education was the most valuable thing a person can have. It's now expensive as hell, but it's still the best predictor of longevity and prosperity. We know the downside of cutting education: it's declining living standards and opportunity. Someone please tell me what the upside of less education is? If Mr. Ryan wants to cut education by half, what does he suggest, we educate half the people not at all or everyone half as much?

Again, the president has the chance to call upon the bipartisan commissions and business leaders of the highest standing to drive the country to a sustained commitment. Even as Simpson-Bowles proposed big cuts in deficits, it declared, "We must invest in education, infrastructure, and high-value research and development to help our economy grow, keep us globally competitive, and make it easier for businesses to create jobs."[16]

When the president met with Steve Jobs during his cancer treatment and later convened a small dinner with Silicon Valley executives, Jobs sat next to the president and stated, "Regardless of our political persuasions, I want you to know that we're here to do whatever you ask to help our country." His top priority was education, the need for engineers, and giving foreign engineering graduates of our schools a visa. In his private conversation, Jobs was very critical of the American education system and teachers' unions, saying teachers should be "treated as professionals" and school should go until 6:00 p.m. every day and eleven months a year.[17]

Maybe if companies like Apple stopped creating phantom main offices in Reno, Nevada (where the corporate tax rate is zero) to avoid paying California taxes, the state could afford to support that level of education.[18]

We are spending about 2.6 percent of GDP on research and development, which is pretty flat in the last decade. The increases have come from business spending, while the federal level has come down to its lowest level, close to .8 percent of GDP. In the United States, government supports mostly defense R & D, while other major countries focus on basic research. Support for R & D has surged in the Asian countries, which in absolute terms is close to matching that of the United States. Meanwhile, U.S. multinationals spend more of their R & D dollars in Asia.[19] The government is abandoning the playing field, failing to find new points to stimulate research while allowing our businesses to focus more on their operations in Asia. This is not a very good formula for the middle class.

We know what role R & D has played in making the United States the leader in the Internet economy, defense, aerospace, and other modern sectors. The National Institutes of Health provide basic research for the pharmaceutical industry and our universities and colleges feed into surging innovation in agriculture, mining, and oil and gas.

Well, we think our country has to recommit to science, not give up the game. So count us in.

James One of the things that you have to remember about Carville, Louisiana, is that the federal government ran the National Leprosarium there. In 1917, they purchased the Louisiana Leper Home, which had been set up in 1894 and did research and treated thousands of inpatients there.

This center was obviously a huge deal in a town of a thousand people. It meant that Carville, Louisiana, had more doctors per capita than anywhere in the country, including Rochester, Minnesota, home of the Mayo Clinic. The place impacted everything in this southern town of a lot of pretty poor folks, including me. I mixed with people I'd never have met if the center wasn't there.

It had a multiplier effect that made us more open—more supportive of government, for sure—but also more open to ideas and figuring that we could improve lives. I'm sure the same formula is true for the country. Before I was born, researchers at the center created the sulfone drugs that form the basis of leprosy treatment today. See, Mr. Ryan, spending money can have good consequences.

The stories from the center were inspirational. As I wrote in a foreword to the book, *Remembering Leprosy in America*, the people who went to the facility in Carville were often broken, humiliated, and outright banished. "But once inside those gates, people began to gain strength, to heal, to find dignity and hope, and in many cases, love."[20]

We are in no position to sort out the debates on how best to improve American education, though we know the country has to debate this issue and affirm a rising national commitment to education, research and technology. The president is already making this a big choice in the election and he needs to win a mandate on this issue.

Today, the United States spends about 5.7 percent of its GDP on education—and we are not doing very well. We have larger per-pupil class size at the primary school level than Europe and OECD countries, and our high schools graduate only three-quarters of its students—again, well below other developed countries. And state education budgets are on the chopping blocks. Three-quarters of the states have cut per-student funding for elementary and secondary grades since the 2010–11 school year. In many states, these cuts have been sharp: more than a third of states have cut per-student funding by at least 10 percent.[21]

Here is our proposal. We think the total amount of federal funding for education must rise each year as a percentage of the overall economy—this commitment is critical to our economic future.

With that kind of mandate, there would be overwhelming demand for a prestigious, bipartisan commission like Simpson-Bowles to set goals and make recommendations for the nation. We will leave it to them to decide how we get higher-quality, accountable, and effective education that grows the middle class.

They will no doubt pay a lot of attention to volumes of research showing zero to three matters a lot, from parental leave to income support and Early Head Start. And while universal pre-kindergarten is less glamorous than K–12 education reform and college, states adopting it would help close the gaps in our society before they spread too wide to close.[22]

We all know our schools need to do dramatically better, so put us down for *school reform*—that is, we're for change that works: "All we want are the facts, ma'am," as Detective Joe Friday on *Dragnet* used to say. We are pragmatists. The country should probably move ahead with elevating the teaching profession, reducing class size, creating charter schools, mandating teacher evaluation and accountability, and instituting a longer school day and year.[23]

James I've been seared by the experience of Katrina in New Orleans, where our public schools were not much good to begin with and got washed away along with 80 percent of the city because of the failure of the flood control systems and the levees. A lot of things failed in New Orleans. Our coastline is eroding at a terrible rate; we lived through the Deepwater Horizon disaster—or, rather, we're still living through it.

In education, though, out of the disaster comes some good news with the grand experiment in charter schools in the city. The disaster left pretty much a clean slate, and charter schools opened to fill the gaps left by the hurricane. Four years after Katrina, and more than half of public school kids were enrolled in charter schools, and test scores went up. It is a big experiment, and it seems charter schools are probably part of the mix for the future.

That leaves me with a "Show me" attitude on education reform. Show me what works in a particular environment, and I'm for it.

Any hope of restoring the dream requires the great majority of Americans realistically thinking that they or their kids can get a college education. So *making college affordable* is the policy battle where Republicans say, literally, "You are on your own"—at a time when we need a comprehensive approach.

Community colleges are flooded with people who have dropped out of the labor force and are struggling to acquire new skills. Despite everything we have written in this book, Americans just believe in their ability to educate themselves and find a way up.

We also would apply the "more" commitment to engineers. Conservatives object to picking winners and losers, but we do when it comes to education. We can best grow the technology sector of the economy by financing the education of new classes of engineers and allowing foreign engineering graduates to remain in the United States.

Support for more engineers, however, is a stopgap when we need to figure out how our country gets behind the skills and professions that enable us to be a middle-class country.

Afghanistan: Zero

That's the number of ground troops we would have in Afghanistan by the end of the year. After eleven years in Afghanistan and so little prospect of success, we need to move quickly to end this war. This country spent a trillion dollars in Iraq after Paul Wolfowitz told us the war would be self-financing from oil revenue. We can no longer afford Iraqi-style adventurism and nation building and should accept reduced defense spending as part of the country's priorities.

The United States maintains 1,800 nuclear warheads. In a new term, the president will have to address such absurd holdovers from the Cold War.

James If we've learned anything from Iraq and Afghanistan, it's that you can't fight a modern war with Cold War tactics and matériel. But I wonder if we have learned anything from Iraq and

Afghanistan—if Republicans think we can pay for these enterprises and hardware with tax cuts. The new F-35 Fighter is going to cost $1.51 trillion in its lifetime. Like a plumbing project in the house, you can bet that's going up. It just did: it was $1.38 trillion a year ago. That's a lot of tax cuts.

Radical Tax Reform: 5

With both parties and leaders all talking about bold, radical tax reform and simplification, we should be entering a 1986 moment like when Senator Bill Bradley and President Reagan came together to pass a bold tax bill that got rid of many tax breaks and loopholes, and simplified and lowered rates—though it was made possible by a starting agreement in common that the bill would be revenue-neutral.[24] We know that it is impossible today, and thus it will be much more difficult to pass tax reform.

In principle, Budget Chair Paul Ryan says he is committed to getting rid of these special interest tax breaks that are worth $250,000 to each member of the top 1 percent, though you can be sure their legion of lobbyists will descend on Washington to make sure all the money they have invested in politics pays off.[25]

If you are going to be radical, then be radical. We favor a new tax code that allows only four widely used exemptions: the number of dependents; mortgage interest on a single home up to $500,000 in value; charitable deductions; and the earned income and child tax credit for low income workers. Any new special tax provision might be reasonable, but it would have to be justified and passed by Congress.

We favor introducing a financial transaction tax like the one that was proposed in the eurozone—though we have proposed dedicating those funds to the new compact on health care.

For the voters, radically simplifying the tax code is the most important element in political reform because it gets rid of the complexity that special interests exploit at the expense of the middle class, who do not have lobbyists of their own. The new rates should obviously maintain the progressivity of the Bill Clinton budget we are committed to.

It is very important that this tax code reward work and make work pay—as a self-conscious goal of tax and public policy. Most of these revisions were introduced on a serious scale under President Clinton, but President Bush made changes as well that are important in meeting this goal. That means battling to keep an expanded earned income tax credit, the higher starting point and new 10 percent tax rate, and the child tax credit, refunded as real dollars for lower-income families. With disdain for the Catholic tradition, the Ryan budget assaults these provisions that aid those of modest means, which conservatives have come to view as giving tax money to people who pay no taxes. But as President Obama made clear, they pay lots of taxes and fees. We cannot begin to make work pay if we fail to defend these policies, which may yet rally the support of conservatives like *New York Times* columnist Ross Douthat, who elevated them in the spirited debate about Charles Murray's book on the state of low-income families.[26] With the challenges facing the middle class, making work pay has to be high on the agenda of liberals and conservatives.

18.

AMERICA: 1?

American voters did not have to read Gideon Rachman's book, *Zero-Sum Future*, to get to his conclusion about where globalization has brought us America and the American middle class.[1] Until the crash brought down this whole edifice, elites assumed that China, India, the former Soviet Union, and Latin America joining the global market would result in a "win-win" world. The bounty would be shared by Americans broadly and by the big emerging economies, too, in a period of American economic, intellectual, and military hegemony. The crash exposed many things, but the most important thing for us is that it also called into question whether the majority of people in the United States were really "winners" sharing in the prosperity.

The public got to that conclusion before the crash. Employees at all levels knew they were increasingly competing with workers from

Mexico and China in a world of declining barriers and diffusing technology. They knew China plays a big role in setting the terms of trade, and Americans have long stopped wondering whether these new global rules work for them.

The crash just increased the urgency of formulating new policies that would reverse the forces that have been eroding the middle class and the American dream for decades. But, to be honest, middle- and working-class Americans are perplexed that no political or business leader has stepped up to interpret what has happened globally and demanded bold action at home and new terms abroad. The elite silence on what has really been happening to America is deafening.

Two-thirds of Americans believe the country is in decline. That would seem to put them in the growing camp of writers who think the odds have gotten harder for Americans and longer for the country—that is, unless we start undertaking the hard work of serious renewal.[2] That does not mean that voters accept Chinese domination or that they lack the will to make America strong again. We have worked in countries all over the world, and it is just true that Americans are more optimistic about the future and have an underlying faith in technology, education and science, human nature, entrepreneurs and small business, and our ability to rally ourselves out of adversity. Wall Street and Washington have made a mess of things, people believe, but their belief in American exceptionalism is still alive.

American voters wonder why America took so long to "get it." They lost confidence in the global order and our intellectual leadership long before the crash. But they also share Rachman's leap of faith that America can get to a global formula that favors American interests and our own people. That starts with rebuilding and strengthening our own economy and society.[3]

That has been the focus of these concluding chapters: how to rebuild and strengthen our own economy and society so that the middle class gains. But the voter also believes that we have been naïve globally and that we have to prioritize America in this new period.

A demagogue like Donald Trump could jump into the race on an anti-China ticket—as economic nationalist Ross Perot did fairly powerfully in 1992. We think voters are pretty sophisticated about the scale of our problems and scale of the solutions required—but they are also pretty impatient with the status quo and the elite's silence on what needs to be done to make America number one again.

Conservatives' Message to America: "You Can't Be Pickin' Winners and Losers"

Stan President Obama pointed to a new direction when he embraced two large initiatives to advance future American industries. The first was the successful rescue of the auto industry; the second was the program to support the growth of a renewable and clean American energy industry. Combined, these programs created or saved 40,000 jobs. Two damn good bets, but Republicans have attacked both as failed efforts by a corrupt government to pick winners and losers:

> We shouldn't be picking winners or losers in Washington. We should be setting the conditions for economic growth so that the private sector can create jobs. Washington is not good at picking winners and losers, so we shouldn't try.[4]

Mitt Romney described the effort to rescue the auto industry as part of a larger scheme: "He's been practicing crony capitalism. And if you want to get America going again you've got to stop the spread of crony capitalism. He gives General Motors to the UAW. He takes $500 million and sticks it into Solyndra."[5]

James Now, tell me what's wrong with picking winners and losers? If we did, maybe we'd have more winners.

The breathtaking hypocrisy. Conservatives don't seem to mind when *they* pick the winners and losers. Anybody notice Exxon? First in line on their subsidies and first in line among Republicans' corporate donors. And agribusiness: I guess they're first in line with tens of billions of subsidies each year—and first at the table when those trade deals got cut. They've been picking winners and losers all along. That is their whole purpose. Their interests win and we lose.

It's time to have a debate about industrial policy and the government playing a catalytic and supportive role in building industries that we think can be successful. Every developed and emerging country— from Germany and Britain, to China and South Korea, to Brazil and South Africa—has an industrial policy that promotes key economic sectors. Germany is the most important, because unlike the United States and Britain, which allowed the market to rule, government and the major manufacturers collaborated to preserve their market share, encourage innovation, discourage strikes, and minimize lay-offs even during the recession in order to protect their skilled labor force. While German manufacturing has stabilized at 25 percent of the economy, it has fallen to 12 percent in the United States and 11 percent in Britain.[6]

Gene Sperling, chair of President Obama's National Economic

Council, took the president's specific initiatives to a much bigger policy and had the nerve to utter the words "industrial policy." The administration committed to advancing policies and tax incentives to prevent a "hollowing out" of our existing manufacturing sector and encourage new plants with the right tax incentives. With no industrial policy, we lost the consumer electronics industry, along with the accompanying skills and technology. But the evidence is that supporting manufacturing comes with a range of "spillover" benefits, including increased R & D and patents, more engineers, suppliers, and consumers. Absent such a policy, individual firms will fail to capture all the benefits: "there is a risk [when] we as a nation under-invest in areas that can be beneficial to the economy at large."[7]

In fact, manufacturing is on the rise in the U.S. While we have mixed feelings about some of the developments—less labor inputs combined with falling energy prices, pro-manufacturing policies and rebalancing in China and other emerging economies—we also know that these developments, with the right choices, could produce more American jobs.[8]

American Innovation

America has had a unique kind of industrial policy centered on large-scale and protected government investment in science and innovation. As Neera Tanden, president of the Center of American Progress, pointed out, the U.S. government has always played a role in promoting large-scale innovation and promoting U.S. industries, even when the government was leading the move toward global integration and breaking down trade barriers. NASA was a massive investment in research and technology that has allowed America to lead in aerospace and spin-off industries that are a large part of our industrial base. The Manhattan Project created our lead in atomic and nuclear capability, and Hyman Rickover was the father of a nuclear navy as well as the father of the nuclear power industry.[9] The Internet was developed under the auspices of the U.S. Defense Department and later supported by the National Science Foundation and a consortium of American universities.[10] The rest is history, including Silicon Valley and the continued leadership of U.S. global high-tech companies.

Jon Gertner's book *The Idea Factory: Bell Labs and the Great Age of American Innovation* is a fascinating account of AT&T's Bell Laboratories and how it organized itself over more than half a century to produce scientific breakthroughs, inventions, and applications, including the transistor that would make possible the computer revolution and American leadership in the area of high technology. At its peak in the late 1960s, 50,000 people and some 1,200 PhDs were employed at the Bell Labs headquarters in Murray Hill, New Jersey, organized in interdisciplinary teams and in dorm- and campus-like settings that somehow worked. Operating under a government monopoly with the grand vision of connecting every American by telephone, they were very open with their findings and freely licensed their inventions to other companies, contributing mightily to America's economic growth and prosperity.[11]

Walter Isaacson hailed the book in the *New York Times*, but also wished Gertner had spent more time writing about how in the world we would advance this kind of innovation today.[12]

The U.S. government invested massively in the Manhattan Project, NASA, and the NIH, as well as negotiating the monopoly that gave Bell Labs the time and freedom to maximize basic research. We can't give up on that kind of innovation.

Energy

For all the acrimony over climate change, gas prices, the Keystone pipeline, offshore oil drilling, and fracturing, we think major players who contest this issue can rally behind an energy policy that promotes a diverse, greener American energy industry that creates American jobs, cuts our trade deficit, and reduces carbon emissions. This is no longer a crazy aspiration, though it will depend on the president, energy companies, and environmental groups coming together to see this unique opportunity.

John Podesta was President Clinton's chief of staff, head of the Obama transition, and founder of the Center for American Progress, and created this opportunity for policy innovation when he published a piece with Tom Steyer in the *Wall Street Journal* that should have been headlined "Americans Are Missing the Big Picture." While conservatives are fighting over things like a pipeline to import oil and offshore drilling, the world is changing. The U.S., Podesta and Steyer write, is "poised to transform its energy portfolio by developing domestic resources—renewable and mineral—that will let it become a net exporter of clean energy and energy technology in this decade."[13] Furthermore, led by President Obama, "we appear to be at the beginning of a domestic gas and oil boom. . . . After a four-decade decline in oil production, the U.S. is now producing more than half of our oil domestically." And as we get the regulation right on fracturing, we are poised to "utilize our dramatically larger and cheaper natural gas reserves." Even Daniel Yergin has had to catch up with the fact that America is emerging as an energy power, with an unequaled set of diverse assets.[14]

But the president of the United States needs to educate the country and also strike the bargain we need to maximize our assets and translate our potential into employment-rich industries. To that end, we join Podesta and T. Boone Pickens in urging the creation of a new energy compact:

- Make permanent the tax credits, investments, and support for research that already make us a leader in clean energy production, especially solar and wind.[15]
- Ensure high regulatory standards and avoid high-risk areas so we can greatly expand our natural gas production.[16]
- Use America's abundant natural gas to replace imported oil as a transportation fuel.[17]
- Build a twenty-first-century backbone electrical transmission grid.
- Provide incentives to home owners and the owners of commercial buildings to upgrade their insulation and increase efficiency.[18]

With all those elements, we can transform how we organize and mobilize our energy resources while escaping the oil domination that has polluted our environment and our politics and made us dependent on the most unstable parts of the world for fuel. Energy independence will soon be one of our greatest economic strengths.

With the president promoting American manufacturing, scientific innovation, and new sources of energy, it's possible to tilt the pendulum in favor of America once more. That new spirit about prioritizing America might put pressure on some of our greatest companies. Companies like Apple, for example, that might feel they need to locate more of their plants, more of their jobs, and pay more of their taxes in the United States. Indeed, the new climate might create pressure on politicians to take away tax breaks from companies that export jobs, and at the same time reward products "Made in America."[19]

Globalization and China

America is also at a presidential moment on globalization and China. We all understand that both Obama and Romney will compete over who is tougher on China. And when it's over, the president will wink, impose some minimal sanctions, and carry forward with a pro-China policy as before. The new secretary of the treasury will put "currency manipulation" on the agenda of the next U.S.–China summit. The elites will explain that any actions against China could have unintended consequences, and that a trade war is a big risk to the global economy.

We understand the risks of a China reaction, but if both presidential campaigns are pushing for a new policy, China may well choose to adapt. This is a different moment. The health of all our economies, including the Chinese, depends on the United States rebuilding, and that starts with new rules that prioritize key American interests. The most global companies and media need to give the new president space to strike a new tone, advance new policies, and align with forces that support "rebalancing" in China.[20]

We will be prioritizing America, and that requires some new, impactful policies.

The truth is, both presidential campaigns will denounce China as a "currency manipulator" that exports to the United States by undercutting American companies.[21] Congress should quickly pass a law declaring such manipulation an "illegal export subsidy," requiring a new administration to take a range of actions to offset it. That's in the cards for 2013, unless the prospect of it leads China to a visibly new direction.

The president should create a new Justice Department bureau to prosecute the massive intellectual property violations that cost key sectors of the American economy $58 billion a year.[22] We know that American global companies deeply invested in China cannot lead the way, so the U.S. government must lead—and all should know: next year will be different. The rules need to change.[23]

In government-funded projects, like large-scale infrastructure improvements, we must establish domestic-content requirements to make sure our economy benefits as much as possible from these investments. In an earlier time, such requirements in the automobile industry led foreign auto companies to locate many of their plants in the United States, and the same could be true in clean energy and transportation. In Germany and France, political leaders acted to ensure that their recovery efforts benefited their own citizens. Again, these measures create the kinds of jobs that are essential to a middle-class economy.

Obviously, the tax code should be changed to reward companies that create jobs in the United States, but let's remember, we ran on this policy in 2008 and never did it when we controlled the executive branch and the Congress. Why? Because the Republicans were deeply opposed, of course. But what are the forces in our own political world that have made this election-year rhetoric rather than real policy?

A key part of prioritizing America and American jobs is making them pay so that they can support the middle-class aspirations key to our identity. That is particularly true for those jobs that are not easily outsourced, including lower-paid service jobs.

We support comprehensive immigration reform that regularizes the position of undocumented workers, improving their legal status and position vis-à-vis their employers while making it tougher to get new visas in areas of less-skilled and lower-paid employment.

And we think this is the time for another presidential moment on the role of unions in the country. In periods when labor unions were consolidated in the 1930s, '40s, and '50s, President Roosevelt and President Truman spoke with pride about the value and importance of unions in our economy, and in building the middle class and the country. It is hard to imagine that we can arrest the decline of incomes, see workers' wages rise with productivity, protect entitlements, and see workers benefit from the changes in health care unless more people say, "Yes, I belong to a union." The stakes are high and this is not the subject of only one speech, but people will notice when the president takes every opportunity to say how important unions are to our future.

Getting the focus on rebuilding and prioritizing America is a great challenge when so many forces work against it. To make America number one again requires a sea-change in thinking that leads us to proactively advance American industry, exports, energy, and innovation that are the sources of new American middle-class jobs.

19.

TRIUMPH OVER POLITICAL DYSFUNCTION

Wang Jisi, Chinese Communist Party and Ministry of Foreign Affairs Adviser, Addressing U.S.-China Strategic Trust.[1]

"[The] United States is seen in China generally as a declining power over the long run. America's financial disorder, alarming deficit and unemployment rate, slow economic recovery, *and domestic political polarization* are viewed as but a few indications that the United States is headed for decline.

"Yet Beijing still sees the lack of confidence and competence of the United States on the global stage and a *quite chaotic picture in U.S. national politics.* . . . It is now a question of how many years, rather than how many decades, before China replaces the United States as the largest economy in the world."

James Stan, you need to read the piece in the *Times* about how the Chinese leadership sees the United States as a declining power. Read it. They think we're "on the wrong side of history" and a declining power because, politically, we're nuts. We're so politically gridlocked, we can't slow the inevitable or stop what's happening.

Stan You didn't have to say anything. I downloaded the Brookings report. It is one of the most stunning and revealing things I've read. It brings home the consequences of taking the country to the edge of default on its debts or to an impasse on every big problem since this Republican Party took over parts of the U.S. government. The Chinese look and see deepening "domestic political polarization" and "a quite chaotic picture in U.S. national politics."

James So tell me what they're missing. Seems like a pretty accurate picture to me. I don't know about the economic stuff. That's above my pay grade, and I'll leave that to the smart economists, like Gene Sperling and the Orszags to figure out. But after working through what we need to do to get America back, it's hard not to retain that underlying confidence in our innovation, our tech companies, our entrepreneurs, our attitude, even the middle class who agree with Joe Biden that "we're tired of being tired." I'm sure people are restless and ready to get moving, I just know it.

I'm not sure the Chinese are wrong about how politically dysfunctional we are and what that means. I think our brand of regulated capitalism has always worked, but only when we control the special interests and don't allow the rich to run the show for their own benefit. Capitalism is too important to be left to the capitalists. It's always produced high-quality goods, it's produced opportunity, and created wealth, but when it gets out of control, it starts to eat itself. It has to be brought back into line, and if we have to do some spanking, then okay.

Stan When I read the report, I was thinking through the China trade issues and whether America will still be the leading economic power. But I stopped on the line and focused in on the political dysfunction. Aren't they right?

James I mean, get the implications of this. If we can't overcome the gridlock, the polarization, the dysfunction, the political chaos, then we can't effect change and do any of what we've been talking about. And if that's the case, ladies and gentlemen, the middle class is screwed. I'm serious. There's no room for debate about what has happened to the middle class over these three decades. Only a flat-earther would dare deny it. And now that has to be the total preoccupation of our politics. There is no other subject. That has to drive what policies we get behind. Is it good for the middle class or not?

But if U.S. politics is the same old, same old after this election, it's not going to happen.

Stan This is very much in line with what Zbigniew Brzezinski is saying in his book. He thinks America can renew itself and remain a big force globally, but among the big obstacles holding us back is "America's increasingly gridlocked and highly partisan political system." While China looks decisive and capable of political decision-making, "political paralysis" in America "often precludes the adoption of needed social remedies."[2] That's us. This is a book of social remedies.

James So there really is a final chapter to this book where you really have to bring an end to the political dysfunction. There is no happy ending for the middle class without doing something about the nut jobs. I have my mission. We have our mission. Without them, this book is dead on arrival too.

Stan The American voter is pretty smart on the political dysfunction, and they've been waving their hands, saying, "Listen to us. We hate this partisan polarization. Work together. Just get it done."

After the 2010 Republican landslide, when the Tea Party took over the House of Representatives and made big gains in the Senate, Democracy Corps conducted post-election polls with both the liberal Campaign for America's Future and the conservative Resurgent Republic, and both drew the same conclusion. The overwhelming majority of voters said they were "dissatisfied." And the top reason why? "Too much party bickering"—higher than the number saying "Too much spending, taxes, and deficits." By a stunning two-to-one margin, these same voters said they wanted their members of Congress and senators to work with President Obama to get things done, not "to mostly oppose President Obama's policies and provide a check on his power."[3]

James   When they said the same thing in our polls after the 2008 Democratic landslide, I said to you—remember?—"Maybe they really mean it this time." I'm usually pretty swayed by data against my position, and I said, "They are serious about this."

Stan   And voters are not confused about who is mainly responsible for the gridlock, polarization, and lack of compromise. This is not reciprocal, where they say, "A pox on both your houses." By far, they thought the Republicans were responsible for the failure to reach an agreement before the debt ceiling deadline and believed the Republicans on the supercommittee were responsible for the failure to reach agreement on additional federal spending cuts. In public polls, just a quarter believe the Republican Party is open to working with the opposing party, 26 points below that for the Democrats.

I talked to Tom Mann, one of the deans of the study of the U.S. Congress, after he spoke at the House Democratic retreat in Cambridge, Maryland, and he told me to watch for his new book, *It's Even Worse Than It Looks*. He and Norm Ornstein have been writing for years about the House of Representatives and they have tried to parse their conclusions to not just blame one party for the problem. In *The Broken Branch*, they note the games being played by both parties, though they mostly put the spotlight on the Republican majority and Speaker Dennis Hastert. Apparently, they are done parsing.[4]

The president should make a big part of his argument for the election that the country needs to elect Republicans who are willing to work together to rescue the middle class, not just get to Washington to make sure he fails. We can only rescue the middle class, the president should say, if the people vote for Republican members and leaders who are ready to work on problems—and send the rest packing. Maybe that gets him an extra punch. Certainly, Democratic House candidates can challenge the Tea Party Republicans who turned Washington into a partisan sinkhole and made it only worse for the middle class.

The grounds on which the election is fought will impact what the political and economic class feels compelled to address afterwards. This is a punch we need to throw.

James I'm at a new point. We have to have an election in 2012 that smashes the political disorder in Washington. When you wake up after the election—if you haven't been up all night on CNN waiting for the Ohio count to go final—then you have to think, *Wow, maybe it will be different.* You have to think positively, otherwise there's no point thinking at all.

Stan The only sure way to get there is for Mitt Romney and the House Tea Party Republicans to be so repudiated by the American voters that Republicans wake up and say, "Maybe we've got to do something different."

James You're right on that. If it is just Mitt Romney that loses, they'll wake up and say, "If we only nominated a genuine movement conservative, we would have won the presidency and stopped Obama's socialism." I know this world. We've seen this before. Their defeat has to be much broader and deeper. It should be so bad, they're going to call the mercy rule. That should be the starting point.

It's going to be hard to get there. The voters view the House Republicans as the lowest kind of human beings with the lowest poll ratings in Washington, D.C., a place populated by the unpopular. But the presidential race is close even if we think the president will probably get there. He needs to be running stronger to get a wave going.

Let's be clear: the best way to sweep out the Republicans is to run on the message of this book, the future of the middle class. That's where the energy of the country is and where voters are ready to say, "No, enough tax breaks for your special-interest, oil company, big-bank friends. It's time for the middle class to get a break."

If President Obama forces this choice in the election, the middle class can emerge with enough traction to get some things done here. He has to point out it is a choice between their way and the right way. It's hard because the crap the Republicans are running on—that deficit reductions accompanied by tax cuts favoring the rich help the economy by creating jobs—has gained ground as a political ideal. Obama has to say, "No, that's wrong. We can do better. We can help the people who need help." Obama is capable of that. He can have a big election, and America can have a landmark election.

Stan   It's ironic, because what we are saying is that we are more likely to overcome the partisan bickering if we have a big partisan election. Winning in 2012 is not like winning in 2008 with a new presidential mandate. Even if Democrats have a big election and hold the Senate and take back the House, they will have small majorities in both. A partisan election does not necessarily produce an intensely partisan outcome: the leaders of both parties will have to take stock to see how to make progress in this new period.

And today's Republican Party is so ideologically extreme—as we have seen in the U.S. House and in Wisconsin, Ohio, and Florida—

that only its repudiation can free up the political system to act again. We need a partisan act in the election to have any chance of bipartisanship.

I suspect a lot of independent voters and some of James's Republican friends, are thinking just that.

And we also need an election about the future of the middle class—based on the president's Kansas and AP speeches—not on the state of the economy and on our competence to manage the economy. Maybe you can squeak by in such an election: in the public polls, voters are pretty evenly split on whether they trust Romney or Obama more to manage the economy.[5] But our only chance for a big election that overturns the political dysfunction is if the campaign is totally about the middle class where voters prefer our approach to the Republicans' by a 14-point margin.[6]

James   They are going to do everything possible to keep us from having this election be about the middle class. They know the stakes.

First, they're going to deny everything. Some of these people think the universe is five thousand years old and they say it with a straight face. If somebody had an explanation saying why they thought the earth was five thousand years old, there's only two possible explanations: you're really stupid or you're really cynical and trying to get really stupid people's votes. One of the most painful things that I've ever seen is the Louisiana legislature passing a piece of creationism legislation.

If people are prepared to sign on for that, then there's no limit to the kind of nonsense they'll buy. There is no income disparity, and even if there is, we have social mobility. And there's no poverty, so people who drop out of the middle class are not actually badly off at all. The middle class is not in crisis. It's doing fine, thanks for asking. It's got iPhones and flat-screen TVs and higher-quality cars and everything a rich person could possibly want.

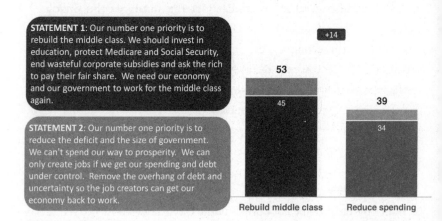

Middle class message defeats spending and deficits message

Now I'm going to read you some pairs of statements. After I read each pair, please tell me whether the FIRST statement or the SECOND statement comes closer to your own view, even if neither is exactly right.

STATEMENT 1: Our number one priority is to rebuild the middle class. We should invest in education, protect Medicare and Social Security, end wasteful corporate subsidies and ask the rich to pay their fair share. We need our economy and our government to work for the middle class again.

STATEMENT 2: Our number one priority is to reduce the deficit and the size of government. We can't spend our way to prosperity. We can only create jobs if we get our spending and debt under control. Remove the overhang of debt and uncertainty so the job creators can get our economy back to work.

+14

53
45

39
34

Rebuild middle class　　　Reduce spending

Source: Democracy Corps National Survey with the Public Campaign Action Fund, January 8 to 11, 2012.

Stan Yes, they will try to deny everything, but the reality of long-term economic problems and the palpable pain of those working hard and struggling to be middle-class just won't allow him to be just a denier. And Mitt Romney has a lot of smart people around him, and he is already starting to utter the words "middle class" and "unfairness."

In his first speeches after establishing himself as the certain Republican nominee, he spoke directly to the dwindling American dream and faltering middle-class aspirations, proclaiming, "So many good and decent people seem to be running harder just to stay in place and, for many, no matter how hard they run, every day puts them just a little bit further behind. . . . The promise of America has always been that if you worked hard, and took some risks, that there was the opportunity to build a better life for your family and for the next generation. . . . Together we'll build the greatest America we have ever known, where prosperity is grown and shared, not limited and divided."[7] He has told reporters to talk with his wife, who knows firsthand about the pressures facing women. He is not very deft at "the middle-class thing," just as he was not when he said, "I'm not concerned about the very poor."[8] Nonetheless, his campaign knows they have to address what is happening to the middle class, even if their answer is to cut taxes, cut funding for education, and end Medicare as we know it.

James You are right, the middle-class-denial crowd won't win out.

But the canary in the coal mine is David Brooks's column in the *New York Times,* "The Two Economies." Mark my words. That is where they are going.

Stan I'm already on it and the economic report that he elaborates on in his column. This is an important piece, because he is saying, in effect, that the long-term crisis of the middle class is real, structural, and cannot be overcome. And while there is inequality, it is part of the productive, dynamic, and successful part of the economy. If you want to know the future, imagine individuals, organizations, and industries trying to figure out how to make the transition to join that dynamic economy. This is a serious conservative argument that does not deny what's happening to the middle class but takes it as given as America moves to a different model for success.

The central point of the argument is the revival of manufacturing and export-oriented industries, what Brooks calls "the creative dynamism of American business," which is both "astounding and a little terrifying"—terrifying because these companies have been relentlessly shedding workers, shifting to software-driven plants with fewer workers and rising productivity, and reducing energy costs in the transition to natural gas. They are now adding workers, and if this analysis is right, Brooks says, "the U.S. is not a nation in decline." Indeed, "we may be in the early days of an export boom that will eventually power an economic revival."

We think this analysis could be right and indeed cite those developments in our support for industrial and energy policies to promote American job growth.

Perceptively, Brooks zeros in on the "growing structural rifts" that may be sorting America into two economies. Economy I faces inexorable global competition and is compelled "to become relentlessly dynamic and very (sometimes brutally) efficient." Companies here are very profitable and create some, though not many, new jobs. Economy II, not nearly subject to such competitive pressures, does not see the same pace of change or productivity gains. Brooks puts health care, education, and government in this economy; he might have added retail and the service sector. This is where you find most of the people and the jobs with stagnant wages.

That analysis is consistent with the case we have been making about the long-term challenges facing the middle class. Maybe David is ready to join the cause, as he doesn't seem all that enthralled with the changes necessary to get himself and the media industry into Economy I.

Nonetheless, we think he gets the politics and society wrong.

We are little surprised about the politics, as he says, "Republicans often live and love the efficient globalized sector and believe it should be the model of the entire society." They like choice in education, the creative destruction and efficiency. What Republicans is he talking about? Maybe the conservative establishment, but Brooks has argued that white non-college graduates disproportionately populate the Republican Party. They are hardly enamored with Economy I.

He says Democrats are "more likely to live in and respect the values of the second sector." But he is wrong on where they live. The export-oriented coasts of the country, cosmopolitan centers, and affluent suburbs are the places trending most Democratic. As we pointed out at the beginning of this book, there are lots of reasons why people have come to support the Democratic Party over the years, reflecting very different values. We have focused on America being a country where hard work is rewarded, but that could be integral to both Economy I and II.

Brooks is probably right that Republicans will speak from the vantage point of Economy I, believing its entrepreneurs should be freed to create the future jobs while associating Economy II with inefficient government. Critically, "government should prepare people to enter that sector but get out of its way as much as possible."

Because Economy I is dynamic and linked to the competitive global economy, and Economy II is not, the structural rift inevitably deepens—and we are left with not many levers other than extraordinary individual initiative to change the course of society. The argument is understandably silent on the American dream.

Maybe the country can live with the political dysfunction, too, if you are not really calling on government to reduce the rifts or come to terms with the society produced by this kind of economy.

He probably gets it right that Democrats will zero in on the "huge profits at the top and stagnant wages at the middle" and want to continue the productivity of the global sectors "while redirecting their benefits" to "subsidize Economy II." Where we part ways is on the word "subsidize," and that's everything. Our book is premised on all of us—whether part of Economy I or II—being prepared to make the changes that will allow the middle to prosper and everyone to rise together. We all have a stake in it. That's the kind of society we want to create and the values we want to honor—and why we are unembarrassed to think that the most fortunate will "get" it, that they have a shared interest in changing the future.

James Look, we have to win the argument. Everyone knows we can't go on like this. If the middle class is shrinking, inequality growing, debt rising, and politics gridlocked, nobody wins. We have to appeal to the spirit of Henry Ford, who doubled workers' pay in 1914 to $5 a day, so that they could aspire to be middle-class and buy automobiles for their families. It could not be more true now. If I'm a businessman, I'm better off if the middle class is growing and has some sense of economic security. Why would I want to elect somebody who wants to take Pell grants away from college kids and take away a new health care law that keeps people from being one illness away from bankruptcy?

I wish the Republicans would lose so badly that the Republican establishment would reclaim the party from the Tea Party and Grover Norquist. But we can't assume that will happen, so they got to wake up after Election Day and have an epiphany.

The U.S. Chamber of Commerce will have just spent over a hundred million dollars to defeat Obama, and the Democrats will have to wake up and say, "We ought to be more than the big-business wing of the Republican Party." Maybe we would do better for our people if we were the business arm of a successful American business community again. Wouldn't that be a nice change? And if they won't wake up, ready to support things that are palpably in the interests of their own members, maybe their own members will walk out on them. We need people at the table ready to talk and get serious about new plans.

Maybe the bishops of the U.S. Catholic Church will wake up and decide that we should rethink being an adjunct of the Republican Party and, heaven forbid, care more about the humble and the poor than getting exercised about how Catholic women pay for contraception or about abortion. That they opposed the health care law that insured 33 million Americans was an outrage: a hell of a lot of them are poor, a hell of a lot of them Latino Catholics.

At the highest level of the hierarchy, there was not a call to arms against Paul Ryan when he took the hatchet to food stamps and aid for the elderly poor. I don't believe the Bible has been rewritten or revised since I was a boy: "Blessed are the 1 percent, for they shall inherit the earth." I don't believe that's in there.

It would make a difference if the Church in all its forms was at the table when we were negotiating a long-term budget deal—making sure the poor were kept whole, not just working to make sure the firewall was high enough as part of some science-fiction scenario where federal funds could end up paying for an abortion. This is my Church, and I know from New Orleans when Archbishop Aymond is at the table, it makes a difference.

I think our great high-tech entrepreneurs have to wake up too. They have built companies and brands that are the envy of the world, and they've said all the right things about what America needs to do and what has to change for us to get back on the road to prosperity, blah, blah, blah. But the time for whining is over and the time for doing is now. If one party is saying "Let's cut funding for science and education," you got to call them out: "You are not a serious party; we're serious people, and we need to work with serious leaders."

With their corporate and individual success and their wealth as their calling card, the business leaders who see the bigger picture have just got to say, "Raise our goddamn taxes!" Sign us up for the 39.6 or the 50-50 deal on revenue that puts us on the path we achieved in the 1990s—the only successful time of these past three-plus decades.

And we want a seat at the table—and not just when Hollywood is trying to protect intellectual property or when Congress is trying to keep kids from getting porn online. We are here to help cut the big deals.

On the face of it, it makes little or no sense they would do that, but sometimes the common sense changes. We need more people like Warren Buffett, people who have been hugely successful who see that they have to give up more of what they have. It can happen. Things change.

In 2013 we need to use our common sense, and bring them to their senses. Does that sound right?

Stan I don't think you're smoking anything. We really are at a moment when everybody recognizes that continued political dysfunction threatens everybody and everything. And more than that— as you think about all the policy initiatives that could be on the table—many sectors and groups have an opportunity to win some big things that could only happen at a moment of change like this.

Many American companies, the Chamber, and conservative think tanks, want to *reform and cut corporate tax rates* and so do many progressives, who seek to purge the code of special-interest breaks.

All have an interest in a more efficient and maybe more progressive corporate tax code. That is what Paul Ryan claims to support, so let's call his bluff.

Many conservatives and liberals want to *simplify the income tax* and get down to fewer exemptions and lower rates that support families with children and encourage work.

With everyone disgusted with the open floodgate of *campaign donations and spending*, maybe corporations will join campaign finance reformers to change the system because they are at risk of becoming arms of the political parties.

The oil companies, the new clean-energy and renewable sector, and the environmental groups have a big mutual interest in an *enduring deal on natural gas* that allows fracturing to go forward with serious environmental protections.

Health insurance is at a crossroads where employers could be shifting health care costs with government subsidies to the individual, but that is only sustainable if there are new revenues, workers paid more, and stronger unions.

Regardless of any Supreme Court decision, health insurance is at a crossroads and the next two years will be an unavoidable period of change, and key players could get critical changes that make it work. Both employers and employees need a big agreement on health insurance.

American industry, agriculture, and the high-tech sector need *comprehensive immigration reform,* but so do the white working-class and Latino communities.

The country can accept a path to citizenship if we open up immigration in highly skilled areas while tightening it in less skilled, while stepping up enforcement in the workplace and on the border.

Both American global companies and American unions have an interest in the U.S. government taking the lead in laying out and *enforcing a new regime on trade with China.*

In so many areas, China has crossed the line in subsidizing state industries, manipulating currency, limiting market access, stealing intellectual property, and sponsoring Internet hacking. Only the U.S. government is in a position to challenge them.

The protracted dysfunction has taken a rising toll in all sectors of the economy, and from the top to the bottom of the socioeconomic ladder, and that has created some uncommon allies. A president with a mandate who understands this moment of change can rally and unite these forces to overcome dysfunction.

Stan Though I believe all that is possible, in the end. The biggest thing we can do is to vanquish those who would grind the system to a halt and empower those who are ready to get to work. We have to keep our focus totally on what's happening to the middle class and the electoral choice that best ensures their future.

James We just have to wake up. Remember, it's still the middle class, stupid!

ACKNOWLEDGMENTS

We wrote this book together in the same way we have worked together almost every day since the Bill Clinton campaign in 1992, talking every morning by 7:00 a.m., bouncing ideas off each other, reacting to events, complaining about and cheering on our party, and trying to impact the debate—whether we were in or out of power.

We would have been just gossiping like old ladies but for Steve Bing and Democracy Corps, which allowed us to conduct national polls every month for over a decade, listen to people in focus groups, and conduct in-depth research right through the Great Recession. We admire Steve's unbelievable enthusiasm, unfailing values, and acute insights—and the fact that he's never asked us to poll on any subject of interest to him.

Fortunately, we have had a core of research partners who care about progressive issues and have made it possible to carry on, always alive and ready to tackle the emerging issues. These include Women's Voices. Women Vote, Campaign for America's Future, Center for American Progress, Public Campaign Action Fund, and others that prefer anonymity. We want to thank Bob Borosage and Roger Hickey, David Donnelly and Nick Nyhart, Page Gardner, David and William Harris, Eric Liu and Nick Hanauer, John Podesta, and Mark Steitz.

David Rosenthal had the idea for this book and approached us about it, and Blue Rider Press (Penguin) has moved with astonishing speed and skill, getting this book into the heated battle during the summer of the presidential election. At Blue Rider we also thank Aileen Boyle, Meighan Cavanaugh, David Chesanow, Vanessa Kehren, Janice Kurzius, Phoebe Pickering, and Linda Rosenberg.

Ian Jackman worked with James in writing this book, and he has been a great collaborator. James wants to thank the interns at Greenberg Quinlan Rosner who produced great transcript prose, despite James's idiosyncratic speech and language. And "Team Stan," as it is known, wants to join James in thanking Caroline Allen and Claire Drake, who are in charge of James, for everything from negotiating James's impossible schedule to accurately relaying his thoughts. They are real professionals.

We don't quite know how to thank Stan's team at Greenberg Quinlan Rosner. Erica Seifert, Matthew Groch, Scott Tiell, Laura Swartz, and Charles Posner took every chapter through to completion, coordinated across the two authors, while carrying the ongoing research of Democracy Corps. Erica is the brilliant and fluent leader of the team, with her own book at a like stage, who took pride of authorship. Dave Walker and Andrew Baumann contributed significantly, and Stan's partners—Al Quinlan, Jeremy Rosner, and Anna Greenberg—made this book possible in untold ways.

We got a lot of help from people who are doing serious work of their own but took this book seriously and contributed mightily to core economic narrative and bold policy options. Larry Mischel and Jody Franklin at EPI (The Economic Policy Institute) accepted our challenge to produce the most compelling set of graphs. We also had the benefit of extended conversations and sometimes supportive memos from Bob Borosage, David Donnelly, Zeke Emanuel, Thomas Friedman, Marcia Hale, David and William Harris, Roger Hickey, John Podesta, Sherle Schwenninger, Doug Sosnick, Neera Tanden, Father Kevin Wildes, John Wilhelm, and Daniel Zeitlin in the Office of Congresswoman Rosa DeLauro. We also thank Charles Murray, who graciously allowed us to include some of his key graphs.

It is customary to thank your parents and family at this point, but they are the story of the book and the reason we got the opportunity to write about the future of the middle class and their values. James acknowledges his parents, and his two brilliant daughters, Mattie and Emma. Stan wants to honor his parents, Sam and Yetta, and his own children and their mates, Kathryn Greenberg and Ari Zentner, Anna Greenberg and John Delicath, and Jonathan Greenberg and Justine Gardner, and the grandchildren, Rigby, Teo, Sadie, and Jasper. They really are the reason we wrote this book.

Our wives, Mary Matalin and Rosa DeLauro, are our partners and toughest critics, best friends, at the heart of our families, responsible for a good part of this history, even as they make their own. They give this all meaning.

We are blessed.

James Carville

Stan Greenberg

NOTES

CHAPTER 2: WHO'S MIDDLE CLASS AFTER ALL?

1. Democracy Corps/Center for American Progress, National Survey, October 15–18, 2011. The survey question was worded: "Generally speaking, would you say that you are wealthy, middle-class, working-class, poor, or something else?" (If the respondent answered, "Middle-class," he or she was then asked: "And would you say that you are upper-middle-class, middle-class, or lower-middle-class?")

2. Survey of 1,000 likely 2012 voters, conducted by Greenberg Quinlan Rosner for Democracy Corps, April 28–May 1, 2012.

3. United States Census Bureau, Table H-1, 2010 data, Income in 2010 CPI-U-RS Adjusted Dollars.

4. *Middle Class in America*, U.S. Department of Commerce, Economics and Statistics Administration, Office of the Vice President of the United States, January 2010, p. 2; David Rohde, "What Does It Mean to Be 'Middle Class'?" *Atlantic*, December 30, 2011.

5. Pew Research Center, "Inside the Middle Class: Bad Times Hit the Good Life," National Survey, April 9, 2008.

6. Shaila Dewan and Robert Gebeloff, "Among the Wealthiest One Percent, Many Variations," *New York Times*, January 14, 2012.

CHAPTER 3: THE MIDDLE CLASS: ISN'T IT THE ENGINE OF AMERICA?

1. Stanley Greenberg, *Middle Class Dreams* (New Haven: Yale University Press, 1996), revised updated edition, p. 42.

2. Woman, white, age 20, non-college-educated.

3. Woman, white, age 30, non-college-educated.

4. Man, Latino, age 25, non-college-educated.

5. Woman, white, age 35, non-college-educated.

6. Woman, Latino, age 20, non-college-educated.

7. Woman, Latino, age 20, non-college-educated.

8. Woman, white, age 40, non-college-educated.

9. Survey of 1,000 likely 2012 voters, with oversamples of 400 youth, unmarried women, and minority voters, conducted by Greenberg Quinlan Rosner for Democracy Corps, May 21–25, 2011.

10. Woman, Latino, age 50, education unknown.

11. Woman, white, age 40, non-college-educated.

12. Man, white, age 35, non-college-educated.

13. Survey of 1,003 adults nationwide, plus 300 additional interviews among first- and second-generation immigrants, conducted by Xavier University Center for the Study of the American Dream, March 5–15, 2011.

14. Gallup, 2001–2011; ABC national survey, September 8–14, 2010; Pew national survey, January 11, 2012; Xavier University survey for the Center for the Study of the American Dream, March 5–15, 2011.

15. Greenberg Quinlan Rosner and Public Opinion Strategies, focus groups conducted for the Pew Economic Mobility Project, January 6–13, 2009, in Atlanta, GA; Baltimore, MD; Chicago, IL; and Phoenix, AZ. In-depth interviews conducted by Greenberg Quinlan Rosner for Democracy Corps Economy Project, March 10–April 13, 2011, and March 29–May 4, 2010.

16. Woman, white, age 40, college-educated; woman, black, age 30, college-educated; woman, white, age 25, college-educated. Focus groups conducted by Greenberg Quinlan Rosner and Public Opinion Strategies for the Pew Economic Mobility Project, January 6–13, 2009, in Atlanta, GA; Baltimore, MD; Chicago, IL; and Phoenix, AZ.

17. Greenberg Quinlan Rosner and Public Opinion Strategies focus groups conducted for the Pew Economic Mobility Project, January 6–13, 2009, in Atlanta, GA; Baltimore, MD; Chicago, IL; and Phoenix, AZ.

18. Woman, white, age 30, non-college-educated; woman, Latino, age 50, non-college-educated.

19. Greenberg Quinlan Rosner and Public Opinion Strategies, survey of 1,000 respondents (2,119 unweighted), with oversamples of African Americans, Hispanic, and youth, conducted for the Pew Economic Mobility Project, January 27–February 8, 2009.

20. Man, white, age 45, non-college-educated.

21. Woman, Latino, age 25, non-college-educated.

22. Woman, Latino, age 35, non-college-educated.

23. Man, Latino, age 35, non-college-educated.

24. Joe Biden, speech to the Democratic Caucus, January 27, 2012.

CHAPTER 4: WHAT'S HAPPENED OVER THE LAST THREE DECADES, AND NOW

1. Sherle Schwenninger and Samuel Sherraden, "The Middle Class Under Stress," New America Foundation Report, April 27, 2011.

2. EPI analysis of Current Population Survey, Annual Social and Economic Supplement, published in *The State of Working America*, Economic Policy Institute, Washington, DC, February 1, 2011.

3. The average cost of a single year of education at a four-year degree-granting institution costs almost 55 percent of the household income for those in the 40th percentile. Even for those who are doing a bit better, the cost is high: for those in the 60th percentile, a single year of college tuition is 40 percent of their household income.

4. U.S. Bureau of Labor Statistics Analysis of Current Population Survey, 1998.

5. Josh Bivens, *Failure by Design: The Story Behind America's Broken Economy*, (Ithaca, NY: Economic Policy Institute/Cornell University, 2011), p. 89. To cope with stagnating incomes, middle-class families aren't just working longer hours, they also have begun saving less and less. From the 1960s to the 1980s, families saved between 8 and 10 percent of their income. But that began to drop in the early 1980s, falling to 2 percent right before the crash.

6. EPI analysis of U.S. Census Bureau, *Income, Poverty and Health Insurance Coverage in the United States: 2010—Historical Income Tables*, "F 7: Type of Family (All Races) by Median and Mean Income," Excel spreadsheet accessed November 23, 2011.

7. See Charles Murray, *Coming Apart* (New York: Crown Forum, 2012). Tables 8.3, 8.4, 8.6, 8.9, 8.11, 11.2, 11.3, 13.1, 14.2, and 15.2.

8. Ibid., Figure 2.2; 3.1.

9. Figures from the Center on Budget and Policy Priorities, Policy Basics: The 2001 and 2003 Tax Cuts, Washington, DC, March 5, 2009.

10. "25 People to Blame for the Financial Crisis," *Time*, February 11, 2009.

11. Rajiv Chandrasekaran, *Imperial Life in the Emerald City: Inside Iraq's Green Zone* (New York: Knopf, 2006), p. 104.

12. David Axelrod, "What Karl Rove got wrong on the U.S. deficit," *Washington Post*, January 15, 2010.

13. John Cassidy, *How Markets Fail: The Logic of Economic Calamities* (New York: Farrar, Straus and Giroux, 2009).

CHAPTER 5: THE ATTACK ON HIGHER EDUCATION

1. At www.lsu.edu/budget, April 26, 2012.

2. James Carville and Henson Moore, "LSU Should Be an Academic Champion, Too," NOLA.com, January 8, 2012.

3. "Big Money: LSU's Economic Impact Estimated at $1.3b," LSU.edu, February 28, 2011.

4. T. Harry Williams, *Huey Long: A Biography* (New York: Knopf, 1979), p. 520.

5. Susan Snyder and Amy Worden, "Corbett to Propose 20% to 30% Funding Cuts for Pa. State Universities," *Philadelphia Inquirer*, February 7, 2012.

6. Kathy Boccella, "Corbett Defends Cuts in Pennsylvania High-Education Budget," *Philadelphia Inquirer*, February 15, 2012.

7. Kaitlynn Riely, "Corbett Defends His Proposed $27 Billion Budget," *Pittsburgh Post-Gazette*, February 18, 2012.

8. California State University press release, "State Cuts Additional $100 Million from California State University Budget," December 13, 2011.

9. Told to reporters, Colorado Springs, CO, February 7, 2012.

10. Speech to Gulf Coast Energy Summit, Biloxi, MS, March 12, 2012.

11. Rebecca Kaplan and Matthew Shelley, "Santorum: Obama Wants to 'Indoctrinate' Students by Boosting College Enrollment," CBSNews.com, February 23, 2012.

12. Sal Gentile and Win Rosenfeld, "Presidentiality: Are Colleges Encouraging Atheism?" PBS.org, February 10, 2012.

13. Felicia Sonmez, "Santorum: Obama Is a 'Snob' Because He Wants 'Everybody in America to Go to College,' " *Washington Post*, February 25, 2012.

14. Frank Donoghue, "How and Why the Humanities Lost Touch," chronicle.com, May 24, 2011.

15. At mittromney.com/issues/education.

16. Travis Waldron, "Romney to College Student: If You Want Affordable College, 'Shop Around' or Join the Military," thinkprogress.org, March 5, 2012.

17. Paul Krugman, "Ignorance Is Strength," *New York Times*, March 8, 2012.

18. Jamie Merisotis, "The Critical Connection Between Higher Education and the American Dream," *Huffington Post,* January 19, 2012.

19. Anthony P. Carnevale, Nicole Smith, and Jeff Strohl, *Help Wanted: Projections of Jobs and Education Requirements Through 2018*, Center on Education and the Workforce (Washington, DC: Georgetown University, 2010), p. 3.

20. Ibid., p. 110.

21. Reeve Hamilton, "Budget Cuts Threaten Underenrolled Physics Departments," *New York Times*, September 15, 2011.

22. "Texas' Decision to Close Physics Programs Jeopardizes Nation's Future," nsbp.org, September 14, 2011.

23. Chris Kirkham, "For-profit College Executives Make Much More Than Their Higher Education Counterparts," *Huffington Post*, January 30, 2012.

24. "Default Rates Rise for Federal Student Loans," Department of Education, September 12, 2011. U.S. Department of Education, Press Release, Washington, DC, September 12, 2011.

25. Senator Harkin press release, May 19, 2011.

26. Eric Lichtblau, "Romney Offers Praise for a Donor's Business," *New York Times*, January 14, 2012.

CHAPTER 6: "A 'SECOND OPINION' ON THE ECONOMIC HEALTH OF THE AMERICAN MIDDLE CLASS"; OR, THE FOG MACHINE AND THE DENIAL OF ALL THEIR PROBLEMS

1. Richard V. Burkhauser, Jeff Larrimore, and Kosali I. Simon, "A 'Second Opinion' on the Economic Health of the American Middle Class," National Bureau of Economic Research Working Paper No. 17164, June 2011.

2. Tom Edsall also underscored our conclusions about the data and the perplexing failure to address the implications. See Thomas Edsall, "The Fight Over Inequality," *New York Times*, April 22, 2012.

3. Burkhauser et al., "A 'Second Opinion,'" p. 4; Stephen Rose, "The Myth of the Declining Middle Class," Statistical Assessment Service, June 9, 2008; Bruce Meyer and James Sullivan, "Sorry, Mr. Biden Most Middle Class Americans Are Better Off Now Than They Were Thirty Years Ago," FoxNews.com, October 24, 2011.

4. Alan Krueger, "The Rise and Consequences of Inequality in the United States," Remarks to the Center for American Progress, Washington, DC, January 12, 2012.

5. Thomas Edsall, "The Fight Over Inequality," *New York Times*, April 22, 2012.

6. EPI analysis of U.S. Census Bureau, *Income, Poverty and Health Insurance Coverage in the United States: 2010—Historical Income Tables,* Table F1: Income Limits for Each Fifth and Top 5 Percent of Families, and Table F 5: Race and Hispanic Origin of Householder—Families by Median and Mean Income," Excel spreadsheet accessed November 23, 2011.

7. Bruce Meyer and James Sullivan, "Sorry, Mr. Biden Most Middle Class Americans

Are Better Off Now Than They Were Thirty Years Ago," FoxNews.com, October 24, 2011.

8. Ron Haskins, "The Myth of the Disappearing Middle Class," *Washington Post*, March 29, 2012; Burkhauser et al., "A 'Second Opinion,'" pp. 2–5.

9. David Rogers, "Republicans to slash food stamps," *Politico*, April 16, 2012.

10. Scott Winship, "Stop Feeling Sorry for the Middle Class! They're Doing Just Fine," *New Republic*, February 7, 2012; Reihan Salam, "Scott Winship on the Real Romney Gaffe," *National Review Online*, February 7, 2012.

11. Scott Winship, "Stop Feeling Sorry for the Middle Class!"

12. Ibid.

13. Andy Kessler, "The Rise of Consumption Equality," *Wall Street Journal*, January 3, 2012.

14. Kessler answers his own question in the story. Larry Page owns a Boeing 767. According to DealBook, in 2010, Page bought a (preowned) yacht called *Senses* for $45 million. And his net worth is $16.7 billion. That's what he has that you don't.

CHAPTER 7. SMARTER THAN YOU THINK: THE FINANCIAL CRISIS

1. Pew Research Center for the People and the Press, National Survey, October 9–12, 2008.

2. ABC News/*Washington Post* Poll, March 26–29, 2009.

3. Based on fifty-five in-depth interviews conducted March 1–May 31, 2010, and thirty in-depth interviews conducted March 1–April 30, 2011. Interviews were conducted by Greenberg Quinlan Rosner for Citizen Opinion and Democracy Corps. Respondents were divided equally among voters in the Rising American Electorate and white non-college-educated voters.

4. Woman, black, age 50, non-college-educated.

5. Man, Latino, age 30, non-college-educated.

6. Man, white, age 45, non-college-educated.

7. Man, Latino, age 30, non-college-educated.

8. Man, white, age 45, non-college-educated.

9. See survey of 1,001 2008 voters conducted by Greenberg Quinlan Rosner for Democracy Corps, January 7–10, 2010. See also a CNN/ORC survey conducted January 12–15, 2009, and February 18–29, 2009, and a survey conducted by Quinnipiac, February 25–March 2, 2009.

10. Democracy Corps Survey, September 11–14, 2010.

11. CBS News/*New York Times* Poll, June 24–28, 2011.

12. *New York Times*/CBS News Poll, April 2010–January 2012. Democracy Corps/Campaign for America's Future survey, July 26–29, 2010.

13. Mike Allen, "Obama, Biden Declare 'Recovery Summer,'" Politico.com, June 17, 2010.

14. From President Obama's remarks at the House Democrats Issues Conference, Cambridge, MD, January 27, 2012, and President Obama's State of the Union address, January 24, 2012.

15. From focus groups in Columbus, OH, composed of non-college-educated men and swing voters, May 10, 2011.

16. Ibid.

17. Ibid.

18. Ibid.

19. From post–State of the Union focus groups in Denver, CO, composed of swing voters, January 24, 2012.

20. In May 2011, 43 percent of all likely voters reported having experienced reduced wages or hours or benefits at work by either themselves or a member of their family. Among white non-college-educated voters, it was 45 percent. From a Democracy Corps survey, May 21–25, 2011.

21. Michael Greenstone and Adam Looney, "Unemployment and Earnings Losses: A Look at Long-term Impacts of the Great Recession on American Workers," Brookings Institution, Hamilton Project, November 4, 2011.

22. Ben Casselman, "Recovery Redraws Labor Landscape," *Wall Street Journal*, January 4, 2012.

CHAPTER 8. SMARTER THAN YOU THINK? THEN WHAT ABOUT KEYNES?

1. Paul Krugman, "How Did We Know the Stimulus Was Too Small?" *New York Times*, July 28, 2010.

2. Nicholas Kristof, "In Athens, Austerity's Ugliness," *New York Times*, March 7, 2012.

3. Survey of 1,000 2008 voters (866 likely 2010 voters). Conducted by Greenberg Quinlan Rosner for Democracy Corps and Campaign for America's Future, July 26–29, 2010.

4. Survey of 1,000 2008 voters (866 likely 2010 voters). Conducted by Greenberg Quinlan Rosner for Democracy Corps and Campaign for America's Future, July 26–29, 2010.

5. Survey of 1,000 2008 voters (866 likely 2010 voters). Conducted by Greenberg Quinlan Rosner for Democracy Corps and Campaign for America's Future, July 26–29, 2010.

6. Results for top two contributors to the national deficit growth: "The wars in Iraq and Afghanistan"—47 percent; "The bailouts of the big banks and auto industry"—36 percent; "Lobbyists and special interests putting unneeded spending in the budget"—32 percent; "President Obama's economic recovery or stimulus plan"—30 percent; "The Bush tax cuts for corporations and top earners"—28 percent; "The economic recession that cut tax revenue and required support for the unemployed"—8 percent; "The cost of the Medicare Prescription Drug benefit"—5 percent. From a survey of 1,000 2008 voters (866 likely 2010 voters). Conducted by Greenberg Quinlan Rosner for Democracy Corps and Campaign for America's Future, July 26–29, 2010.

7. Survey of 1,000 2008 voters (866 likely 2010 voters). Conducted by Greenberg Quinlan Rosner for Democracy Corps and Campaign for America's Future, July 26–29, 2010.

8. In October 2011, 57 percent gave "a plan to invest in new industries and rebuild the country over the next five years" a warm, favorable rating on our zero-to-100 thermometer scale, while only 49 percent gave "a plan to dramatically reduce the deficit over the next five years" a warm rating. In July 2010, 60 percent gave a plan to invest a warm rating and 61 percent gave a plan to reduce the deficit a warm rating. Results from a survey of 1,000 2008 voters (866 likely 2010 voters), conducted by Greenberg Quinlan Rosner for Democracy Corps and Campaign for America's Future, July 26–29, 2010, and from a survey of 1,000 likely 2012 voters conducted by Greenberg Quinlan Rosner for Democracy Corps and the Center for American Progress, October 15–18, 2011.

CHAPTER 9. SMARTER THAN YOU THINK?
CORRUPTED GOVERNMENT

1. Greenberg Quinlan Rosner conducted six focus groups for the Inequality Working Group in the early spring of 2011. Groups were conducted in Milwaukee on February 23, 2011; in Houston on February 28, 2011; and in Philadelphia on March 14, 2011. The Milwaukee group was composed of white, non-college-educated men and women. Houston hosted one group of Hispanic voters and one group of mixed-race youth (under age 30). The Philadelphia group was recruited among college-educated, upper-income suburban voters. All groups were screened for "swing" and middle-of-the-road voters.

2. Findings from six focus groups conducted by Greenberg Quinlan Rosner for the Inequality Working Group. Groups were conducted in Milwaukee on February 23, 2011; in Houston on February 28, 2011; and in Philadelphia on March 14, 2011. The

Milwaukee group was composed of white, non-college-educated men and women. Houston hosted one group of Hispanic voters and one group of mixed-race youth (under age 30). The Philadelphia group was recruited among college-educated, upper-income suburban voters. All groups were screened for "swing" and middle-of-the-road voters.

3. Ibid.

4. Focus group among swing voters in Milwaukee, WI, February 23, 2011.

5. Findings from six focus groups conducted by Greenberg Quinlan Rosner for the Inequality Working Group. Groups were conducted in Milwaukee on February 23, 2011; in Houston on February 28, 2011; and in Philadelphia on March 14, 2011. The Milwaukee group was composed of white, non-college-educated men and women. Houston hosted one group of Hispanic voters and one group of mixed-race youth (under age 30). The Philadelphia group was recruited among college-educated, upper-income suburban voters. All groups were screened for "swing" and middle-of-the-road voters.

6. Sara Murray, "Romney Tries to Fill His Coffers in Florida," *Wall Street Journal Washington Wire*, posted April 15, 2012.

7. Lawrence Lessig, *Republic, Lost: How Money Corrupts Congress—and a Plan to Stop It* (New York: Twelve, 2011), p. 7.

8. Ibid., p. 83.

9. Ibid.

CHAPTER 10: THE ELITES DEPLORE CLASS WARFARE, BUT WHAT ABOUT THE VOTERS?

1. Based on surveys of 1,000 likely voters conducted by Greenberg Quinlan Rosner for Democracy Corps and the Center for American Progress, July 26–29, 2010, and October 15–18, 2011.

2. Based on results from a national survey of 1,000 adults conducted October 6–9, 2011, by Princeton Survey Research Associates for the *Washington Post* and Bloomberg News. Other polls confirm these results. For example, every April for the last several years, Gallup has conducted a survey on taxes. In 2011, just a quarter of all respondents said that "upper-income people" were paying a "fair share" of taxes and just a fifth said that "corporations" paid their fair share, based on a survey of 1,077 adults nationwide conducted April 7–11, 2011, by Gallup. For other polls on this topic see the CBS News/*New York Times* survey of 1,185 adults conducted January 20–23, 2012. See also Pew Research Center for the People and the Press survey conducted December 7–11, 2011.

3. Nicolle Wallace, "This Week," ABC News Transcript, March 11, 2012, on abcnews .com.

4. Mark Mellman was quoted in the *New York Times* on November 8, 2010, as saying, "An election that's dominated by the tax issue is a bad election for Democrats everywhere, anywhere and always."

5. Survey of 1,000 2008 voters conducted by Greenberg Quinlan Rosner for Democracy Corps, August 30–September 2, 2010.

6. Bill Clinton, Acceptance Speech to the Democratic National Convention, New York, NY, July 16, 1992.

7. Bill Clinton, "A Partnership for Opportunity," remarks by Governor Clinton at Montgomery College, Rockville, MD, September 2, 1992.

8. "Ad Watch: Campaign '92," *Los Angeles Times*, September 19, 1992, and May 23, 1992.

9. Al Gore, remarks at Portland Community College, October 31, 2000.

10. Survey of 1,000 likely 2008 voters conducted by Greenberg Quinlan Rosner for Democracy Corps, October 21–23, 2008.

11. Remarks by the president on the Economy, Osawatomie, KS, December 6, 2011.

12. This is a mélange of quotes that we have taken some license with in order not to be in a debate with any specific person. That would get in the way of the larger point. See Patrick H. Caddell and Douglas E. Schoen, "Our Divisive President," *Wall Street Journal*, July 28, 2010; Mark Penn, "Obama—Don't Bring Back Class Warfare," *Huffington Post*, September 18, 2011; John Judis, "Why Democrats Must be Populists," *American Prospect*, August 19, 2002; Bill Galston, "Why Obama's New Populism May Sink His Campaign," *New Republic*, December 17, 2011; Jim Kessler, quoted in "Campaigning on the Equity Card," Joseph J. Schatz, *Congressional Quarterly*, December 22, 2011.

13. Al Gore, campaign event in Chicago, IL, July 6, 2000.

14. David Gergen, "Gore Peppers Speech with Old-Line Themes," ABC News, http:// abcnews.go.com/Politics/story?id=123079&page=1, August 18, 2000.

15. Survey of 952 voters nationwide conducted August 1–3, 2000. This statement beat the Republican offer by a 37-point margin (62–27).

16. Al Gore, acceptance speech to the Democratic National Convention, August 17, 2000.

17. Kenski, Hardy, and Jamieson, *The Obama Victory*, Chapter 9: "Period Four: The McCain Surge" (New York: Oxford University Press, 2010), pp. 203–32.

18. Democracy Corps survey of 1,000 2008 voters conducted on November 2, 2008. See also *Washington Post*–ABC News tracking poll conducted October 30–November 2, 2008, among a random national sample of 2,762 registered voters, including 2,470 likely voters.

19. Democracy Corps National surveys conducted October 5–November 2, 2008.

20. The authors of the study are making a more nuanced case: that after the third debate, the percentage saying Obama (and not McCain) would raise your taxes went up from about 29 to 34 percent and, controlling for other factors, that pushed up favorable views of McCain. He also pushed up the confidence in his ability to handle the economy over this two-week period by 5 points to the hardly impressive 38 percent. Their modeling showed that gain could be explained by the increased perception that Obama would raise your taxes, that he would give checks to the undeserving who pay no taxes, and that he had a socialist plan.

21. Kenski, Hardy, and Jamieson in *The Obama Victory* study asked instead whether Obama would raise your taxes, but that wording accepts the conservative terms of the debate. That could shift perceptions of what he would do but not necessarily shift voters to support the Republican approach to taxes. A more neutral wording— "better job on taxes"—allows the respondent to champion their overall posture on taxes, including the prospect of increased taxes. Sure, McCain's distortion of Obama's tax plans produced more people saying he would raise their taxes, but not their posture on taxes overall. There was no surge on this more neutral wording.

22. Democracy Corps surveys conducted October 30–November 2, 2008.

CHAPTER 11: THE DISASTER OF 2010

1. Based on a combined dataset of three national post-election surveys conducted by Greenberg Quinlan Rosner for Democracy Corps, Resurgent Republic, Campaign for America's Future, and Women's Voices. Women Vote. The surveys were conducted November 2–3, 2010.

2. Ross Colvin, "One Year on, Obama Cites Struggle with Bush Legacy," Reuters, November 5, 2009.

3. Based on a combined dataset of three national post-election surveys by Greenberg Quinlan Rosner for Democracy Corps, Resurgent Republic, Campaign for America's Future, and Women's Voices. Women Vote. Surveys conducted November 2–3, 2010.

4. Remarks by the president in the 2011 State of the Union address, January 25, 2011.

5. Based on a combined dataset of three national post-election surveys by Greenberg Quinlan Rosner for Democracy Corps, Resurgent Republic, Campaign for America's Future, and Women's Voices. Women Vote. Surveys conducted November 2–3, 2010.

6. President's weekly address, December 3, 2011; remarks by the president at a DNC event, October 4, 2011; remarks by the president in Toledo, OH, June 3, 2011.

7. Stan Greenberg, James Carville, David Walker, and Erica Seifert, "A Path to Democratic Ascendency on the Economy: Report on the Economy Project," June 2, 2011,

www.democracycorps.com. Memo based on results from research conducted by Greenberg Quinlan Rosner for Democracy Corps, including 30 in-depth interviews conducted from March to April 2011, four focus groups in Denver, CO, and Columbus, OH, on May 10 and 12, 2011, and a national survey of 1,481 likely 2012 voters conducted May 21–25, 2012.

8. Address by the president to the nation, July 25, 2011.

9. Based on a combined dataset of three national post-election surveys by Greenberg Quinlan Rosner for Democracy Corps, Resurgent Republic, Campaign for America's Future, and Women's Voices. Women Vote. Survey conducted November 2–3, 2010.

10. Matt Bai, "The Game Is Called Chicken," *New York Times Magazine*, April 1, 2012.

11. Data from Larry M. Bartels, "Partisan Politics and the U.S. Income Distribution," February 2004. During Democratic administrations, unemployment averaged 4.84 percent; during Republican administrations, unemployment averaged 6.35 percent. GDP growth averaged 4.08 percent during Democratic administrations; GDP growth averaged 2.86 percent during Republican administrations.

12. Brian Beutler, "Government Jobs Buoyed Bush's Economy and Sink Obama's," TalkingPointsMemo.com, March 21, 2012.

13. Bob Drummond, "Stocks Return More with Democrats in White House," Bloomberg News, February 22, 2012.

CHAPTER 12: WHY DO YOU FEEL BETTER ABOUT 2012? BECAUSE WE HAVE A STORY TO TELL

1. Remarks by the president on the economy in Osawatomie, KS, December 6, 2011.

2. President Barack Obama, Associated Press lunch, Marriott Wardman Park, Washington, DC, April 3, 2012.

3. Remarks by the president at the House Democrats Issues Conference, Cambridge, MD, January 27, 2012.

4. Mark Landler, "On Jobs, Obama and Romney Argue Over Fullness of the Glass," *New York Times,* April 6, 2012.

5. Democracy Corps national survey with Women's Voices. Women Vote. Survey conducted February 11–14, 2012.

6. Remarks by the president to UAW Conference, Washington, DC, February 28, 2012.

CHAPTER 13: PAUL RYAN HAS THE ANSWER

1. "Paul Ryan Talks About Pre-empting a Debt Crisis and the Choices of Two Futures," *Face the Nation*, CBS, March 25, 2012.

2. Jeff Zients, "The Ryan-Republican Budget: The Consequences of Imbalance," whitehouse.gov, March 21, 2012.

3. Robert Greenstein, "CBO Shows Ryan Budget Would Set Nation on Path to End Most of Government," cbpp.org, March 20, 2012.

4. "Statement of Robert Greenstein on Chairman Ryan's Budget Plan," cbpp.org, March 21, 2012.

5. "Spending Cuts and Entitlement Reform," ricksantorum.com.

6. Rasalind S. Helderman, "Santorum: Ryan's Budget Plan 'a Great Blueprint,' but Doesn't Cut Enough," washingtonpost.com, March 21, 2012.

7. Z. Byron Wolf, "Illinois Exit Polls," ABCnews.com, March 20, 2012.

8. Henry Aaron and Austin Frakt, "Why Now Is Not the Time for Medicare Premium Support," Brookings, brookings.edu, January 25, 2012; Ezra Klein, "Wyden-Ryan Is Not a Compromise Proposal," *Washington Post*, December 15, 2011; Paul Van de Water, "Ryan-Wyden Premium Support Proposal Not What It May Seem," Center on Budget and Policy Priorities, cbpp.org, December 21, 2011.

9. "2013 Ryan Budget Proposal Program Impacts," Office of Management and Budget, March 2012.

10. United States Congressional House Budget Committee, "The Path to Prosperity: A Blueprint for American Renewal," March 20, 2012, p. 7.

11. Paul Ryan, "A Blueprint for Renewal: An Address by House Budget Committee Chairman Paul Ryan," American Enterprise Institute, March 20, 2012.

12. Paul Ryan, Fox News, Sunday, March 25, 2012.

13. Paul Krugman, "Moochers Against Welfare," *New York Times*, February 16, 2012.

14. Christopher Beam, "The Trouble with Liberty," *New York Magazine*, December 26, 2010.

15. "The Truth About GOP Hero Ayn Rand," video at thinkprogress.org.

16. "Paul Ryan and the Republican Vision," by Jonathan Chait, *New Republic*, March 11, 2010.

17. Ayn Rand, *The Voice of Reason* (New York: Plume, 1990).

18. Matt Taibbi, *Griftopia: A Story of Bankers, Politicians, and the Most Audacious Power Grab in American History* (New York: Spiegel and Grau, 2010).

19. "Paul Ryan Challenged on Budget by Georgetown Faculty," *Huffington Post*, April 24, 2012.

20. "Ryan Shrugged," by Robert Costa, *National Review Online*, April 26, 2012.

21. "Audio Surfaces of Paul Ryan's Effusive Love of Ayn Rand," by Elspeth Rieve, *Atlantic Wire*, April 30, 2012.

22. Gus Schumacher, Michel Nischan, and Daniel Bowman Simon, "Healthy Food Ac-

cess and Affordability: We Can Pay the Farmer or We Can Pay the Hospital," *Maine Policy Review,* Winter/Spring 2011, pp. 124–39.

23. Ibid., pp. 128–31.

24. United States Department of Agriculture, Office of Research and Analysis, "Benefit Redemption Patterns in the Supplemental Nutrition Assistance Program," Final Report, February 2011.

25. Sabrina Tavernise, "Food Stamps Helped Reduce Poverty Rate, Study Finds," *New York Times,* April 9, 2012.

26. Census Bureau Supplemental Poverty Measure, reported in speech by Congresswoman Rosa DeLauro, Washington, DC, February 2, 2012.

27. Schumacher et al., "Healthy Food Access and Affordability," p. 125.

28. Jason DeParle, "Welfare Limits Left Poor Adrift as Recession Hit," *New York Times,* April 7, 2012.

29. Dorothy Rosenbaum, "Ryan Budget Would Slash SNAP Funding by $134 Billion over Ten Years," Center on Budget and Policy Priorities, March 21, 2012; Ryan budget, pp. 35, 39–44.

30. David Rogers, "Republicans to Slash Food Stamps," *Politico,* April 16, 2012.

31. Dottie Rosenbaum, "Ryan Budget Would Slash SNAP Funding by $134 Billion over Ten Years," Center for Budget and Policy Priorities, March 22, 2012.

CHAPTER 14: AND DO YOU THINK YOU CAN REALLY DO SOMETHING ABOUT IT? SURE DO

1. Rick Perry, *Fed Up! Our Fight to Save America from Washington* (New York: Little, Brown, 2010).

2. Brad Johnson, "Rick Perry Thinks Texas Climate Scientists Are in a 'Secular Carbon Cult,'" ThinkProgress.org, August 15, 2011.

3. "Climate Change Statement" at atmo.tamu.edu.

4. "Perry shoots the messenger on climate change," *Houston Chronicle,* September 2, 2011.

5. "Koch Brothers Exposed," by C. Gibson, Greenpeaceblogs.com, April 2, 2012.

6. Seth Bornstein, "Richard Muller, Global Warming Skeptic, Now Agrees Climate Change Is Real," *Huffington Post,* October 30, 2011.

7. Justin Gillis, "Study Affirms Consensus on Climate Change," *New York Times,* June 22, 2010.

8. Brad Johnson, "Climate Scientists Rebuke Rupert Murdoch . . . ," ThinkProgress.org, February 1, 2012.

9. Suzanne Goldberg, "Wall Street Journal Rapped over Climate Change Stance," *Guardian*, February 1, 2012.

10. Bill McKibben, "The Great Carbon Bubble," TomDispatch.com, February 7, 2012.

CHAPTER 15: THE ELITE CONSENSUS ON ENTITLEMENTS AND DEFICITS

1. Survey of 1,000 likely 2012 voters nationwide conducted by Greenberg Quinlan Rosner for Democracy Corps, November 16–20, 2011.

2. *The Moment of Truth: Report of the National Commission on Fiscal Responsibility and Reform*, December 1, 2010.

3. Debt Reduction Task Force, *Restoring America's Future: Reviving the Economy, Cutting Spending and Debt, and Creating a Simple, Pro-Growth Tax System*, Bipartisan Policy Center, November 2010.

4. Stuart M. Butler, Alison Acosta Fraser, and William W. Beach, eds., "Saving the American Dream: The Heritage Plan to Fix the Debt, Cut Spending, and Restore Prosperity," Special Report No. 91, Heritage Foundation, www.heritage.org, May 10, 2011.

5. The Bipartisan Policy Center's Rivlin-Domenici plan had almost a one-to-one balance of revenue and cuts. The Bowles-Simpson plan had a cuts-to-revenue ratio of about two to one.

6. Remarks by the president, "Weekly Address: A Unique Opportunity to Secure Our Fiscal Future," White House, July 16, 2011.

7. Matthew Dowd, "Sunset to Sunrise: Politics Today," *National Journal*, September 10, 2011.

8. Brian Hamilton, "Can Shared Sacrifice Really Save the Economy?" *Washington Post*, January 23, 2012.

9. Interviewed on *Fareed Zakaria GPS*, January 9, 2012.

10. Jeremy Pelzer, "Al Simpson Speaks Out Against Debt Committee Critics, Political Climate," *Casper* (WY) *Star-Tribune*, November 24, 2010.

11. *The Moment of Truth: Report of the National Commission on Fiscal Responsibility and Reform*, Part III; Debt Reduction Task Force, *Restoring America's Future: Reviving the Economy, Cutting Spending and Debt, and Creating a Simple, Pro-Growth Tax System*, Bipartisan Policy Center, p. 17.

12. Stuart M. Butler et al., "Saving the American Dream," Heritage Foundation, May 10, 2011, p. 18; and Joseph Antos, Andrew Briggs, Alex Brill, and Alan D. Viard, "Fiscal Solutions: A Balanced Plan for Fiscal Stability and Economic Growth," American Enterprise Institute, www.aei.com, May 25, 2011, p. 5.

13. January Angeles, "Ryan Medicaid Block Grant Would Cause Severe Reductions in

Health Care and Long-term Care for Seniors, People with Disabilities, and Children," Center on Budget and Policy Priorities, May 3, 2011.

14. Karl Rove, "Obama Targets Medicare Advantage," *Wall Street Journal*, August 26, 2009.

15. Crossroads GPS television ads, "Wake Up," July 7, 2011.

16. Survey of 1,000 2008 voters by Greenberg Quinlan Rosner for Democracy Corps, July 26–29, 2010. See also Democracy Corps survey of 1,000 likely 2012 voters in Republican battleground districts conducted September 14–19, 2011. An extraordinary 70 percent said that ending "Medicare as we know it, forcing seniors to pay 6,400 dollars more out of pocket every year, and us[ing] that money to continue tax breaks for those earning over 200,000 dollars and special interest subsidies for oil companies" raised very serious or serious doubts.

17. According to analysis by the EPI, Demos, and the Century Foundation, "the system is fundamentally sound under its current structure and . . . the projected 75-year shortfall is modest and could be fixed without reducing benefits" or raising the retirement age. Ross Eisenbury of the Economic Policy Institute has argued that because income has risen at the top since 1983, and because the payroll tax cap has prevented the Social Security system from capturing these income gains, the system can be easily returned to solvency by restoring the balance that was projected when the system was reformed in 1983.

18. Survey of 1,000 2008 voters by Greenberg Quinlan Rosner for Democracy Corps and Campaign for America's Future, July 26–29, 2010. See also survey of 1,000 2010 voters by Greenberg Quinlan Rosner for Democracy Corps and Campaign for America's Future, November 2–3, 2010.

19. *The Moment of Truth: Report of the National Commission on Fiscal Responsibility and Reform*, Part V; Debt Reduction Task Force, *Restoring America's Future*, pp. 18–19.

20. Survey of 1,480 likely 2012 voters by Greenberg Quinlan Rosner for Democracy Corps and Campaign for America's Future, conducted January 9–11, 2011.

21. In 2011, the Social Security Administration estimated that Social Security benefits accounted for about 41 percent of the income of the elderly. Dependence is more pronounced among unmarried beneficiaries; 54 percent of married couples and 73 percent of unmarried persons receive 50 percent or more of their income from Social Security.

22. In a poll we conducted in July 2010, 66 percent said they opposed raising the retirement age and 67 percent opposed any cuts to Social Security.

23. Survey of 1,480 likely 2012 voters by Greenberg Quinlan Rosner for Democracy Corps and Campaign for America's Future, conducted January 9–11, 2011.

24. Other polls show declining resistance to raising the retirement age over time. In just

the last six years, opinion has shifted almost 10 points on this issue. In 2005, an ABC News/*Washington Post* poll found that two-thirds opposed raising the retirement age to sixty-eight. When ABC News/*Washington Post* asked the same question in 2011, 57 percent opposed the idea.

25. See the Report of the National Commission on Social Security Reform (Greenspan Commission), January 1983. In our poll, which fielded from July 26–29, 2010, 61 percent of all voters said that we should "eliminate the cap on Social Security payroll taxes so those earning more than $107,000 pay the same rate as everyone else." We found the same result in a survey of 1,480 likely 2012 voters by Greenberg Quinlan Rosner for Democracy Corps and Campaign for America's Future, conducted January 9–11, 2011.

26. Several proposals have recommended calculating cost-of-living adjustments in a new way to more accurately reflect inflation.

27. Thomas Friedman, "American Voters: Still Up for Grabs," *New York Times,* January 21, 2012.

28. Ibid.

CHAPTER 16: LET'S GET SERIOUS ABOUT WHAT REALLY MATTERS: HEALTH CARE

1. Kaiser Family Foundation, "Health Care Spending in the United States and Selected OECD Countries," http://www.kff.org/insurance/snapshot/oecd042111 .cfm, April 2011.

2. Josh Bivens, *Failure by Design: The Story Behind America's Broken Economy* (Ithaca, NY: Economic Policy Institute/Cornell University, 2011), p. 81; Economic Policy Institute, *The State of Working America*, "Growth of Health Insurance Premiums Far Outpaces Workers' Earnings and Overall Inflation: Growth Rate Index of Family Health Insurance Premiums, Workers' Earnings, and Overall Inflation, 1999– 2009" (chart), http://stateofworkingamerica.org/charts/growth-rate-of-premiums-earnings-and-inflation.

3. Economic Policy Institute, *The State of Working America*, "Eroding Health Insurance Coverage, 2000–2010" (chart), http://stateofworkingamerica.org/charts/any-insur ance-vs-employer-sponsored-health-insurance.

4. "Health-Care Law's Many Unknown Side Effects," *Wall Street Journal*, March 23, 2012.

5. "Why Now Is Not the Time for Medicare Premium Support," Brookings, brookings .edu, March 31, 2012.

6. Kasie Hunt and Billy House, "CBO Estimates Show Public Plan with Higher Savings Rate," *National Journal*, September 25, 2009.

7. Walid F. Gellad, Sebastian Schneeweiss, Phyllis Brawarsky, Stuart Lipsitz, and Jennifer S. Hass, "What If the Federal Government Negotiated Pharmaceutical Prices for Seniors? An Estimate of National Savings," *Journal of General Internal Medicine* 23, no. 9, September 2008.

8. Valerie C. Melvin, "Fraud Detection Systems: Centers for Medicare and Medicaid Services Needs to Expand Efforts to Support Program Integrity Initiative," United States Government Accountability Office, December 7, 2011; Richard Sorian, Assistant Secretary for Public Affairs, "Keeping the System Clean: Fighting Medicare Fraud," www.healthcare.gov, June 17, 2011.

9. New America Foundation, "Realigning U.S. Health Care Incentives to Better Serve Patients and Taxpayers," June 12, 2009.

10. Among the employed population (excluding those who lost health insurance as a result of unemployment), the percent of individuals covered by employer-sponsored health insurance declined 6.6 percent from 2000 to 2009 (Elise Gould, "Employer-Sponsored Health Insurance Erosion Accelerates in the Recession," EPI Briefing Paper No. 283, November 16, 2010).

11. Conversation with Zeke Emanuel, March 22, 2012.

CHAPTER 17: DOING SOMETHING ABOUT IT: NUMBERS

1. David Frum, "Coming Apart: The Review," *The Daily Beast*, Five-part review of Charles Murray's book *Coming Apart: The State of White America, 1960–2010*, February 6–8, 2012; George Packer, "Poor, White and Republican," *New Yorker*, February 14, 2012; Ross Douthat, "Can the Working Class Be Saved?" *New York Times*, February 11, 2012; Jonathan Chait, "Inequality and the Charles Murray Dodge," *New York Magazine*, January 31, 2012.

2. Thomas L. Friedman and Michael Mandelbaum, *That Used to Be Us: How America Fell Behind in the World* (New York: Farrar, Straus and Giroux, 2011).

3. Richard Burkhauser, Jeff Larrimore, and Kosali Simon, "A 'Second Opinion' on the Economic Health of the American Middle Class," NBER Working Paper Series, June 2011.

4. Pat Garofalo, "Reagan Called for an end to 'Crazy' Tax Loopholes . . ." ThinkProgress, October 3, 2011.

5. Matt Bai, "Obama vs. Boehner: Who Killed the Debt Deal?" *New York Times Magazine,* March 28, 2012.

6. Stanley Greenberg, *Dispatches from the War Room* (New York: Thomas Dunne Books/St. Martin's Press, 2009), p. 94.

7. 2009 Report Card for American Infrastructure, American Society of Civil Engi-

neers; Building America's Future Educational Fund, "Falling Apart and Falling Behind: Transportation Infrastructure Report 2011," http://www.infrastructurereport card.org.

8. Leo Hindery and Leo Gerard, "The Task Force on Job Creation: A Vision for Economic Renewal," New America Foundation, July 2011, pp. 42–43; and The State of American Business, 2012 Address by Thomas J. Donohue, President & CEO, U.S. Chamber of Commerce, January 12, 2012.

9. H.R. 402: National Infrastructure Development Bank Act of 2011, 112th Congress, sponsored by Rosa DeLauro.

10. Congresswoman Rosa L. DeLauro, Comments, New America Foundation I-Bank Event, "A Bank to Renew America," June 8, 2011.

11. Michael Stewart, "To Boost Sustainable Growth, Let Private Capital Help Rebuild Aging Infrastructure," McKinsey & Company, Draft memo.

12. 2009 Report Card for American Infrastructure, American Society of Civil Engineers; Building America's Future Educational Fund, "Falling Apart and Falling Behind: Transportation Infrastructure Report 2011," http://www.infrastructurereport card.org.

13. Remarks by the president in Osawatomie, KS, December 6, 2011.

14. Adam Hersh and Sarah Ayres, "New Ryan Budget Disinvests in America," Center for American Progress, http://www.americanprogress.org/issues/2012/03/ budget_disinvestment.html, March 20, 2012.

15. Motoko Rich, "Federal Funds to Train the Jobless Are Drying Up," *New York Times*, April 8, 2012.

16. *The Moment of Truth: Report of the National Commission on Fiscal Responsibility and Reform*, December 2010, p. 12.

17. Walter Isaacson, *Steve Jobs* (New York: Simon & Schuster, 2011), pp. 544–46.

18. Charles Duhigg and David Kocieniewski, "How Apple Sidesteps Billions in Taxes," *New York Times*, April 28, 2012.

19. National Science Foundation, Science and Engineering Indicators 2012, Chapter 4: "R&D: National Trends and International Comparisons," Appendix figures 4-10, 4-13, 4-19, 4-28, 4-31.

20. Marcia Gaudet, *Carville: Remembering Leprosy in America* (Jackson: University Press of Mississippi, 2004).

21. Phil Oliff and Michael Leachman, "New School Year Brings Steep Cuts in State Funding for Schools," Center on Budget and Policy Priorities, http://www.cbpp .org/cms/?fa=view&id=3569, October 7, 2011.

22. Jon Baron and Isabel V. Sawhill, "Federal Programs for Youth: More of the Same Won't Work," Brookings, brookings.edu, April 3, 2012.

23. David Ravitch, "How, and How Not, to Improve the Schools," *New York Review of Books*, March 22, 2012.

24. Michael Crowley, "On Reagan's 101st Birthday, Republican Revisionism," *Time*, February 7, 2012.

25. United States Congressional House Budget Committee, "The Path to Prosperity: A Blueprint for American Renewal," March 20, 2012, p. 60.

26. Ross Douthat, "What Charles Murray Gets Right," *New York Times*, February 14, 2012.

CHAPTER 18: AMERICA: 1?

1. Gideon Rachman, *Zero-Sum Future: American Power in an Age of Anxiety* (New York: Simon & Schuster, 2011).

2. Zbigniew Brzezinski, *America and the Crisis of Global Power* (New York: Basic, 2012).

3. Gideon Rachman, *Zero-Sum Future*, p. 282.

4. Paul Ryan, *Fox News Sunday*, September 18, 2011.

5. Mitt Romney, Republican primary debate in Charleston, SC, January 21, 2012.

6. Robert Scott, "Memo to the *Times*: Hold the Funeral March for U.S. Manufacturing," *Economic Policy Institute*, April 10, 2012. See also Department for Business Innovation & Skills, Economics Paper No. 10B, "Manufacturing in the UK: Supplementary Analysis," December 2010.

7. Remarks at the Conference on the Renaissance of American Manufacturing, March 27, 2012.

8. Ibid. See also Tyler Cowen, "What Export-Oriented America Means," *American Interest*, May/June 2012.

9. Daniel Yergin, *The Quest: Energy, Security, and the Remaking of the Modern World* (New York: Penguin Press, 2011).

10. National Science Foundation, "A Brief History of NSF and the Internet," August 13, 2003.

11. Jon Gertner, *The Idea Factory: Bell Labs and the Great Age of American Innovation* (New York: Penguin Press, 2012).

12. Walter Isaacson, "Inventing the Future," *New York Times*, Sunday Book Review, April 6, 2012.

13. Tom Steyer and John Podesta, "We Don't Need More Foreign Oil and Gas," *Wall Street Journal*, January 24, 2012.

14. Daniel Yergin, *The Quest;* and Daniel Yergin, "America's New Energy Security," *Wall Street Journal*, December 12, 2011.

15. Tom Steyer and John Podesta, "We Don't Need More Foreign Oil and Gas," *Wall*

Street Journal, January 24, 2012. Also, "The Pickens Plan," http://www.pickensplan
.com/theplan.

16. John Podesta and Timothy Wirth, "Natural Gas: A Bridge Fuel for the 21st Century," Center for American Progress, August 10, 2009.

17. "The Pickens Plan," http://www.pickensplan.com/theplan.

18. Ibid.

19. Conversation with Neera Tanden, president of the Center for American Progress, March 28, 2012.

20. Martin Wolf, "Two Cheers for China's Rebalancing," *Financial Times,* April 3, 2012.

21. Robert E. Scott, "Revaluing China's currency could boost US economic recovery," Briefing Paper #318, Economic Policy Institute, June 17, 2011.

22. MPAA Statement on Strong Showing of Support for Stop Online Piracy Act, December 16, 2011.

23. Leo Hindery and Leo Gerard, "The Task Force on Job Creation: A Vision for Economic Renewal," New America Foundation, July 2011, pp. 38–39.

CHAPTER 19: TRIUMPH OVER POLITICAL DYSFUNCTION

1. Kenneth Lieberthal and Wang Jisi, *Addressing U.S.-China Strategic Distrust,* John L. Thornton China Center, Brookings, brookings.edu, March 2012, p. 9.

2. Brzezinski, *Strategic Vision: America and the Crisis of Global Power* (New York: Basic Books, 2012), pp. 52–53.

3. Based on a combined dataset of three national post-election surveys by Greenberg Quinlan Rosner for Democracy Corps, Resurgent Republic, Campaign for America's Future, and Women's Voices. Women Vote. Surveys conducted November 2–3, 2010.

4. Thomas Mann and Norman Ornstein, *The Broken Branch* (New York: Oxford University Press, 2006). See also Thomas Mann and Norman Ornstein, *It's Even Worse Than It Looks* (New York: Basic Books, 2012).

5. ABC News/*Washington Post* survey, conducted among 1,003 adults nationwide from April 5–8, 2012.

6. Survey of 1,000 likely 2012 voters nationwide, conducted by Greenberg Quinlan Rosner for Democracy Corps, January 8–11, 2011.

7. Mitt Romney, Wisconsin victory speech, April 3, 2012.

8. Mitt Romney on *Starting Point with Soledad O'Brien,* CNN, February 1, 2012.